Entanglements, or Transmedial Thinking about Capture

A John Hope Franklin Center Book

Entanglements, or Transmedial Thinking about Capture

REY CHOW

Duke University Press Durham and London 2012

GN
357
.C4

CARDIFF UNIVERSITY
16 MAY 2012
PRIFYSGOL CAERDYDD

© 2012 Duke University Press
All rights reserved
Printed in the United States of America on acid-free paper ♾
Designed by C. H. Westmoreland
Typeset in Minion Pro with Twentieth Century display
by Tseng Information Systems, Inc.

Library of Congress Cataloging-in-Publication
Data appear on the last printed page of this book.

Frontispiece: Julian Rohrhuber, *Vogelscheuche*
(detail, one of four photographs, 1995).
Courtesy of the artist.

Contents

Note on Translations

With the exception of cases in which I believe it would help readers to see the original quotations, words and passages from languages other than English are provided in the official English translations or in the conventional Romanized formats.

Acknowledgments

For the successful completion of and opportunity to publish this book, I am indebted to numerous people, but I must begin by expressing my gratitude to Ken Wissoker, my editor, and the advisory board members and production team in charge of my manuscript at Duke University Press. Their warm and effective assistance at each stage made the experience of preparing the book a privilege. Two anonymous readers who reviewed the book proposal and final manuscript gave me invaluable advice and concrete suggestions as well as confidence; I thank them for their immense generosity and enthusiasm. The book's chapters have also benefited from constructive feedback from audiences in Western Europe, East Asia, and North America.

Several sources of institutional support enabled me to write and to travel and allowed me the time I needed to adjust to a new work environment. These include the Andrew W. Mellon Professorship of the Humanities at Brown University, which I held in 2000–9; a Fulbright Distinguished Lectureship from the Japan–United States Educational Commission for the Nagoya American Studies Summer Seminar in 2008; a Class of 1932 Professorship in English and a Visiting Fellowship from the Council of the Humanities at Princeton University in 2008; and teaching relief from the Program in Literature at Duke University during my relocation there in 2009–10.

Although they may not remember it, Timothy Bewes, Jim Dennen, Rachel Greenspan, Calvin Hui, Kien Ket Lim, and Robyn Wiegman kindly provided the help I asked of them at specific stages.

Chris Cullens and Ken Haynes gave me the most affirmative intellectual and emotional support during many a dysfunctional moment. They humble me with their erudition, intelligence, and wit, all of which

I have come to depend on, shamelessly, like potent nutrients. As always, Austin Meredith spoils me with his unswerving devotion and magnanimous spirit. He creates the domestic environment that makes it possible for me to do my work. For what I owe him, there are simply no words.

A special note of thanks to Julian Rohrhuber for contributing to the text of chapter 2 and for permitting his photographic work to be reproduced in the frontispiece, postscript, and on the paperback cover. He was the one who taught me to think philosophically with traps, knots, masks, mazes, parasites, shadows, and other figures of entanglement. This book has been an endeavor to pursue that line of thinking, both in response to the charm with which he led me to it and in conjunction with some of the work I had been doing over the years. I give the book to Julian as a token of love, in return for the many gifts he has brought me.

An earlier and shorter version of chapter 1 was published in *Theory after "Theory,"* ed. Jane Elliott and Derek Attridge (New York: Routledge, 2011), 135–48. An earlier version of chapter 2 was published in *Reading Rancière*, ed. Paul Bowman and Richard Stamp (London: Continuum, 2011), 44–72. An earlier version of chapter 3 was published in *Critical Inquiry* 28.1 (2001), 286–304. An earlier and shorter version of chapter 4 was published in *Representations* 94 (Spring 2006), 131–49. An earlier version of chapter 5 was published in *differences* 20.2–3 (2009), 224–49. An earlier version of chapter 6 was published in *Nanzan Review of American Studies* 30 (2008), 47–61. An earlier and shorter version of chapter 7 was published in *Deleuze and the Postcolonial*, ed. Paul Patton and Simone Bignall (Edinburgh: Edinburgh University Press, 2010), 62–77. An earlier version of chapter 8 was published in *PMLA*, May 2011, 555–63. These previous versions are reproduced here with permission from the original publishers. All of them have been revised and updated or expanded for the purposes of this book.

Introduction

> The task of philosophy today could well be, What are these relations of power in which we are caught and in which philosophy itself . . . has been entangled?
>
> —MICHEL FOUCAULT, *Dits et ecrits*

The essays collected in this volume were written for various occasions during the decade 1999 to 2010, and most of them within the second half of that period.[1] Rather than with a preemptive unitary focus, they are presented here in the fundamental sense of the word "essay," as attempts at thinking through a series of recurrent, overlapping issues: the status of the mediatized image in relation to reflexivity; capture and captivation; mimetic violence, victimization, and forgiveness; and the place of East Asia in globalized Western academic study. This condition of overlapping recurrences is indicated by the term "entanglement," which is invoked, first and foremost, to suggest a topological looping together that is at the same time an enmeshment of topics. Beyond this intimation of a tangle, of things held together or laid over one another in nearness and likeness, my aim is to ask if entanglement could not also be a figure for meetings that are not necessarily defined by proximity or affinity. What kinds of entanglements might be conceivable through partition and par-

1. The French-language original of the epigraph: "La tâche de la philosophie aujourd'hui pourrait bien être: qu'en est-il de ces relations de pouvoir dans lesquelles nous sommes pris et dans lesquelles la philosophie elle-même s'est . . . empêtrée?" Michel Foucault, "La Philosophie analytique de la politique" (1978), *Dits et écrits, 1954–1988*, ed. Daniel Defert and François Ewald with Jacques Lagrange, 4 vols. (Paris: Gallimard, 1994), 3:541; English translation quoted in Arnold I. Davidson, "Structures and Strategies of Discourse: Remarks towards a History of Foucault's Philosophy of Language," *Foucault and His Interlocutors*, ed. and intro. Arnold I. Davidson (Chicago: University of Chicago Press, 1997), 3.

tiality rather than conjunction and intersection, and through disparity rather than equivalence?[2]

From these two series of convolutions—one could perhaps think of them as conceptual out-foldings superimposed on conceptual in-foldings—a certain contour of the entangled may be conjured, across a number of medial and cultural forms, with capture as artifice, force, and momentum.

Loops

Brecht's Scissors, Benjamin's Copy-images, Our Image-capturings ♦ As a point of departure, the essay "When Reflexivity Becomes Porn" revisits some of modernism's prominent legacies, pondering the direction in which reflexivity as a theoretical practice has been heading. Walter Benjamin's work on Bertolt Brecht is exemplary of the conceptual innovations that continue to bear an impact on theoretical and artistic thinking in the twenty-first century. Brecht, contrasting the dramatic with the epic, was fond of citing Alexander Döblin's idea of using a pair of scissors to cut up a narrative into pieces, with the pieces remaining fully capable of life.[3] To cut up, to subdivide, to render into parts: if art since

2. These questions are inspired to some extent by scientific inquiry such as quantum physics, in which the term "entanglement" designates mysterious connections between particles, which are said to be entangled due to simultaneous reactions they produce, reactions that are not the results of proximity (that is, of particles drawing close to one another). For an informative work in this area by a feminist theoretical physicist, see Karen Barad, *Meeting the Universe Halfway: Quantum Physics and the Entanglement of Matter and Meaning* (Durham: Duke University Press, 2006). In the area of biosemiotics, the behaviors of animals and organisms which coevolve by mysterious patterns of symmetry, down to the precise details of their bodily formations, could perhaps be considered another instance of this kind of ecological or cosmological entanglement. For a classic study, see Jakob von Uexküll, *A Foray into the Worlds of Animals and Humans*, with *A Theory of Meaning* (originally published in German in 1934 and 1940), trans. Joseph D. O'Neil, introduction by Dorion Sagan, afterword by Geoffrey Winthrop-Young (Minneapolis: University of Minnesota Press, 2010). The physical and biological sciences are well beyond the scope and concerns of this book, but it is worth noting the cross-disciplinary dynamism of the queries involved.

3. See Bertolt Brecht, *Brecht on Theatre: The Development of an Aesthetic*, ed. and trans. John Willett (New York: Hill and Wang, 1964), 70: "The bourgeois novel in the last century developed much that was 'dramatic,' by which was meant the strong centralization of the story, a momentum that drew the separate parts into a common relationship. A particular passion of utterance, a certain emphasis on the

modernism has been about a heightened sense of estrangement (or defamiliarization), estrangement itself is often a result of the intensification—one could say infinitization—of the part and the partial, and of partitioning. The actions of the scissors from which Brecht derived revolutionary thinking about narrative are also the actions of the camera. Montage, which in the Chinese language is often translated as 剪接 *jianjie* (literally, cutting-reconnecting), may in this light be rethought not simply as an event in the history of cinema but also as a key operation in twentieth-century theoretical thinking. This is the operation of scattering a (purported) previous continuum into fragments, which are then soldered or sutured together and distributed anew. We perform montage whenever we move things around from one context into another in the realm of thought, producing unanticipated, unsuspected relations—oftentimes triggering a crisis and a new situation—through the very gesture of juxtaposition. (To this extent, the contemporary image-editing procedure known as Photoshop, sometimes derided as fakery, is simply a continuation and implementation of montage by digital means.)

This new order of things—technical, artistic, and political—as triggered by cinematographic maneuvers of space and time is the focus of Benjamin's widely read essay "The Work of Art in the Age of Mechanical Reproduction."[4] For centuries, Benjamin reminds us, artists tried to perfect techniques of representation in order to reproduce reality in as accurate a manner as possible. That centuries-old effort was rendered obsolete by the advent of daguerreotypy, as a mere click on a machine, the camera, can replicate reality with a kind of resemblance no human hand, however skilled, ever could have. Although it was written in the mid-1930s, Benjamin's argument remains a landmark for reasons that go far beyond the empirical invention of photography and film. His thesis is really about a paradigm shift in the way replication is, or can be, conceptualized. No matter how well made, the artistic image was, before the arrival of photography, simply an imperfect copy, a reproduction that was deemed secondary in status to the source, which was reality itself. Mechanical automatism, Benjamin suggests, has fundamentally overturned

---

clash of forces are hallmarks of the 'dramatic.' The epic writer Döblin provided an excellent criterion when he said that with an epic work, as opposed to a dramatic, one can as it were take a pair of scissors and cut it into individual pieces, which remain fully capable of life."

4. Walter Benjamin, "The Work of Art in the Age of Mechanical Reproduction," *Illuminations*, ed. and introduction by Hannah Arendt, trans. Harry Zohn (New York: Schocken, 1969), 217–51.

this hierarchy by ushering in an era in which an image's replicability is to be grasped in its infinite extendability or generatability both from within and from without (the frame). This is how the copy-image supersedes the original as the main action or event. While the original may remain confined to the particular place and time of its making, the copy-image, by virtue of becoming (re)producible in forms that were previously unimaginable, lives a life of versatility and mobility, enabling even the most distant and exotic sights to be held in one's hand, visually pried open, and examined up close, at the same time that they are disseminated far and wide.

If we consider the copy-image as a part that has been cut out from the original, Benjamin's thesis can also be rethought as a thesis about the afterlife of the part and the partial: technically reproducible copy-images are so many sections from an original "whole" that can henceforth no longer be reassembled into one piece. As the parts take on lives of their own, multiplying tens of thousands of times in unexpected locales and dimensions, before unexpected audiences, the original is by contrast trapped in its own aura, imprisoned in the specificity of its "natural" time and place. By calling attention to the copy-image as an endlessly multipliable and endlessly movable part, *Benjamin has in effect inaugurated a reconfiguration of the conventional logic of capture*: rather than reality being caught in the sense of being contained, detained, or retained in the copy-image (understood as a repository), it is now the machinic act or event of capture, with its capacity for further partitioning (that is, for generating additional copies and images ad infinitum), that sets reality in motion, that invents or makes reality, as it were.[5]

This modernist ambience of cutting, capturing by copy-images, and partition-as-ever-renewable-productivity—an ambience that resonates both with the Marxian commodity fetish and with the psychoanalytic partial object—is one framework in which the chronologically later work of Michel Foucault and Gilles Deleuze on visibilities may also be understood. An important moment in this theoretical loop is Foucault's

5. For related interest, see the discussion of the paradigm shift in memory brought about by digitization in Viktor Mayer-Schönberger, *Delete: The Virtue of Forgetting in the Digital Age* (Princeton: Princeton University Press, 2009). Mayer-Schönberger makes the important point that there has been an irreversible change in the economics driving the storage (memory) of information—namely, that unlike in ages past, it is now much cheaper to save (that is, remember) than to discard (that is, forget). This is an interesting parallel to, and update of, Benjamin's point about the fundamental change in the economics of image-distribution made possible by technological reproducibility.

powerful work on incarceration by light, in which he famously asserts, "Full lighting and the eye of a supervisor capture better than darkness, which ultimately protected. Visibility is a trap."[6] Beyond the popularized reading of *Discipline and Punish* as a treatise on surveillance (with surveillance being a manmade form of transcendent violence), however, Foucault's work on visibility can in fact lead in a quite different direction. To see this, we need to read that work in conjunction with Deleuze's and follow the possible lines of flight into the contemporary discursive terrain of image-capturing and redemption. As explored in the essay "Postcolonial Visibilities," in reference to the work of Helen Grace as well as Foucault and Deleuze, what is at stake is no longer the coupling of visibility and incarceration or surveillance, on the one hand, or even simply the deterritorialization and becoming-mobile of technologized images, on the other. Rather, it is the collapse of the time lag between the world and its capture. What happens to memory when images, in which past events are supposedly recorded and preserved, become instantaneous with the actual happenings? When conventional time shifts vanish as a result of the perfecting of the techniques of image-capturing? When time loses its potential to become fugitive or fossilized—in brief, to become anachronistic?

Captivation, Identification ◆ The second theoretical loop that runs through this collection involves another, sentient dimension of capture, in which the affective rather than purely mechanistic ramifications of capture come to the fore. These workings are implicitly present in all the essays and explicitly addressed in "On Captivation." Juxtaposing the work of Jacques Rancière with that of the cultural anthropologist Alfred Gell as well as with readings of theory, literature, and film, that essay approaches capture and captivation through the debate on the indistinction of art and nonart. In advancing his admirably democratic thesis about the indistinction between art and everyday artifacts, Gell, for instance, puts an intriguing spotlight on the trap, a device for catching and killing animals, as a major example of such indistinction. And yet the trap is, to all appearances, the opposite of indistinction and, by implication, the opposite of a liberalization of boundaries: its art or cunning lies in an aggressive potential to take another being captive and bring it into submission. What makes a trap a trap is a state of arrest and enclo-

6. Michel Foucault, *Discipline and Punish: The Birth of the Prison*, trans. Alan Sheridan (New York: Pantheon, 1977), 200.

sure, coinciding with the prey's loss of mobility, autonomy, and perhaps life. How, then, to explain the centrality of the trap in a nonelitist consideration of art and artifacts? Is the trap in the end simply an account of history as told by the victors, the captors? Can the trap be thought of as a special part, both in the foregoing medial terms and in terms of Rancière's specific sense of *partage*, which pertains both to sharing and to distribution? It is by following the lead of these questions that this essay arrives at the suggestion of capture and captivation as a type of discourse, one that derives from the imposition of power on bodies and the attachment of bodies to power, and that contains the makings of what may be called a heteronomy or heteropoeisis.

At the same time, capture and captivation constitute a critical response, however untimely, to the disconnect(ing) of identification as a perceptual mode, a disconnect(ing) that underlies many examples of modernist art and theory, including feminist film theory of the 1970s and 1980s. As is well-known, this too is an important legacy of Brecht's teaching: at the heart of Brecht's attack on traditional Western dramaturgy is the aesthetic effect, crucial to Aristotle's theory, of what may be called audience identification with the dramatic spectacle. Making-strange, for Brechtian critics, essentially means rejecting wholesale the emotion of tragic inevitability that makes dramatic action cohere and enables the identificatory entanglement with fiction. Instead, in an anti-Aristotelian mode, the audience is invited—not the least through the cutting-up of a narrative (continuum) into different characters' perspectives—to adopt critical positions in relation to the dramatic spectacle, so as to interrupt and puncture its illusionism as based on aesthetic unity, which in psychological terms would correspond to the illusionism of a secure founding of the self, of a fully integrated selfhood. In retrospect, it is possible to say that such programmatic dismantling of identification, and with it the conscious disengagement from binding emotions such as empathy and compassion, has become instrumental not only to subsequent innovations in the modern theater and cinema but also to the ongoing, contemporary politicization of identities by way of class, gender, race, culture, sexual orientation, and other social partitions and divisions.

But ghosts of identification refuse to die, and typically return to haunt scenarios involving loyalty and betrayal and the pain and pleasure that accompany the pursuits of objects, be these objects human or nonhuman. In a number of essays ("On Captivation," "Fateful Attachments," and "Framing the Original"), we encounter fictional characters who can easily be labeled mad but whose madness, or state of being captivated, lends the stories their perverse psychological textures. A bored housewife in the nineteenth-century French countryside who squanders her life in addictions to cheap romances and consumerist spending; a Stasi functionary in East Germany who, at the risk of his own career, opts to guard the people he is supposed to catch and incriminate; a minor collector in mid-twentieth-century Republican China who, the pressure of public opinion notwithstanding, surrenders to Japanese invaders in order to save his own collection of bric-a-brac; a woman spy in the same period in China who participates in a patriotic plot to seduce and catch a national traitor live, only to end up letting him off at a critical moment, at the expense of her own and her allies' lives . . . By what exactly are these characters so captivated—knotted together, tangled up—that physical survival seems negligible, indeed beside the point? Is it sheer coincidence that these memorable tales of captivation, with their protagonists' characteristic propinquity toward bondage, masochism, and self-annihilation, have emerged amid modern contexts of conflicting allegiances, East and West, and alongside a modernist (anti-) aesthetics of anti-identification? Should such bondage, masochism, and self-annihilation be taken for a final enclosure or an anarchical opening, a recoiling of the self into . . . the infinite?

Victimhood ◆ With the essay "Sacrifice, Mimesis, and the Theorizing of Victimhood," a third theoretical loop can be traced, one that intersects with copying and capturing through the dynamics of mimesis. The work of René Girard, with its critique of the presumed originariness of desire and its emphasis on the mimetic nature of cultural violence, provides the main argumentative intervention here. In Girard's focus on mimesis as a sociological phenomenon, we hear resonances with feminist and postcolonial criticisms. At the same time, insofar as feminist and postcolonial criticisms tend to posit masculinity and whiteness as the definitive sources for women's and colonized people's acts of imitation, they tend to leave intact a presupposition of origins that carries with it the implication of mimesis as a derivative form of action. By contrast, in an argumentative move that recalls Benjamin's thesis about the potency of the copy-image, Girard asserts mimetic violence as the very mechanism—or the first term—of collective cultural existence. His unapologetic observation of mindless iteration or repetition in human behavior can be discomfiting, for the simple reason that it refuses to idealize or prettify humanity, individual or collective. Apart from the sacred rituals and the artworks that, in the course of human civilization, have helped exorcize mimetic violence through the sacrifice of surrogate victims, the only viable exit suggested by Girard's work seems to be religion. Hence, we surmise, his investment in such radical Judeo-Christian figures as Job and Jesus.

Another kind of Judeo-Christian response to cultural violence is forgiveness. From Hannah Arendt to Jacques Derrida, theorists have embraced forgiveness as the essential form of transcendence that can liberate or salvage us from being held captive to the spell of past injuries and sufferings. In Derrida's rendering of forgiveness as translation, and of translation ultimately as a kind of Hegelian *Aufhebung*, the question of suffering and victimhood takes on a thought-provoking lingual significance: suffering and victimhood are at once intractably untranslatable and what strives for, what demands translation. (To quote Derrida's words from another context: "Only that which is untranslatable calls for translation.")[7] These issues are discussed in the essay "'I insist on the Christian dimension,'" in which Derrida's advocacy of Christian forgiveness (in the context of a reading of *The Merchant of Venice*) is juxtaposed with two fictional characters' self-destructively intransigent behavior in the form of a refusal or inability to forgive without the reward of power. Insofar as they cast these characters outside the borders of what is acceptably human, the experiences of abjection undergone by Shylock in Shakespeare's play and by Shin-ae Lee in the Korean film *Secret Sunshine* leave the piety of Christian forgiveness, rather than as a satisfactory answer, as an unresolved aporia, an epistemic snarl. Against such piety, these stories ask, how should we come to terms with victimhood, which for many victims and their descendents is a singular, impassable, and nontranscendable occurrence?

The essay "American Studies in Japan, Japan in American Studies" serves as a rejoinder to these issues from a historically different perspective. Occasioned by a meeting on American studies in Japan, this essay examines two films, *No Regrets for Our Youth* and *Rhapsody in August*, both by Akira Kurosawa and both having to do with the fraught history of the Second World War in the Pacific. In *Rhapsody in August*, in particular, we encounter the compelling figure of a grandmother who lost her husband to the atomic bomb that was dropped on Nagasaki in August 1945, who in her old age seems courageously willing to move on

7. See Mustapha Chérif, *Islam and the West: A Conversation with Jacques Derrida*, trans. Teresa Lavender Fagan, with a foreword by Giovanna Borradori (Chicago: University of Chicago Press, 2008), 81.

in peace, in spite of a lifetime's suffering caused by an irreparable personal loss. As is evident in the politics of translation, there is an intimate relation suggested here among victimhood, redemption, and language (as in the notion of heterolingualism, borrowed from Naoki Sakai). If the frail old woman's ability to move on is the result of a letting-go, of what exactly has she let go? How might such letting-go be understood when compared with the transcendent, redemptive impulse of Christian forgiving?

The Far East of the West ◆ The essay "Fateful Attachments" focuses on a little read text by Lao She, an eminent writer who, in the summer of 1966, was hounded into suicide during the Chinese Cultural Revolution. Exploring a minor collector's obsession with objects against a background of competing forces of commodity fetishism, patriotism, and nihilism, this story offers a small preview of China's full-scale embrace of capitalist consumerism in the age of globalization, in the wake of its dogmatist communist era. The essay "Framing the Original" features the story "Lust, Caution" by Eileen Chang, on which the contemporary director Ang Lee's controversial film of the same title is based. Be the experience of captivation through collected objects or illicit sexual partners, Lao She's and Eileen Chang's works demonstrate how the presence of the national enemy, Japan, cuts into such experience with a prohibitive divide—the divide between "us" and "them" that, in accordance with Girard's logic of collective mimetic violence, cannot be crossed. In both stories, the main characters' failure to adhere to this prohibitive divide is fatal, yet it is such failure, caused by the insistence of other forms of fidelity—eccentric, masochistic, unpatriotic, metaphysical—that constitutes the inexhaustible narrative interest in each case.

The presence of Japan in these stories about China during the 1930s and 1940s, together with the films by Kurosawa mentioned earlier, evokes the difficult question of the changing status of the modern Far East in the Western, in particular the U.S. academy after the Second World War. If, as China ascends to the position of an economic superpower, it is no longer possible to approach China as a subaltern nation, by way of a line from a primer such as "I am hungry" (see the opening discussion in "Framing the Original"), how should the clichés, the stereotypes, and the myths as well as the proper scholarly knowledge about the modern Far East be reassembled? How to come to terms with the history of Japan's imperialist aggression against China and other Asian countries, even as we come to terms with the history of U.S. militarism in Japan, the rest of Asia, and elsewhere in the postwar world? And how might this discursive loop of "the Far East of the West," now complicated by various technologies of framing, including but not limited to film, be extendable in an encounter with the cosmopolitan Christian aspirations toward an ethically tolerant world literature, aspirations shared by theorists such as Erich Auerbach, Edward Said, and others in the discipline known as comparative literature (as discussed in the essay "'I insist on the Christian dimension'")?

Scenes of Entanglement, Dreams of Enlightenment

By bringing to the fore uncharted and potential connections among discourses and disciplines, these essays, when read as an assemblage, demonstrate what is perhaps the most obvious sense of entanglement: the sense of a contemporary horizon in which relationships among things, among things and humans, and among different media have become increasingly an issue, in part because of the steady relativization, in modernity, of once-presumed stable categories of origination and causation such as author, owner, actor, mind, intention, and motive. Such relativization of agency is compounded, in the age of digitization, by the rapid disappearance of time-honored intervals, be those intervals temporal, geographical, or personal. (In this respect, the transmediality of the web or the net, so felicitously named, is a nonnegligible operator in our thoroughly entangled daily environment.) As Bruno Latour suggests, many ideas tend to make sense only when they are kept segregated from one another as distinct, specialized domains of knowledge; once they are put side by side, the very sense that they have been making in isolation begins to evaporate.[8] One outcome of entangled relationships, then, would be the fuzzing-up of conventional classificatory categories due to the collapse of neatly maintained epistemic borders. The state of an intermixing, of a diminution of distances among phenomena that used to belong in separate orders of things, necessitates nothing short of a recalculation and redistribution of the normativized intelligibility of the world, includ-

8. See the opening pages of Bruno Latour, *We Have Never Been Modern*, trans. Catherine Porter (Cambridge: Harvard University Press, 1993). These pages notably recall the beginning of Foucault's *The Order of Things: An Archaeology of the Human Sciences*, trans. Alan Sheridan (London: Tavistock, 1970), with the deranged list of classifications from Borges's fantastical Chinese encyclopedia.

ing a realignment of the grids, sets, and slots that allow for such intelligibility in the first place.

Against this epistemic sense of entanglement (that is, of entanglement as a derangement in the organization of knowledge caused by unprecedented adjacency and comparability or parity), scholars of the literary humanities will note that the word "entanglement" also carries the more familiar connotation of being emotionally tied to a person or an object, from whom or from which one cannot extricate oneself. As Gaston Bachelard, writing about the "cogito" of the dreamer, declares, "The night dream (*rêve*) does not belong to us. It is not our possession. With regard to us, it is an abductor, the most disconcerting of abductors: it abducts our being from us."[9] Alternatively, describing how a poet writes about the angles of moldings on a ceiling, Bachelard suggests, "If we 'listen' to the design of things, we encounter an angle, a trap detains the dreamer." He concludes, "Even when the criticisms of reason, the scorn of philosophy and poetic traditions unite to turn us from the poet's labyrinthine dreams, it remains nonetheless true that the poet has made a trap for dreamers out of his poem. / As for me, I let myself be caught. I followed the molding."[10] As is evident in some of these essays, this precarious situation of losing oneself in an other, a situation that at times culminates in self-destruction, is often the stuff of art and fiction. Paradoxically, it is in the realm of such sticky, sentimental entanglements, which can be both blockages and throughways, that the old-fashioned but ever relevant question of art's and fiction's relation to (metanarratives of) social progress tends to linger.

In a nutshell: the democratization of society typically calls for and witnesses a gradual elimination of elitist distinctions (the leveling of categories of knowledge in modernity, as observed by Latour, is a good instance of such democratization); entanglements in the affective or aesthetic form of capture and captivation, on the other hand, tend to be experiences of becoming sensorially *overtaken* and *overpowered* that bear the persistent constitutive markings of hierarchical distinctions (such as domination and submission). When politically progressive intellectuals think the democratization, indistinction, and liberalization of social boundaries, in a kind of conceptual fluidity between art and the every-

9. Gaston Bachelard, *The Poetics of Reverie: Childhood, Language, and the Cosmos*, trans. Daniel Russell (Boston: Beacon Press, 1971), 145.

10. Gaston Bachelard, *The Poetics of Space*, trans. Maria Jolas, foreword by Etienne Gilson (Boston: Beacon Press, 1969), 144–45.

day, between the modern and the primitive, between the West and the non-West, and so forth, they typically run up against some populations' embodied states of captivity, including the intangible but phenomenologically registered effects of enchantment, subordination, unevenness, vulnerability, desperation, servitude, and deprivation of existential autonomy—in short, all the basic issues of terror and freedom, and (often sadomasochistic) pleasure and pain that, in refracted manners, surface in art and fiction. The latter demand engagement, therefore, in their antagonistic materiality as much as in their open-ended ideality.

Entanglements: the linkages and enmeshments that keep things apart; the voidings and uncoverings that hold things together. The essays in this collection can be read as so many scenes of entanglements, in multiple valences of the term "scene"—as situation, dramatization, staging, picture, frame, window, and above all as the assemblage or installation of a critical aperture, a supplemental time-space in which perhaps even the roughest crossings can be approached with a sense of innovation and creativity, and the most painful entanglements understood, if somewhat counterintuitively, as evolving states of freedom.

In Mandarin, the character for "entanglement," 纏 (*chan*), happens to be a homonym with the character for "Buddhist meditation," 禪 (*chan*), a practice, it is believed, that has the potential to lead toward spiritual enlightenment. In the gap between these conceptually disparate yet aurally indistinguishable phenomena, is there some whimsical relation to be dreamt? Some other loop, as yet unthought, that awaits being made intelligible?

1

When Reflexivity Becomes Porn

Mutations of a Modernist Theoretical Practice

> It is . . . better to shift the vocabulary of reflexivity, and to suggest that all acts are not so much reflexive and self-conscious as they are already proto-dramatic.
>
> —FREDRIC JAMESON, *Brecht and Method*

"The Crudest Example"

A striking image appears repeatedly in Walter Benjamin's discussions of Bertolt Brecht's epic theater. Many of us will remember the cultural politics behind Benjamin's reading, a cultural politics that is in line with Brecht's own radical, nonmimetic investments and aimed at destroying the Aristotelian aesthetic illusionism from which Western drama has derived its modus operandi for centuries. To begin the present exploration of reflexivity, let me dwell momentarily on Benjamin's image—a family row—to which he returns several times in his various accounts on Brecht:

> The task of the epic theater, Brecht believes, is not so much to develop actions as to represent conditions. But "represent" does not here signify "reproduce" in the sense used by the theoreticians of Naturalism. Rather, the first point at issue is to *uncover* those conditions. (One could just as well say: to *make them strange* [*verfremden*].) This uncovering (making strange, or alienating) of conditions is brought about by processes being interrupted. Take the crudest example: a family row. Suddenly a stranger comes into the room. The wife is just about to pick up a bronze statuette

> and throw it at the daughter, the father is opening the window to call a policeman. At this moment the stranger appears at the door. "Tableau," as they used to say around 1900. That is to say, the stranger is confronted with a certain set of conditions: troubled faces, open window, a devastated interior. There exists another point of view from which the more usual scenes of bourgeois life do not look so very different from this.[1]

This remarkable passage was first published in German in 1939, but the picture Benjamin depicts, together with the types of agency involved, exemplifies a modernist mode of theoretical thinking that has remained with us to this day.[2]

A number of words in the passage pinpoint the emphases characteristic of such thinking. First and foremost is the rendering of a familiar situation as *strange*: the point of such estrangement is to allow for a rational *uncovering* (*Entdeckung*, usually translated as "discovering") of conditions that have become automatized and thus unnoticeable, even as these conditions precipitate a crisis. Second is the presence of a *stranger*, whose appearance on the scene transforms the dynamics involved in the interior. Positioned in the *doorway*, between the inside and the outside, the stranger turns the happenings inside into an astonishing sight, with bits and pieces of visual information caught as though they were frozen in a still photograph or *tableau*. Third, the setting involved is that of a *family*, in a society where *policemen* may be called to restore domestic order. (!) Fourth, the more usual scenes of the middle class can look similarly astonishing to yet another point of view, that of *the epic dramatist*.[3] Whereas the emotional core of Aristotelian drama depends for its effect on the audience's cathartic identification with the spectacle of

1. Walter Benjamin, "What Is Epic Theatre? [Second version]," *Understanding Brecht*, trans. Anna Bostock, introduction by Stanley Mitchell (London: Verso, 1998), 18–19; emphases Benjamin's. A somewhat different translation by Harry Zohn of the same essay can be found in *Illuminations*, ed. and with an introduction by Hannah Arendt, trans. Harry Zohn (New York: Schocken, 1969), 147–54 (the quoted passage is on 150–51). See also Benjamin's slightly reworded versions of the same scene in "What Is Epic Theatre? [First version]," *Understanding Brecht*, 4–5; "The Author as Producer," *Understanding Brecht*, 100. The original, German versions of these texts can be found in Walter Benjamin, *Versuche über Brecht* (Frankfurt am Main: Suhrkamp Verlag, 1966).

2. Stanley Mitchell: "There are . . . strong indications that the ideas and implications of 'epic theatre' were common to them both [Brecht and Benjamin] before they met" (*Understanding Brecht*, viii).

3. This last point is made clear by Benjamin in "The Author as Producer," *Understanding Brecht*, 100.

closely knit *kinship networks in crisis*, the "crudest example" (*das primitivste Beispiel*) named here to demonstrate how the epic theater works is also that of kinship in crisis—in the updated version of the *middle-class* family in disarray—but kinship now appears for the purpose of soliciting *observation and change* rather than compassion and identification.

Even in a small example such as this, Brecht's well-known principle of alienation (*Verfremdung*), a principle he considers necessary to all understanding,[4] is amply evident. If the hallmarks of the dramatic in the Aristotelian tradition are "the strong centralization of the story, a momentum that [draws] the separate parts into a common relationship," and "[a] particular passion of utterance, a certain emphasis on the clash of forces," in the case of epic theater "*one can as it were take a pair of scissors and cut it [a story] into individual pieces, which remain fully capable of life.*"[5] Accordingly, with the cutting impulse of the epic work, the aim of the alienation effect, produced by artistic means such as acting, is "to make the spectator adopt an attitude of inquiry and criticism in his approach to the incident."[6]

Staging: A Mediatized Theoretical Practice

As has often been noted, Brecht's theory of alienation shares affinities with the notion of art as argued by the Russian Formalist Victor Shklovsky, who in his famous essay of 1917, "Art as Technique," advocated an art of "making strange" (*ostranenie*) as the means to disrupt habitualization and refresh perceptibility of the world. As Shklovsky writes, "Art exists that one may recover the sensation of life; it exists to make one feel things, to make the stone *stony*. . . . The technique of art is to make objects 'unfamiliar,' to make forms difficult, to increase the difficulty and length of perception because the process of perception is an aesthetic end in itself and must be prolonged."[7] Although their political orien-

4. Bertolt Brecht, *Brecht on Theatre: The Development of an Aesthetic*, ed. and trans. John Willett (New York: Hill and Wang, 1964), 71. See also Bertolt Brecht, *The Messingkauf Dialogues*, trans. and ed. John Willet (London: Methuen, 1965).

5. Brecht, *Brecht on Theatre*, 70, my emphasis. Brecht is paraphrasing the epic writer Alexander Döblin's criterion for the epic.

6. Brecht, *Brecht on Theatre*, 136. Fredric Jameson has argued that the term *Verfremdungseffekt* should be translated as "estrangement effect" rather than "alienation effect"; see Jameson, *Brecht and Method* (New York: Verso, 1998), 85–86n13.

7. Victor Shklovsky, "Art as Technique," *Russian Formalist Criticism: Four Essays*,

tations were by no means identical, what Shklovsky and Brecht had in common, it is fair to say, was a predilection for estrangement, and in particular for locating in artistic practice a capacity for defamiliarizing and making conscious conventions (literary, historical, or social) that have become so conventionalized as to be unrecognized.[8] As is well-known, Brecht was also inspired by Chinese acting, which he saw in a performance by the Beijing Opera actor Mei Lan-fang's company in Moscow in 1935. In this non-Western art form, he found affirmation for the rationality of his own theatrical methods, aimed as they were at the nonfusion and nonintegration between audience and actor, between actor and fictional character, and between spectacle and emotion.[9] Elsewhere, Brecht sums up the moral of these methods in this manner: "Non-aristotelian drama would at all costs avoid *bundling* together the events portrayed and presenting them as an inexorable fate, to which the human being is handed over helpless despite the beauty and significance of his reactions; on the contrary, it is precisely this fate that it would study closely, showing it up as of human contriving."[10]

Rather than being the synonym for social isolation, therefore, alienation in Brecht is attributed a specific kind of agency, namely, the ability to *de-sensationalize* the emotional effects of Aristotelian drama by puncturing its well-wrought illusionism, a piece of fiction premised on transcendent unities and coherent relations. As Stanley Mitchell puts it, "To be anti-bourgeois or proletarian was to show how things worked, while they were being shown; to 'lay bare the device' (in the words of the Rus-

---

translated and with an introduction by L. Lemon and M. J. Reis (Lincoln: University of Nebraska Press, 1965), 12, emphasis his.

8. For a helpful, informative discussion of the relationship between Shklovsky's term *ostranenie* and Brecht's term *Verfremdung*, see Stanley Mitchell, "From Shklovsky to Brecht: Some Preliminary Remarks towards a History of the Politicisation of Russian Formalism," *Screen* 15.2 (1974), 74–81. For a discussion that argues the significance of the First World War as the formative background behind Shklovsky's advocacy of estrangement as artistic innovation, see Galin Tihanov, "The Politics of Estrangement: The Case of the Early Shklovsky," *Poetics Today* 26.4 (2005), 665–96.

9. See Brecht, "Alienation Effects in Chinese Acting," *Brecht on Theater*, 91–99. What might not have been apparent to Brecht in his radical mindset, however, was the determinism of hierarchical role classification in traditional Chinese acting: an actor playing a specific type of operatic role is normally expected to perform, for his entire career, only in that role; the role, in other words, typecasts the actor by consigning him to a fixed identity, which defines his lifelong social positioning as well as his part on stage. For this important point, I am indebted to a conversation with Dr. Young-suk Kim on 23 July 2009.

10. Brecht, *Brecht on Theatre*, 87, my emphasis.

sian Formalists). Art should be considered a form of production, not a mystery; the stage should appear like a factory with the machinery fully exposed."[11] Obviously, the stranger in Benjamin's example of the family row is a personification of this kind of interruptive work. Alienation may thus, logically, be equated with the camera, whose capacity as a relatively new scientific and artistic apparatus still held the promise, as of the late 1930s, of a revolutionary aesthetics. The stranger's foreign body, accordingly, is the artificial device—a prosthesis—by which the procedure of estrangement is formalized; such formalization is technologically commensurable with the possibilities brought about by the then-novel medium of film.

What remains provocative, however, is perhaps less the felicitous fit between alienation effects as such and the medium of film—a point that is, in retrospect, easy enough to make—than the unfolding, within Brecht's method, of an ambitious conceptual experiment, one that takes the form of an aggressive stilling: the tableau. Roland Barthes's description of the tableau may be borrowed here for clarification:

> The tableau (pictorial, theatrical, literary) is a pure cut-out segment with clearly defined edges, irreversible and incorruptible; everything that surrounds it is banished into nothingness, remains unnamed, irreversible and incorruptible; while everything that it admits within its field is promoted into essence, into light, into view. . . . The tableau is intellectual, it has something to say (something moral, social) but it also says that it knows how this must be done; it is simultaneously significant and propaedeutical, impressive and reflexive, moving and conscious of the channels of emotion. The epic scene in Brecht, the shot in Eisenstein are so many tableaux.[12]

By the sheer force of its abruptness (to which theorists such as Benjamin would attribute sensations of shock and astonishment), the tableau captures an existing situation at the same time that it renders it fluid and movable, and hence no longer entirely coincident with itself. What makes the tableau in Brecht's method so interesting to consider from today's point of view is not simply that it is cinematic but also, and more impor-

11. Mitchell, "Introduction," *Understanding Brecht*, xv–xvi.

12. Roland Barthes, "Diderot, Brecht, Eisenstein," *Music-Image-Text*, essays selected and translated by Stephen Heath (Glasgow: Fontana/Collins, 1977), 70–71. Jameson writes that Barthes's Brechtian origins have often been neglected and that his classic *Mythologies* paved the way for the success of the estrangement or alienation effect in French theory (poststructuralism); see Jameson, *Brecht and Method*, 38, 40, 41, 49–51, 172–73.

tant, that it works by incorporating the technicality of a newer medium into an older one. The techniques of film—in particular the principle of montage, as Benjamin stresses—are used by Brecht to form a vision of theatrical productivity that is simultaneously a demand for thinking, a demand that occurs in the interstice between (two or more) different media. This is how I would define reflexivity in this context: as it appears in Brecht's method, reflexivity is a conscious form of staging (what Jameson, as cited in the epigraph, calls a "proto-dramatic" act),[13] which materializes as an intermedial event, in ways that far exceed the genre of drama.

Although Benjamin is ostensibly discussing the specifics of Brecht's epic theater, then, he is really exploring a larger, more difficult aesthetic question: How does thought—and more precisely, thought's critical self-consciousness—emerge, and how can such emergence be grasped, in ways that do not simply collapse back into the ruts of idealism? To this extent, it is possible to see epic theater as a medium (or more precisely, an intermedium) designed for the articulation of epistemic thresholds and hence, utopically, for the mobilization of thought away from mentation's tendency toward transcendence. As the process in which thought becomes aware of its own activity, reflexivity takes place, in Brecht's hands, in concretely mediatized terms—indeed, as an intermediatized staging. Going further still, we might argue that the Brechtian imprint, which eventually found its way into studies of literature and art as well as theater, film, and performance in a broad sense, has to do with turning reflexivity itself into a perceptible object. In such a process of objectification, the abstract operation of thinking, rather than being seamlessly woven into the fabric of the production (as the actant that motivates what happens but remains itself invisible), is made to assume protruding forms, most noticeably as gests or gestures but also as titles, scenes, captions, posters, parables, verses, songs, and other visible and perceptible bits and pieces.[14] *Thought, in other words, has been made ex-plicit through*

13. Fredric Jameson, *Brecht and Method*, 83.

14. As is well-known, the word *gestus*, translated into English as "gest," is an important part of Brecht's theory and method. In the notes he provides, the translator John Willet writes that *gestus* means "both gist and gesture; an attitude or a single aspect of an attitude, expressible in words or actions" (*Brecht on Theatre*, 42). For Brecht's own elaborations, see *Brecht on Theatre*, in particular 42, 86, 104–105, 198–201. For a wide-ranging discussion of *gestus* not only in Brecht's work but also in reference to major literary-historical, theatrical, and philosophical concepts, see Jameson, *Brecht and Method*, 89–130. Jameson writes that "*gestus* is the operator of an estrangement-effect in its own right" (99).

staging: rather than drawing things into itself by unifying them, it splits them up, moves them apart, and gives them independence, in a series of sensuous ex-plications (out-foldings).

It is also possible to state all this in the language of space, and argue that the special theoretical or speculative event embedded in Benjamin's description of the epic theater is that of (re)conceptualization through spatialization. Space is, in this instance, not a matter of an already existent physical environment but rather an insertion, into a continuum, of an interval, gap, and area of noncoincidence, such as the deliberate implantation of an outsider perspective in a familiar or familial interior. Space is thus a *phenomenological field* in which a movement of doubling-cum-dis-alignment may occur, in turn enabling the epistemic limit of an existing set of conditions to become palpably perceptible—and marked off in their historical particularity. Defined in this manner, the epic theater anticipates much of the way conceptual art continues to work in our contemporary contexts. The practice of installation art, for instance, is a good case in point. Often the result of an intermixing of things—an intermixing that comprises uncertainty of origination, disparateness of collected objects, politics of display, and diversity of reception—installation art, it may be said, exhibits the (otherwise imperceptible) noncongruities that, when apprehended phenomenologically, serve as the means to draw attention to reflexivity as an ongoing process. And insofar as space signifies a discursive-relational production or reception of knowledge, the epic theater also anticipates much of poststructuralism's way of deconstructing epistemic boundaries.[15]

Reflexivity, Artistic Form, and the Senses

If what we call "theory" in the late twentieth century is inextricably bound up with the ramifications of reflexivity, then the protrusion or ex-plication of thought in sensuous forms and the practice of reconceptualization through spatialization may well be theory's predominant maneuvers. To that extent, we can begin to understand Benjamin's statement that "Brecht has attempted to make the thinking man, or indeed

15. In the context of French philosophy and literature, the phenomenological works on space and knowledge production by Maurice Blanchot, Gaston Bachelard, Maurice Merleau-Ponty, and the early Michel Foucault would be obvious interlocutors here. A fully fledged exploration of this complex linkage will need to be deferred until another occasion.

the wise man, into an actual dramatic hero. And it is from this point of view that his theatre may be defined as epic. . . . Following Brecht's line of thought, one might even arrive at the proposition that it is the wise man who . . . is the perfect empty stage [*den vollkommenen Schauplatz*] [on which the contradictions of our society are acted out]."[16] This conscious attempt to mediatize reflexivity as a thinking that is sensuous but unsensational, and that appears as a rational rather than tragic performance, is one of the most widely adopted, if largely unacknowledged, of Brecht's legacies. For exactly that reason, Brecht's method has not only been influential in the study of drama proper but, arguably, even more so in transdisciplinary theoretical practice on the left. In his magisterial account of Brecht's continuing relevance and contemporaneity, Fredric Jameson offers an invigorating formulation of this method:

> It is tempting to suggest that it is precisely Brecht's well-known slyness that is his method, and even his dialectic: the inversion of the hierarchies of a problem, major premiss passing to minor, absolute to relative, form to content, and vice versa—these are all operations whereby the dilemma in question is turned inside out, and an unexpected unforeseeable line of attack opens up that leads neither into the dead end of the unresolvable nor into the banality of stereotypical doxa on logical non-contradiction.[17]

Any examination of theory after the heyday of theory must, I believe, take the legacy of this method into account.

Consider, for instance, the trend-setting intervention in ideology made by Louis Althusser in the 1960s and 1970s, in particular the oft-cited essay "Ideology and Ideological State Apparatuses." Although Althusser's formulation of ideology, as the representation of the imaginary relationship of individuals to their real conditions of existence,[18] was inspired by Lacan's psychoanalytic writings on subjectivity, his approach to art bears unmistakable marks of a Brechtian tactic of reading. In essays such as "The 'Piccolo Teatro': Bertolazzi and Brecht," "A Letter on Art in Reply to André Daspre," and "Cremonini, Painter of the Abstract,"[19] Althusser implements the equivalent of the alienation effect when he invokes an

16. Benjamin, *Understanding Brecht*, 17.

17. Jameson, *Brecht and Method*, 25.

18. Louis Althusser, *Lenin and Philosophy and Other Essays*, trans. Ben Brewster (London: Monthly Review Press, 1971), 162.

19. The first two essays are found in Althusser, *Lenin and Philosophy*, 221–27 and 229–42; the third essay is found in Louis Althusser, *For Marx*, trans. Ben Brewster (London: New Left Books, 1977), 129–51.

internal distance or dissociation that gives art (such as theater, painting, and literature) a privileged relationship to ideology, a relationship that is yet distinct from scientific knowledge.

Whereas Althusser's analysis of ideology underscores how various institutional agencies (such as the church, the school, the police, and so forth) stabilize and perpetuate the functioning of bourgeois society by recruiting (in his words, interpellating) the individual subject into a conforming and rewarding pattern of behavior, in his approach to artistic media Althusser suggests a rather different set of procedures at work. Unlike the situation in which an individual is interpellated by ideological state apparatuses, in the case of art, reflexivity is possible through a space opening from within the artwork: the function of art, Althusser writes, is "to make *visible* (*donner à voir*), by establishing a distance from it, the reality of the existing ideology (of any one of its forms)."[20] The spectator, in other words, is not solicited by art in the same way the subject is interpellated by ideology. Instead, according to Althusser, *some* art provides a potentiality for something similar to Brecht's alienation, the point of which, he argues, is to demystify the identification model of consciousness, so that the spectator, placed at a distance from the performance, would have to become "an actor who would complete the unfinished play, but in real life."[21] Just as the stranger's entry (in Benjamin's description of the family row) introduces a break within the bourgeois family's dynamics, so does a painter such as Cremonini remove, in a process that Althusser calls *determinate deformation*, all the coherent expression of individuality and subjectivity from human faces that is part of a mystifying, ideological function of humanistic art. Such deformation means that spectators cannot simply recognize themselves in his pictures, and only thus (in the negative space of nonrecognition) come to know themselves.[22]

In the realm of literature, Pierre Macherey offers a comparable endeavor to articulate a staged reflexivity to the work of literary criticism. Macherey's analysis is marked by his insistence that "the emergence of thought institutes a certain distance and separation,"[23] and that such distance and separation is a way to reconceptualize the utterances of narrative fiction. Thus literary criticism, in which thought about literature

20. Althusser, "Cremonini," 241–42.

21. Althusser, "Bertolazzi and Brecht," 146.

22. Althusser, "Cremonini," 238–40.

23. Pierre Macherey, *A Theory of Literary Production*, trans. Geoffrey Wall (London: Routledge and Kegan Paul, 1978), 6.

emerges, is an autonomous discourse that "brings out a *difference* within the work by demonstrating that it is *other than it is*."[24] In a homologous fashion, the literary text itself provides an internal distance from ideology: rather than being a mimetic reproduction or reflection of a preexisting, ideological reality, the literary text is where contradictory social relations confront one another, and where ideology is made visible by refraction, as though in a broken mirror (Macherey's major example being the work of Leo Tolstoy).[25] Notably, Macherey too invokes "Brecht's notion of a dialectic of the theatre" to elaborate the phenomenon of doubling, slippage, and noncoincidence that constitutes the possibility of a politicized reception.[26] In such reception, both the literary text and literary criticism are made part of a process of discursive production, which takes place through the staging of parallel but nonintegrated relations.

In British feminist film studies of the 1970s, the work of the theorist Laura Mulvey similarly seeks to unplug the illusion of the dominant, classical narrative cinema by revealing its ideological—that is, patriarchal—underpinnings.[27] Mulvey's influence on Anglo-American film studies is too well-known to require repeating, but what may be said in the current context is that the feminist insistence on dislocating classical film narrative should also be seen as part of a collective theoretical effort, enabled by Brechtian alienation, to pry open existing epistemic foreclosures. A deliberate estrangement of women's traditional role as beautiful objects, together with an elaboration of women spectators as thinking subjects, becomes for Mulvey and subsequent generations of feminist critics a means of staging—and hence undercutting—the previously unproblematized vision constructed in accordance with masculinist interests.

These few examples have been brought up in an admittedly schematic fashion, but they suffice to help establish two points. First, if alienation may be understood as a demand to think in the terms I have outlined, it seems fair to conclude that much of contemporary theory has been a systemic response to, and a continued enactment of, the key Brechtian legacy. It is, however, when the demand to think is entangled with specific

24. Macherey, *A Theory of Literary Production*, 7.

25. See the chapter "Lenin, Critic of Tolstoy," *A Theory of Literary Production*, 105–35.

26. Macherey, *A Theory of Literary Production*, 129.

27. Laura Mulvey, "Visual Pleasure and Narrative Cinema," *Movies and Methods*, vol. 2, ed. Bill Nichols (Berkeley: University of California Press, 1985), 303–15. The essay was originally published in *Screen* 16.3 (1975).

artistic media—as for instance, theater, painting, literature, or film—that things become the most challenging: How is reflexivity possible when a particular form is involved, or, to put it somewhat differently, how does thought's self-awareness (or self-distancing) take shape in conjunction with prescribed formal parameters? Staging, understood as a phenomenological rather than simply empirical process, is, I propose, one way in which these questions have been answered. Importantly, the epistemic space that is opened up from within an aesthetic spectacle, the space in which reflexivity can be staged, is also a steadily widening gap—and noncorrespondence—between the presence of a work as such and the way "it" may be activated in reception. Precisely on account of its status as phenomenon rather than as actuality, therefore, staging remains an abstract operation. And it is such abstractness, which is also a quality of incompleteness and openness, that lends staging its political potential. At the same time that it signifies the mediatization of reflexivity, staging shows theoretical practice to be *in process*.

Second, in Brecht's method, the leaning toward science and experimentation (in contrast to the fixity and fossilization of convention) goes hand in hand with the suspension, if not evacuation, of empathetic identification in response to artistic representation. This move, which may be called a move to de-sensationalize, is traceable in the analyses of drama, painting, literature, and film as undertaken by theorists such as Althusser, Macherey, and Mulvey. Even though their objects of inquiry remain sensuous, the sense that has become dominant as a result of the Brechtian way of mediatizing reflexivity is rationality—that is to say, the capacity for cool-headed observation, experiment, pedagogy, didacticism, and wisdom.[28] This leaves a fraught issue unresolved: What exactly is the status of the senses in relation to mediatized reflexivity? Walter Benjamin was still writing at a time when relaxation and distraction could be embraced as emancipatory sense modalities, as opposed to the contemplation and absorption necessitated by traditional, bourgeois cultural forms such as the novel and painting. But as alienation is followed to its logical conclusion, sensuous pleasure in the form of emotional involvement becomes, increasingly, politically suspect. The heightened alarm of mystification and delusion (that is, false consciousness) sounded around (the yielding to) aesthetic illusionism means that the Brechtian legacy, in spite of Brecht's own often entertaining, sensuously

28. This point is thoroughly explored by Mitchell, "Introduction," *Understanding Brecht*, as well as by Benjamin.

pleasing stage productions, has led to the prevalence of a puritanist austerity in certain theoretical practices. As Mulvey sums it up revealingly in her landmark essay, "It is said that analysing pleasure, or beauty, destroys it. That is the intention of this article."[29]

These two intimately linked dimensions in the entanglement of reflexivity and artistic media—the phenomenon of staging and the increasing *disconnect between production and receptivity*, on the one hand, and on the other, the residual ineluctability of the senses and with it, *the unresolved question of pleasure*—are among the difficult philosophical issues confronting us in the afterlife of theory. How viable might staging remain as a theoretical practice? How might the senses be (re)distributed after the critical censuring of illusionism, identification, empathy, and other sensuous pleasures?[30]

By displacing the gravitational pull of dramatization onto the spectator as a thinking person, the Brechtian method has in effect dethroned the transcendent mind and distributed or divided it up among the ordinary masses. The point of the alienation effect is to politicize reflexivity by making it *vulgar*: thought is no longer deep and refined but crude; it sticks out where you least expect it to; it takes on unsubtle, obtrusive shapes, like the petty, biased habits and behaviors of the uneducated classes (a good example: Brecht's Mother Courage). At the same time, the agency that accompanies this vulgarization of reflexivity—the ability or potentiality to think otherwise, to stage the familiar through an alternative, phenomenological space, to produce the new through multiplication into segments and component parts—is increasingly faced with a certain impasse, namely, its own im-plication (in-folding), through the rational processes of distribution and division, in the endless fragmentation and reification of thought.[31]

If reflexivity was, once upon a time, associated with freedom (think of the trajectory imagined by Hegel for the Western historical Spirit), in the days of hypermediatization it seems rather caught between becoming impotent under circumstances of ubiquitous technological surveillance, and having to let the practice of staging multiply ad infinitum (in the

29. Mulvey, "Visual Pleasure and Narrative Cinema," 306.

30. I take the notion of the distribution of the senses from Jacques Rancière; see *The Politics of Aesthetics: The Distribution of the Sensible*, trans. with an introduction by Gabriel Rockhill (London: Continuum, 2004), 7–45.

31. See Jameson, *Brecht and Method*, 43–51, for a lucid discussion of the significance of reification in Marxist thought and in Brecht's dramatic and representational method.

sense of an infinite reiteration of the breaking-up of mediatized spectacles into ever newer units). Staging defined in these terms now occurs not only in the form of the arrested tableau, collage, montage, conceptual art, installation art, and so forth but also in the form of various screening and framing possibilities, produced with sophisticated apparatuses and circulated everywhere as the daily fare of social interaction (consider the framing and cropping techniques of Photoshop, for instance, or the multitasking capabilities of a device like the iPhone).

In the days of proliferating, hypermediatized screens and frames, is staging, which belongs to an older, modernist way of objectifying reflexivity, still meaningful? And even if it is, has not staging lost its once utopic function now that it seems to have been thoroughly assimilated into facets of what Guy Debord has famously named the society of the spectacle,[32] from museum art exhibits to television talent shows, to real estate marketing strategies? In terms of the senses, what has reflexivity, once staged and mediatized in the form of estranged thought and roughened perception, become in the new regime of the abstract touch—the pinch, the click, the tap, the slide, and the finger swipe, all characteristic of digital technologies? Has not the speed and smoothness, the so-called flow, of the microcomputer, so ostentatiously always already reflexive in its basic modes of operation, paradoxically reintroduced a sense of illusionism and automatism, exactly the kind of sensation that the earlier generations of media theorists such as Brecht and Benjamin were keen on dispelling?

Pornographic Intensities

Recall now how Benjamin describes the resilience of the Brechtian dramatic scene: "It can happen this way, but it can also happen quite a different way."[33] The fundamentally empty, because open, nature of Brecht's epic theater (as Benjamin writes, the wise man is a perfect empty stage) suggests that the most radical gestures of change, precisely because they are so radical, *can* turn into their opposites. Herein lies the danger of reversibility, whereby a different kind of revolution—capitalist, rather than

32. Guy Debord, *Society of the Spectacle*, ed. and trans. Donald Nicholson-Smith (New York: Zone Books, 1994). Debord's book was first published in the 1960s. By "spectacle" Debord means not a collection of images but a situation in which relations among people are mediated by images.

33. Benjamin, "What Is Epic Theatre? [First version]," *Understanding Brecht*, 8.

socialist—can overtake the global scene with an invincible logic of exchange and substitution. Benjamin's "this way, [or] . . . a different way" is, in this light, fully montage-able as a slogan for the consumer's choice, with as many spaces, breaks, gaps, and variations introduced into a previously simple and restricted process. Nowadays, to satisfy even our most basic daily needs—think of fluids, for instance—there is often a limitless spectrum of options.

Beyond the specter of capitalist consumerism, there is a larger epistemic conundrum underlying the mediatization of reflexivity through estrangement and alienation. To see this, we need to return briefly to the notion introduced by Shklovsky alongside that of art as device—the notion of laying bare. While "art as device" defamiliarizes an object in such a way as to make us notice its perceptible quality (such as the stoniness of a stone), "laying bare" suggests, rather, a return to an original condition lying behind a set of numbing habits or automatized conventions—an original condition, that is, of *unadorned nakedness*. This is evident in Shklovsky's emphasis on the result of seeing something "for the first time": "Tolstoy makes the familiar seem strange by not naming the familiar object. He describes an object as if he were seeing it for the first time, an event as if it were happening for the first time."[34] "The purpose of imagery in erotic art can be studied even more accurately; an erotic object is usually presented as if it were seen for the first time."[35] Inscribed in Shklovsky's aesthetics of renovation and renewal is thus, ironically, a preoccupation with the old and the timeless (what has, regrettably, been veiled or fogged up). With defamiliarization defined as laying bare, it may be argued, comes the nostalgic longing for an implicit authentic norm, a "first time" (both at the level of objects and at the level of perception) to which artists awake us from the mechanicity and repetitiveness of routine. As Galin Tihanov writes, "Any successful act of estrangement . . . rests on a paradox: the end product is meant as a piece of innovation—arrived at through various artistic devices—that serves, however, to revive and make more palpable the old (and constant) substance of things. To conduct the procedure of estrangement properly and to the desired end means to bring the old to the fore in and through the new, thus reasserting what is presumed to be the object's timeless substance."[36]

34. Shklovsky, "Art as Technique," 13.
35. Shklovsky, "Art as Technique," 18.
36. Tihanov, "The Politics of Estrangement," 686.

Critics who have explored the connections between Shklovsky and Brecht tend to see Shklovsky's concept of making strange as lacking in the dialogical possibility, embedded in the spectator's reaction, of historical change that is offered by Brecht's alienation effect.[37] Although I share this view, a word in Benjamin's description of the family row—"uncovering" or "discovering" (*Entdeckung*)—gives me pause. The point is not to debate the instabilities of translingual traffic (in this case, among Russian, German, and English) but rather to heed a predicament typical of the modernist gesture of making present and making new.[38] Like the metaphor of laying bare, the rhetoric of uncovering underlying conditions is intended to call attention to what has become unthinking (that is, mindless), but when examined closely, the potential for change (supposedly an endless and unpredictable process), attributed in this instance to art, is undergirded by an opposite kind of wish, the wish to recuperate an as yet untouched, primitive state. This wish, which is in concert with the violence of display and exposure—indeed, with display and exposure as necessary forms of violation—may be termed pornographic.

What is at stake, in the imagined and (in some cases) literal acts of uncovering, taking things off, minimizing, dispensing with ornamentation, and so forth that are typical of modernist artistic practices, is a vision of purification that seeks to revive a certain before—before the onset of corruption, before the loss of innocence. To convey the moral severity of such a vision, some have found it necessary to borrow the licentious moves of a striptease. Noteworthy examples include André Bazin's reading of the photographic image (whose "aesthetic qualities . . . are to be sought in its power to lay bare the realities," as the cinematic lens strips from the object "that spiritual dust and grime with which my eyes have covered it" and lets it be seen "in all its virginal purity"), and Jacques Derrida's reading of Antonin Artaud's theater of cruelty (which, in Derrida's description, "lays bare the flesh of the word, lays bare the word's sonority, intonation, intensity—the shout that the articulations

37. See Tihanov, "The Politics of Estrangement," 686–91 for a discussion of how Brecht and Herbert Marcuse assessed and critiqued Shklovsky's aesthetic notion of estrangement as insufficient for coping with reification and alienation, which are complex and durable products of history.

38. Paul de Man's deconstructive analysis of modernity's desire for a new origin—a desire that is haunted by history—remains instructive at this juncture. See de Man, "Literary History and Literary Modernity," *Blindness and Insight: Essays in the Rhetoric of Contemporary Criticism*, 2nd edition, revised, introduction by Wlad Godzich (Minneapolis: University of Minnesota Press, 1983), 142–65.

of language and logic have not yet entirely frozen, that is, the aspect of oppressed gesture which remains in all speech").[39]

Such a tendency toward the pornographic seems at first quite at odds with the rational and experimental tone toward the production of thought that was intended by Brecht and Benjamin. Only when one ponders the evocative set of associations that runs from cruelty (and violence) to crudeness and primitiveness (as in Brecht's crude thinking [*plumpes Denken*] and Benjamin's "crude" or "primitive" example of the family row), and, more recently, to what is termed "bare life," whose somber transhistorical reality the philosopher Giorgio Agamben seeks to restore to global biopolitics[40]—only then does the close affinity between pornography's denuding conventions and the logic of mediatized reflexivity become evident.

Could this be a reason the staging of reflexivity tends, in the hands of some contemporary media artists, to become synonymous with the violence of medial exhibitionism?

As a brief example, consider the work of the Austrian film director Michael Haneke, whose self-conscious staging of mediality is often simultaneously a staging of physical violence. In films such as *Benny's Video* (1992) and *Funny Games* (1997), Haneke offers chilling portrayals of German-speaking bourgeois society in the most ordinary and peaceful settings. In *Benny's Video*, a teenager, obsessed with computers, invites a girl home to watch videos and ends up killing her and capturing the incident on camera. His parents, on discovering the crime, collaborate in covering it up so as to preserve the decorum of the status quo, only to find themselves being reported to the authorities by their son, who has secretly taped their private conversations in which they reveal their culpability. In *Funny Games*, soon after a nuclear family arrives at its vacation home in an upscale countryside neighborhood, two polite male adolescents, claiming to be houseguests at a neighbor's, show up to borrow some eggs. The incident quickly spirals into a succession of abusive acts inflicted on the family, whose members are trapped and tortured until they die. The two villains then move on to their next set of targets, another family on vacation. In both films, there is a conspicuous play

39. André Bazin, "The Ontology of the Photographic Image," *What Is Cinema?*, vol. 1, trans. Hugh Gray (Berkeley: University of California Press, 1967), 15; Jacques Derrida, *Writing and Difference*, trans. with an introduction and additional notes by Alan Bass (Chicago: University of Chicago Press, 1978), 240.

40. Giorgio Agamben, *Homo Sacer: Sovereign Power and Bare Life*, trans. Daniel Heller-Roazen (Stanford: Stanford University Press, 1998).

on mediality, either involving the use of machines such as video cameras, computers, tape recorders, and the like, or, as in the case of *Funny Games,* a literal rewinding of moments of the film itself in the midst of the atrocities befalling the family.

Such medially self-referential citations are reminders of how contemporary life is saturated with media technology. Rather than staging a "tableau" that invites the audience to become actors and complete the action in real life (as Althusser suggests), however, Haneke's films seem more intent on simply exhibiting the extreme, yet pointless, nature of physical as well as ideological malice. This conjunction of the extreme and the pointless is fetishized precisely through its equation with reflexivity itself, as though self-conscious critical thought must now be staged in such a manner as to stretch the mediality of the medium to its limits—*by ripping off the medium's clothes, as it were.* To my mind, it is such insistent, aggressive gestures of laying bare or uncovering—in what may be termed an (anti-) aesthetics of subtraction—that put Haneke in the lineage of Shklovsky and Brecht, in ways that magnify the pornographic reasoning of modernist mediatized reflexivity in general. As is indicated by the title of Haneke's widely acclaimed film *Caché* (2005), what needs to be laid bare or uncovered is none other than a history of violence, the degree-zero reality or ground that is intimated as "hidden" because it has been repressed. (Hidden-ness and repression are also featured in Haneke's more recent film *White Ribbon* [2009], set in early twentieth-century Germany before the official rise of Nazism.) Art-as-thought is still, or so we are led to believe, a matter of stripping things naked so as to reveal the deep dark secrets lurking underneath. But even such extreme revelations may be pointless, the films seem to say, for they may well mean *nothing* to those who are watching.

With an intellectual director like Haneke, thus, the relationship of reflexivity to mediatization has become thoroughly tormented. As thought can no longer proceed without mediatization and yet mediatization cannot be trusted, an obsessive-compulsive dependency on media technologies now goes hand in hand with what comes across as a frigid human environment in Haneke's stories, in which interpersonal relations are often characterized by suspicion, cynicism, noncommunication, and lack of compassion. In *Benny's Video* and *Funny Games,* the indifference shown by the adolescent protagonists—upper middle-class youths, human society's potential future leaders—to the pain and injury experienced by other people (be they the nearest kin or anonymous strangers) underscores an additional dimension to the pornographic, namely, spectatorial apathy in face of representations of extreme cruelty and suffering.[41] Porn, in other words, has to do not only with the obscenity of laying or being laid bare; it also has to do with the seemingly "normal," yet in fact shocking, disconnect between spectacle and spectatorship, between the extreme staging of trauma and the nonchalance of audience reaction.

But isn't such a disconnect precisely the point of the Brechtian project of estrangement, designed as it was to make us suspend embodied fellow feelings such as pity and fear, and unlearn the identificatory habits that typically accompany catharsis?

As dramatized in Haneke's stylistically "cool" works, such nonaffect (or affect of nonresponse) is symptomatic of one dominant direction in which reflexivity as a modernist theoretical practice has mutated in postmodernity from its earlier and more optimistically utopian cast. Does this mutation signal the exhaustion, as well as perfection, of the performativity of estrangement-as-laying-bare? It remains to be seen whether and how the philosophical capaciousness and playful adaptability of this performativity, such as have been associated with the work of Brecht, can find some means of reasserting themselves. This would be a formidable task, as the opponent is an ever pervasive metaphysical yearning for the purity of the void, a purity that is, perhaps, the ultimate lure of porn.

41. For an informative discussion of the widespread use of the term "pornography," since the mid-twentieth century, to mark the increasing loss of empathy among audiences toward representations of other people's suffering, see Carolyn J. Dean, "Empathy, Pornography, and Suffering," *differences* 14.1 (2003): 88–124.

2

On Captivation

A Remainder from the "Indistinction of Art and Nonart"

(written with Julian Rohrhuber)

What is a border or boundary? It is, first of all, the line that is drawn, let us call it its "ridge"; its significance is one of definition. This boundary, this line, always has two sides. If I trace around me a closed contour, I keep myself in and defend myself against. One side of the line protects me and the other side excludes others.—MICHEL SERRES,
"The Geometry of the Incommunicable: Madness"

The greater part of "thinking" consists of abductions of one kind or another.—ALFRED GELL, *Art and Agency: An Anthropological Theory*

[A] *charnière* . . . This word can be taken in the technical or anatomical sense of a central or cardinal articulation, a hinge pin . . . or pivot. A *charnière* or hinge is an axial device that enables the circuit, the trope, or the movement of rotation. But one might also dream a bit in the vicinity of its homonym, that is, in line with this other *artifact* that the code of falconry also calls a *charnière*, the place where the hunter attracts the bird by laying out the flesh of a lure.
—JACQUES DERRIDA, "'To Do Justice to Freud':
The History of Madness in the Age of Psychoanalysis"

The Question of Boundaries in Relation to Art

Much of contemporary French thought is preoccupied with boundaries. The first and last epigraphs, taken respectively from Michel Serres's and Jacques Derrida's responses to Michel Foucault's first major work, *Folie et déraison: Histoire de la folie dans l'age classique* (*History of Madness*),[1] are but two instances of a vast reserve of critical deliberations on this elusive topic, which has had enormous impact on the conceptualizations of knowledge production and circulation worldwide. Few discussions of knowledge production and circulation today can proceed without some attempt at addressing boundaries, if only (as is often the case) to reestablish and reinforce them.

Jacques Rancière's work may be approached similarly in light of these contemporary philosophical concerns with boundaries. One of Rancière's compelling notions about aesthetics, for instance, is that genuine art is what indistinguishes art and nonart: in such capacity for indistinction lies art's transformative power and potential to bring about a new humanity.[2] In many ways, the extensive spectrum of modern and postmodern art—from surrealism and cubism to pop art, documentaries, performance art, and the contemporary new media installations, reenactments, and exhibits using human bodies as well as everyday objects—attests to this ongoing process of the morphing—and transgression—of proper artistic boundaries.[3] A classic example of such morph-

1. The full source citations are Michel Serres, "The Geometry of the Incommunicable: Madness," in *Foucault and His Interlocutors*, ed. and intro. Arnold Davidson (Chicago: University of Chicago Press, 1997), 42, and Jacques Derrida, "'To Do Justice to Freud': The History of Madness in the Age of Psychoanalysis," in *Foucault and His Interlocutors*, 64.

2. See in particular Jacques Rancière, "The Distribution of the Sensible," *The Politics of Aesthetics: The Distribution of the Sensible*, trans. and with an introduction by Gabriel Rockhill (London: Continuum, 2004); "Politics and Aesthetics: An Interview" (conducted in 2002), trans. Forbes Morlock, introduction by Peter Hallward, *Angelaki: Journal of the Theoretical Humanities* 8.2 (2003), 191–211; "Problems and Transformations in Critical Art/2004," trans. Claire Bishop, assisted by Pablo Lafuente, *Participation* (Documents of Contemporary Art Series), ed. Claire Bishop (Cambridge, Mass.: MIT Press, 2006), 83–93; "A Few Remarks on the Method of Jacques Rancière," *Parallax* 15.3 (2009): 114–23.

3. For a helpful introduction to conceptual art, see the essay "Ideas, Systems, Processes," *Conceptual Art*, ed. Daniel Marzona and Uta Grosenick (Köln: Taschen, 2005), 6–25. For an influential discussion, see also Nicolas Bourriaud, *Relational Aesthetics*, trans. Simon Pleasance and Fronza Woods with the participation of Mathieu Copeland (Dijon: Les presses du réel, 2002).

ing and transgression, Marcel Duchamp's "art" exhibit *Fountain*, we remember, features the mundane object of a urinal. (Indeed, the *tout-fait* or readymade, as exemplified by the bottle dryer, the bicycle wheel, the comb, the coat rack, and other found objects, is Duchamp's consciously good-humored, avant-garde way of experimenting with boundaries, both in the sense of what may function as art and in the sense of how art may remain ambiguous.) Whereas in an earlier moment, theorists were fascinated with such boundary mutation in terms of the evolution in technology and belief (one thinks, for instance, of Walter Benjamin's oft-cited artwork essay of 1936, with its description of the interruption and decline of the aura—the magical, religious quality of the artwork bound to location and beholden at a distance—in the secular age of reproducible photographic and filmic images),[4] Rancière's investment in the indistinction of art and nonart is consistent with his attempt to find a critical idiom that would represent the excluded others on the other side of the line, as alluded to by Serres, above—an attempt that is traceable to Rancière's break from Louis Althusser, his teacher, of whom he published a spectacular critique (*La Leçon d'Althusser*) in 1974.[5]

For many French-speaking intellectuals after the Second World War, language has served as the privileged setting for the confrontations between various kinds of subjects (poets, leftist philosophers, workers, women, mental patients, and colonized people), on the one hand, and, on the other, reason's claim to sovereignty: language is where the often perilous crossings of epistemic thresholds leave their material traces. Likewise may Rancière's rejection of Althusser be described as a relation to language, in the sense that it is a rejection not only of the master himself but also of the masterly pose (or dogmatism) of the language of theory and the language of institutionalized knowledge. Not surprisingly, one of the major influences on Rancière is Foucault's *The Archaeology of Knowledge*.[6] Foucault's explorations of the subterranean discursive strata

4. Walter Benjamin, "The Work of Art in the Age of Mechanical Reproduction," in *Illuminations*, ed. with an intro. Hannah Arendt, trans. Harry Zohn (New York: Schocken, 1969), 217–51.

5. See Rancière's account of his relations with Althusser in "Politics and Aesthetics," 194–96; see also Peter Hallward's introduction to the same interview, 191.

6. "If, among the thinkers of my generation, there was one I was quite close to at one point, it was Foucault. Something of Foucault's archaeological project—the will to think the conditions of possibility of such and such a form of statement or such and such an object's constitution—has stuck with me" (Rancière, "Politics and Aesthetics," 208–9). See also Rancière's description, in Foucauldian terms, of how he approached the question of the worker in Marxism after 1968: "Being a

that underlie knowledge formation may, in retrospect, be understood as a type of research into what Rancière terms the silent witnesses of history, witnesses whose anonymity and wordless speech constitute a form of participation and partaking (in the French, *partage*, sharing). As in his work on madness, Foucault's special imprint here is that of an invitation to destabilize and declassify thought from within the apparatuses and institutions that give thought its constraining positivity and normativity. As Foucault puts it, "It is reflection, the act of consciousness, the elucidation of what is silent, language restored to what is mute, the illumination of the element of darkness that cuts man off from himself, the reanimation of the inert—it is all this and this alone that constituted the content and form of the ethical [in Western thought in modernity]."[7] Rancière's attention to the questions of equality, justice, disagreement, and commonality involved in the writing of history is recognizably akin to Foucault's politics and ethics;[8] likewise, we may surmise, is his argument about the indistinction of art and nonart, which is historically specific and inextricable from the emergence of such indistinction in modern French art and literature. Borrowing from Rancière's description of his own method, we may say that art, as much as democracy, is for him "characterized by the fact of determining a specific experience without defining any border separating art from non-art." What interests him about any historical relation, including that pertaining to art, is "the polemical nature that makes it an object of thinking, that situates it in a field of tensions," and the possibility of constructing from the situation "a dramaturgy of politics, conceived out of its limits."[9] (Note that the metaphor of staging is found in many of Rancière's discussions.)

'worker' wasn't in the first instance a condition reflected in forms of consciousness or action; it was a form of symbolisation, the arrangement of a certain set of statements or utterances. I became interested in reconstituting the world that made these utterances [énonciations] possible" ("Politics and Aesthetics," 196).

7. Michel Foucault, *The Order of Things: An Archaeology of the Human Sciences*, trans. Alan Sheridan (London: Tavistock, 1970), 328.

8. See the many discussions in Rancière's works, such as *The Ignorant Schoolmaster: Five Lessons in Intellectual Emancipation*, trans. and with an introduction by Kristin Ross (Stanford: Stanford University Press, 1991); *The Names of History: on the Poetics of Knowledge*, trans. Hassan Melehy, foreword by Hayden White (Minneapolis: University of Minnesota Press, 1994); *Disagreement: Politics and Philosophy*, trans. Julie Rose (Minneapolis: University of Minnesota Press, 1998); *The Philosopher and His Poor*, ed. Andrew Parker, trans. Andrew Parker, Corinne Oster, and John Drury (Durham: Duke University Press, 2004).

9. Rancière, "A Few Remarks on the Method of Jacques Rancière," 116 (first two quotes); 119 (third quote).

At the same time, as in the case of Foucault's many interventions (in particular his interventions in the history of sexuality), once the forces of liberalization are set into motion, the questions of ontology, finitude, and infinitude return, often with a vengeance. That is to say, once the vertical axis of metaphysical transcendence is displaced onto the horizontal one of empirical practices, the older questions of dominance and subordination, which may have been temporarily bracketed during that process of displacement, tend to persist and hover around the empirical practices in the form of epistemic limits. Rancière's endeavor to democratize art is, arguably, similarly haunted. For one thing, such democratization seems readily assimilable to the fashionable talk about "flows" that is characteristic of our postmodern globalist culture, in which catchwords such as dispersion, circulation, migration, and so forth have together produced a facile form of progressive thinking, capitalist and otherwise. Is the indistinction Rancière advances about art and nonart definitively different from such contemporary valorization of flows? How might it be perceived as definitively different?

As a first step in responding to these questions, a closer look at the notion of indistinction is in order.

How "Madame Bovary, c'est moi" Becomes le Mot Juste: Medial Liberalization and Reflexivity as a Problematic in Art

In a good-humoredly ironic essay on the nineteenth-century novel *Madame Bovary*, Rancière argues that Emma Bovary, the heroine, has to be killed by Gustave Flaubert, the novelist, because she is unfaithful to the pure sensation that belongs in the then-new regime of art.[10] In mid-nineteenth-century France, as the social hierarchy of the ancien régime gave way to a new, democratic order of life, and as the border between art and everyday experience became porous—or so goes Rancière's argument—this story of a peasant's daughter and poor country doctor's wife is typical of the masses getting caught up in the excitement of "the multitude of aspirations and desires, cropping up everywhere in all the pores of modern society" ("Emma Bovary," 236). Rancière, skillfully ventriloquizing and satirizing the attitudes of the learned classes

10. Jacques Rancière, "Why Emma Bovary Had to Be Killed," *Critical Inquiry* 34 (Winter 2008), 233–48. Hereafter page references to this essay, abbreviated as "Emma Bovary," will be included in parentheses in the text.

of that time, including Flaubert's, sees Emma's predicament in terms of a common folk's way of pursuing democracy. Emma turns her fleeting sensations of pleasure (culled from romance novels, natural and architectural surroundings, and other mundane associations) into real things and people to be desired and possessed; she repeatedly seeks to solidify her daydreams in both sentimental and practical ways, in the form of extramarital affairs, beautiful clothes and jewelry, and fashionable furniture. Rather than condemning Emma for being deluded, Rancière traces in her behavior the symptoms of what he calls a redistribution of the sensible, a process in which art and life have become ever more equivalent and interchangeable.[11] Emma's proliferating objects of desire are, as Rancière comments, serially replaceable and substitutable: "When she has resisted her love for Leon, she thinks that she deserves a reward. She buys a piece of furniture. And not only any piece of furniture: a gothic prie-dieu. This is what respectable persons perceive as the law of democracy, the law of universal equivalence: anybody can exchange any desire for any other desire" ("Emma Bovary," 236). In terms of the history of art and literature, Emma may thus be seen as practicing a form of "kitsch": her habits of mixing—and mixing up—art and nonart may be said to foreshadow the high modernist principle of juxtaposition or collage, a principle that is alternately manifest in literary writing (consider what T. S. Eliot, in his study of the affinities between the metaphysical poets and modernist writers such as himself, alludes to as the violent yoking-together of the most heterogeneous ideas),[12] in painting (consider Salvador Dali's way of gathering distinct mundane objects in dreamlike proximity), and in early film (consider Lev Kuleshev's montage experiments whereby unrelated images were assembled in different sequences, each generating a disparate narrative).

According to Rancière, Flaubert too was infected with Emma's disease of democratic equivalence and equality ("Emma Bovary," 237). As a novelist, Flaubert understood that "there is no border separating poetic matters from prosaic matters, no border between what belongs to the poetical realm of noble action and what belongs to the territory of prosaic life"

11. See also his amplification of this point in "A Few Remarks on the Method of Jacques Rancière."

12. T. S. Eliot, "The Metaphysical Poets (1921)," *Selected Prose of T. S. Eliot*, ed. and with an introduction by Frank Kermode (New York: Harcourt Brace Jovanovich, 1975), 60. Eliot is quoting Samuel Johnson, who remarks of poets such as Donne, Cleveland, and Cowley that "the most heterogeneous ideas are yoked by violence together."

("Emma Bovary," 237). Hence, perhaps, Flaubert's well-known confession, "Madame Bovary, c'est moi!" Rather than handling the equivalence between art and nonart in Emma's vulgar manner, however, Flaubert comes to terms with it by developing a distinctive style—one that specializes in precision and exactitude, and in enjoying sensations as pure sensations, disconnected from the sensorium of ordinary experience and from the chains of individuality ("Emma Bovary," 241)—so as to foreground the specificity and purity of art itself. Style, in other words, is "the way in which the writer disappears, the way in which the writer tries to reach a kind of impersonal view."[13] For Flaubert, Rancière writes, the task of literature, as a new regime of writing, consists in none other than inscribing the difference between these two ways of making art similar to nonart ("Emma Bovary," 243). *Madame Bovary* is, in this respect, "the first antikitsch manifesto" ("Emma Bovary," 240).

Rancière's reading asks us to think of *Madame Bovary* as the scene of a disagreement (to borrow an important term from him), a disagreement that takes the form of divergent, or irreconcilable, approaches to the same words—such as "democracy" and "equality"—and that results, in this case, in a death sentence for Emma. Despite his identification with the heroine, the artist must kill her off in order that (his) art may live. Flaubert's signature dedication to *le mot juste*, then, needs to be understood as the outcome of a struggle for domination—a kind of violence, in fact—which Rancière implicitly restores to Art, with a capital A. Although Flaubert has won, this violence means that Art will henceforth survive only as an eccentric (off-centered) practice with its own rules and criteria, often at the expense of universal communicability and accessibility. With a form of "speech" that is increasingly fastidious, solipsistic, self-referential, and intransitive, and a potency achieved only through a persistent withdrawal from the world,[14] the emergence of Art as such thus stands as one of the ironic historical effects of the liberalizing of the boundaries between art and life. Art is now a form of self-imposed quarantine: if Emma soils art with life, a circle has to be drawn around her (and her type of personal behavior).

The example of Flaubert highlights what, in today's terminology, we would call medial reflexivity. Once Art takes on a specificity of its

13. Jacques Rancière, "Aesthetics against Incarnation: An Interview by Anne Marie Oliver," *Critical Inquiry* 35 (Autumn 2008), 189.

14. In *The Order of Things*, Foucault discusses the historical emergence of literature in modern Western Europe in similar terms, as a type of language that becomes increasingly self-referential and intransitive (see 294–300).

own, the question of boundaries becomes complex: boundaries are no longer simply the demarcations externally imposed but must involve as well differentiations internal to the artwork itself. When rethought in terms of medial reflexivity, the putative killing of Emma can be understood as part and parcel of a process by which an artistic medium (in this case, novel writing) becomes self-conscious, in the sense of having a heightened awareness of its own activity, capability, and limits. On this point, some classic examples come to mind by way of contrast. Gotthold Ephraim Lessing's analysis of *The Laocoön*, in which a visual medium (sculpture) and a linguistic medium (poetry) are said to operate each on the awareness of their own semiotic limits as well as capacities, would be one instance of such reflexive self-observation. Friedrich Schiller's analysis of the distinction between naïve and sentimental poetry (on the basis of the poet's becoming-conscious of a loss, the loss of the plenitude that is nature) would be another. As Rancière points out, the implicit assumption underlying such classical discussions of aesthetics is that there *can be* an appropriateness or correspondence between content and form—that the appropriate medium, deemed suitable for a particular kind of subject matter, still exists—whereas such an assumption has been rendered meaningless by the antirepresentational nature of modern avant-garde art, for which there is, simultaneously, no longer a form that is definitively appropriate to a particular type of content and no longer any medial constraint or limit to what can be represented.[15]

Although there is not sufficient space to offer a fully fledged discussion of medial reflexivity here, it is noteworthy that Rancière's reading of *Madame Bovary* in effect places the novel in an interesting discursive interstice, in which an older notion of artistic or medial reflexivity (or self-understanding), still operating on the premise of formal constraints, must now give way to the disappearance of such constraints and, with them, the possible disappearance of any harmonious correspondence between medium and subject matter. Faced with the liberalization of the limits previously imposed on art, medial reflexivity becomes, in Flau-

15. Jacques Rancière, "Are Some Things Unrepresentable?," *The Future of the Image*, trans. Gregory Elliott (New York: Verso, 2007), 109–38. See also his comments in "Why Emma Bovary Had to Be Killed," 237. An interlocutor who springs to mind here is Clement Greenberg, who defended the adequacy of certain art forms precisely in terms of an avant-garde notion of medium specificity, emphasizing in particular the antisculptural, two-dimensional character of painting. In other words, art is art because it is self-referential, because it is an investigation and purification of itself (its medium specificity). Clement Greenberg, "Towards a Newer Laocoön," *Partisan Review* 7 (July–August 1940), 296–310.

bert's hands, reconfigured as a new particularity, le mot juste, which, as a kind of medial agency, is defined as much by its political ineffectualness and impotence to change the world as by its stylistic singularity. Despite being chronologically closer to our time, much of the hyperperformativity of contemporary conceptual artworks may be seen as genealogically akin to Flaubert's handling of artistic and medial reflexivity, whereby art, in defiance of a thoroughly instrumentalist world, folds upon itself narcissistically with its own set of semiotic gestures, including a consciously reiterated display of—and often ironic play on—its conditions of possibility, conditions under which art's autonomy is constantly assailed by other dominant social forces, such as commercialism. Accordingly, as everything in the world has become construed in terms of exchangeability and market value, art needs, by default, to make its mark of distinction in the form of uselessness. Formulated in these terms, modern artistic and medial reflexivity tends always to be a matter of dis-ease (with the world), a self-consciousness of its own futility and social inconsequentiality. Rancière's advocacy of the indistinction of art and nonart, it seems, has simply crystallized such dis-ease (itself an ongoing historical situation) by bringing it up to date.[16]

For Rancière, the politics of *contemporary* art is constituted by a fundamental undecidability among contradictory attitudes shown by various aesthetic paradigms, all of which bear witness to a common world.[17] This emphasis on the world as common means that Rancière tends to be equivocal on the question of mediality. Even as he speaks sympathetically to the impersonality of style (the quarantining of art from the messiness of the personal and the subjective), as exemplified by Flaubert, for instance, he is (in contrast to proponents of technical medium specificity such as Friedrich A. Kittler) in favor of an expansive rather than restrictive approach to the medium as such: "A medium cannot be reduced to a specific materiality and a specific apparatus. A medium also means a milieu or a sensorium, a configuration of space and time, of sensory forms and modes of perception."[18] Hence, also, his equivocal reading of

16. For an important earlier discussion of this ongoing historical situation and the controversy over the status of art in modern European society, see Peter Bürger, *Theory of the Avant-Garde*, trans. Michael Shaw, foreword by Jochen Schulte-Sasse (Minneapolis: University of Minnesota Press, 1984).

17. See his comments in "Problems and Transformations in Critical Art."

18. Rancière, "Aesthetics against Incarnation," 185. By contrast, Kittler has written, for instance, that "[a] medium is a medium. Therefore it cannot be translated. To transfer messages from one medium to another always involves reshaping them to conform to new standards and materials." Friedrich A. Kittler, *Discourse Net-*

Flaubert: "Flaubert writes 'against' Madame Bovary and the 'democratic' confusion of art and life, but, at the same time, he writes from the 'democratic' point of view which affirms the equality of subjects and intensities. It is this tension that interests me."[19]

At this juncture, it would be productive to shift gears and broaden the parameters of our discussion by introducing another type of discourse, cultural anthropology, so as to probe further the ramifications of Rancière's provocation. This shift to cultural anthropology enables a certain "unthought" (to use a phrase from Foucault) to come into view,[20] not only because the cultural frame of reference for thinking about art and politics is extended beyond France and Europe but also because, in a comparable democratic movement toward indistinction and social equity, another type of border and hierarchy unexpectedly reasserts itself.

The Trap as Artwork

Cultural anthropologists have long observed that non-Western societies' practices of art can be quite different from those familiar to Euro-American audiences, who are by convention more accustomed to a specific distinction between art and nonart. James Clifford's critique, in *The Predicament of Culture*, of the dichotomization between art museums and ethnographic museums in the West, and Michael Taussig's account, in *Mimesis and Alterity*, of the artful creativity of non-Western cultural rituals are but two prominent examples published in recent decades.[21] Indeed, the signs are that the field of cultural anthropology itself is undergoing a remarkable discursive transformation in regard to the status of artistic practices.[22]

The work of the British anthropologist Alfred Gell provides an instructive point of intersection with the issues at hand. In *Art and Agency*, a

works 1800/1900, trans. Michael Metteer, with Chris Cullens, foreword by David E. Wellbery (Stanford: Stanford University Press, 1990), 165.

19. Rancière, "Aesthetics and Politics," 205.

20. See the section "The Cogito and the Unthought" in Foucault, *The Order of Things*, 322 and following.

21. James Clifford, *The Predicament of Culture: Twentieth-century Ethnography, Literature, and Art* (Cambridge: Harvard University Press, 1988); Michael Taussig, *Mimesis and Alterity: A Particular History of the Senses* (New York: Routledge, 1992).

22. Michael M. J. Fischer, *Anthropological Futures* (Durham: Duke University Press, 2009).

series of essays defining what constitutes an anthropology of art, Gell challenges, and rejects, the universalizing tendencies of Western aesthetics on account of its Eurocentricity and ideological presumptions, including its acceptance of a purely institutional notion of art.[23] In contrast to an aesthetics that serves Western art in the form of a cult, Gell proposes a general anthropology of art on the basis of relationships between participants in social systems of various kinds. In his words, this would be an "action-centred approach to art" that is "preoccupied with the practical mediatory role of art objects in the social process" (*Art and Agency*, 6). Such action, he argues, is itself uncentered, and the places of "the agent" and "the patient" (or the recipient) may swap. Importantly, then, "nothing is decidable in advance about the nature of this [art] object" (*Art and Agency*, 7), but, as is characteristic of anthropologists' way of solving problems about the apparent irrationality of human behavior, the point is that of "locating . . . behaviour . . . in the dynamics of social interaction, . . . a real process, or dialectic, unfolding in time" (*Art and Agency*, 10).

To underscore the distributed nature of agency (*Art and Agency*, 22) at play within such situations, Gell invokes the interesting notion of abduction—a term used, as he reminds us, by logicians and semioticians to designate the inference of meanings that are not established or provable, but hypothetical and derived from a particular case under consideration (*Art and Agency*, 14–16). By stressing abduction, Gell intends to depict the contingency of agency in situations in which agency can only be grasped as effect, as the outcome of interactions between agents who or which are seeking to realize their life projects through their relations with others: "The spaces of anthropology are those which are traversed by agents in the course of their biographies, be they narrow, or, as is becoming increasingly the case, wide or even world-wide" (*Art and Agency*, 11). These agents may fit into classical categories of personhood, such as artist, recipient, a portraited person, or the patron who instigates the work, but they may just as well be technical objects, ancestors, spirits, or hybrid entities. In their function of being an index to one or the other kind of agency, *artifacts* are pivotal in that they bring about

23. By "institutional," Gell refers to views according to which art is simply what circulates as art; that is, views that do not consider what artistic meaning may be immanent to the work. Alfred Gell, *Art and Agency: An Anthropological Theory* (Oxford: Clarendon Press, 1998). Hereafter page references to this work will be given in parentheses in the text (this chapter's second epigraph is from p. 15). For a related discussion, see George Dickie, *The Art Circle: A Theory of Art* (New York: Haven, 1984).

(and do not result from) differences between inwardness (mind) and externality (what is physical or social; *Art and Agency*, 126 and following). This is why abduction is a remarkably well-chosen term, poised as it is between the experience of personhood and the impersonality of causation. In any given situation (what Gell calls a "causal milieu"), agency is ultimately the trace of an anomaly, an aberrant cause. Rather than being attributable, unambiguously, to semiotic conventions or laws of nature, agency is what must be inferred or abducted (into being or existence; *Art and Agency*, 20).

Gell's democratic approach to art resonates most suggestively with Rancière's in the essay "Vogel's Net," in which he argues against the Hegelian differentiation between art and artifacts, as recalled by the art historian Arthur Danto, whereby art's superiority is seen as residing in its superfluous, noninstrumental value.[24] In a way that echoes Flaubert's stylization, as discussed earlier, this differentiation may be paraphrased as follows: art is more because it is less—more artistic (read: superior) because it is less utilitarian (read: vulgar). To deconstruct Danto's age-old aesthetic assertion as one steeped in elitism, Gell introduces a cross-cultural scenario, by observing that the so-called artifacts in certain "primitive" societies have in common with Western avant-garde art the key attribute of obscuring the more stable distinction between art and everyday objects. This observation allows Gell to argue that such artifacts are, de facto, art, which is now defined not so much by sensuous beauty as by conceptuality and reflexivity. Whereas Rancière articulates art's alterity to the working or lower classes, the masses, the country as opposed to the metropolis, and so forth, Gell does so by way of life worlds beyond the bounds of Euro America and Western aesthetics. Notwithstanding their different cultural frames of reference, however, the two authors obviously share an ethicopolitical interest in the liberalizing of boundaries of sensibility, identity, and agency in the modern world.

Even so, the most intriguing part about Gell's argument is not exactly the point about the indistinguishability of art and artifacts. It is rather the key example he picked to illustrate such indistinguishability: the trap, a device for capturing animals. (To repeat, Gell's point is that as an artifact, the trap is really a kind of—that is, equivalent to—conceptual art.)

The trap is, to all appearances, the opposite of freedom: its "art" or

24. Alfred Gell, "Vogel's Net: Traps as Artworks and Artworks as Traps," *The Art of Anthropology: Essays and Diagrams*, ed. Eric Hirsch (London: Athlone, 1999), 187–214.

cunning lies in an aggressive potential to take another being captive and bring it into submission. It is the state of arrest and closure, coinciding with the prey's loss of mobility and autonomy, that makes the trap a trap. If the artwork is reconceptualized in the cross-cultural—and globally sensitive—manner that Gell proposes, with its attendant conceptuality and reflexivity, and if such reconceptualization, much like some of Rancière's formulations, is aimed at a certain social emancipation (the emancipation from the rigidity of classification and hierarchical distinctions, and above all from the stable differentiation of experiences), how come it is the trap that occupies such a strategic place in this emancipatory thinking? What exactly is the status of the trap in relation to art?

As an example of the emancipation of the distinction between art and artifacts, the trap in Gell's text makes it imperative to ask: Whose or what emancipation are we talking about? Whose or what mind, consciousness, or thought is being liberated in the conceptual flow between art and nonart? Is it that of the designer of the trap, that of the philosopher who discerns its cunning, or that of the trap itself? Yet such conceptual mobility and fluidity would not be possible (that is, realized) without the prey's abduction and participation. It is only in the prey's entanglement and, finally, its embodied state of captivity that the intent or intelligence of the trap's design is fulfilled and becomes intelligible.

What begins as a democratic attempt on the part of the cultural anthropologist to dissolve the distinction between art ("Western") and everyday objects ("non-Western") has, in other words, reintroduced into the scene a crucial type of distinction—the hierarchy between the hunter and the prey, a hierarchy that underwrites the zone of contact as a site of cruelty, domination, subordination, and asymmetrical power dynamics. The non-Western example Gell picked to instantiate a radical epistemic break with conventional Western aesthetics, it appears, is precisely what threatens to throw his ethical project off course, intercepting (abducting!) it from its erstwhile movement toward cultural equality.[25]

Albeit salutary, then, the philosophical and social scientific attempts to realign art with freedom (especially in the form of the artwork or artifact that renders the distinction between art and nonart indistinguishable) tend to run into a paradox, one that revolves around the (knotty figure of the) trap in the terms outlined. This paradox leads to the contentious

25. The arguably unresolved sketch of what Gell terms an extended mind, which makes up the second part of *Art and Agency*, shows that this issue is indeed, to use his own words, "unfinished business" (80–81).

conjecture that *what remains of art* in the age of medial liberalization is perhaps less a relation to freedom as such than a relation to capture and captivity, a field of discursivity that, as will be suggested in what follows, has an arguably irreducible linkage to art and literature. (Let it be noted that even when making its appearance in a supposedly nonartistic and nonliterary realm such as cultural anthropology, the trap returns us in an uncanny fashion to a literary form—Western tragedy, to be exact—as Gell's passing comments illuminate.)[26]

The Artwork as Trap and the Force of Captivation

At one level, what the trap conjures, together with what Gell alludes to as the abduction of the indexes of meaning in processes of social interaction, is of course none other than the tradition of literary and artistic representations of phenomena of capture and imprisonment, phenomena that have long inspired authors across cultures. The memorable image, described by Henry David Thoreau, of the American muskrat repeatedly chewing off a paw if the paw is caught, until it can no longer walk because it has chewed off all its paws this way, is simply one among many examples of a literary fascination with entrapment and its thematic associations of escape, resistance, endurance, sacrifice, and survival.[27] Another example might be Vladimir Nabokov's *Lolita*, which, according to the author, had its germ in a news item about an ape in the Paris Zoo. When encouraged to draw a picture, the ape, it was said, drew the bars of his cage.[28] In our time, Foucault's influential discussions of confinement—in the form of the institutional compartmentalization of madness, criminality, education, sexuality, reproduction, and so forth—may

26. At one point, Gell compares different trapped animals to "tragic heroes" such as Faust and Othello: "The fact that animals who fall victim to traps have always brought about their downfall by their own actions, their own complacent self-confidence, ensures that trapping is a far more poetic and tragic form of hunting than the simple chase. The latter kind of hunting equalises hunters and victims, united in spontaneous action and reaction, whereas trapping decisively hierarchises hunter and victim. The trapper is God, or the fates, the trapped animal is man in his tragic incarnation" ("Vogel's Net," 202).

27. Henry David Thoreau, *Walden* (1854) (Princeton: Princeton University Press, 2004), 66.

28. See Dominic Pettman, *Love and Other Technologies: Retrofitting Eros for the Information Age* (New York: Fordham University Press, 2006), 66. Pettman offers an illuminating analysis of the important allusions to spider webs in Nabokov's novel.

also be understood as contiguous with a long-standing philosophical preoccupation with entrapment as a type of limit experience, which for Foucault culminates not in spaces of darkness (as in the dungeon) but in spaces of visibility (as in Bentham's Panopticon).[29] Foucault's summary statement on panopticism is that "visibility is a trap."[30] The examples of Thoreau, Nabokov, Foucault, and other writers and artists suggest that the trap is, arguably, an archetypal epistemic or representational device, a *dispositif* (in Foucault's terms), perhaps, that has been central to what may be called a parapoetics.[31] In the years since September 11, 2001, as incidents of arbitrary arrest and torture, forced detention, unjust execution, and other varieties of physical coercion become routines of the global order of terror, the ramifications of the trap have acquired ever more profound degrees of poignancy.

At the same time, this marked semiotic kinship between the trap and art and literature should not be restricted to the level of represented content. In terms of discursive formations, what the figure of the trap accentuates is a structure of unevenness—an uneven distribution of forces, to be precise—whose injurious effect is, by definition, *borne by the prey* (the recipient of the trap's negative impact). The trap is an index to a type of social interaction in which one party takes advantage of another by being temporally preemptive, by catching the other unawares. This time differential between the hunter's and the prey's contacts with the trap, it follows, is an implicit division of labor, one that rewards the former's (premeditated) action of deceiving, disabling, and disempowering the latter. To talk about the trap as a clever device, an intelligent artifact, a sophisticated conceptual artwork, and so forth, is to talk about this process of one-upmanship. This fundamental structure of unevenness is the reason the trap, as much as being an archetypical device for portraying suffering, can also be a source of comic relief. Duchamp's readymade *Trébuchet* (*Trap*) provides an excellent case in point: a coat rack lying on the floor, which the artist kicks every time he walks past it, is transformed into avant-garde Art by being nailed permanently to the floor. The *showing* of the visual object is henceforth encoded with a narrative *telling* of

29. For a study of the theme of incarceration in French literature, see Victor Brombert, *The Romantic Prison: The French Tradition* (Princeton: Princeton University Press, 1978).

30. Foucault, *Discipline and Punish*, 200.

31. Steve McCaffery, "Parapoetics and the Architectural Leap," *A Time for the Humanities: Futurity and the Limits of Autonomy*, ed. James J. Bono, Tim Dean, and Ewa Plonowska Ziarek (New York: Fordham University Press, 2008), 161–79.

how it all happened over time: the artist, initially in the position of an unsuspecting fool who repeatedly stumbles on the coat rack, in the end masters the situation and makes his escape by deliberately staging the process of trapping and thus turning the joke back on the coat rack itself, which is now, literally, stuck.[32] Whether in the form of tragedy (with a kind of heroism defined by suffering and endurance) or comedy (with a kind of heroism defined by slapstick humor and ironic distance), however, the trap tends to be treated as a unified discursive plane, one that is organized strictly by the binary, mechanistic determinism of openness and enclosure, and oriented toward the interest of the hunter—that is to say, the winner—when, ontologically and epistemically speaking, no such unity exists.

To put this in more formal terms: the trap, by virtue of its binary operation (open or shut), is a line of pressure, constraint, and blockage. Before the prey is caught, the trap lies in waiting, carrying the potentiality of the hunter's imaginary like a blueprint. Once a prey is caught and the trap snaps shut, however, the trap's formal structure of obstruction and inhibition sets into motion a new process that becomes, strictly speaking, indeterminate. Like the *charnière* mentioned by Derrida in the third epigraph at the beginning of the present essay, the trap may therefore be analogized or approximated to a hinge or pivot, around which multiple planes rotate in perpetual slippage from one another, in such ways as to conjoin mobility with enclosure, and alterity with capture. How so?

The missing link is the prey's experience of *being* captured: How to *count* this experience without simply collapsing it back into the intent or intelligence of the trap's design, which is complete only when the prey gets caught? For, once caught, the prey's existence renders the trap more than just the elegant design understood from the sovereign command perspective of the hunter, who can henceforth no longer monopolize the terms of the interaction. The hunter's carefully conceived, preemptive plan, as embodied in the open trap, is now folded into another space and time that comes into being through entrapment, while the prey's past and present actions take on, belatedly, a new, additional significance as self-entanglement. Gell's aforementioned allusion to tragedy (note 26) is an attempt to account for this temporal knot of suspense and *anagnorisis*.

This discursive excess, at once inarticulate and indispensable, at once

32. For an informative discussion of this and other readymades of Duchamp's, see Helen Molesworth, "Work Avoidance: The Everyday Life of Marcel Duchamp's Readymades," *Art Journal* 57.4 (1998), 51–61.

outside and informing the economy of the trap's instrumentalist functioning, is what makes the trap such an inexhaustibly evocative object for literary and artistic contemplation. Such discursive excess means that a supplementary plane of articulation, the plane of articulation of an other, ensnared in but not coinciding with the hunter's, philosopher's, or conceptual artist's, and oscillating between the shock of ensnarement and the pain of possible annihilation, now slides into place to rupture, from within, the trap's presumed discursive unity. Entangled, vulnerable, and delirious, this supplementary discursive plane comes into being—"appears," as it were—only as the trap snaps shut, yet has the potential of tilting the trap toward a radically heteronomous affective assemblage, one in which a reactive relation to the world (in the form of being caught, being struck, being touched, being infected, and so forth), which is situationally entwined with but also phenomenologically disjointed and discontinuous from an active relation (as in catching, striking, touching, infecting, and so forth), is a primary, rather than simply derivative, sensation.

In the English language, this heteronomous affective assemblage (rather than the straightforwardly mechanistic, open-or-shut determinism that allows the trap to function) is invoked whenever we speak of being "captivated" in the sense of being lured and held by an unusual person, event, or spectacle. To be captivated is to be captured by means other than the purely physical, with an effect that is, nonetheless, lived and felt *as* embodied captivity. The French word *captation*, referring to a process of deception and inveiglement by artful means, is suggestive insofar as it pinpoints the elusive yet vital connection between art and the state of being captivated.[33] But the English word "captivation" seems more felicitous, not least because it is semantically suspended between an

33. For an astute discussion of *captation* in the contexts of economics and sociology, in particular in relation to strategies for marketing commodities, see Franck Cochoy, "A Brief Theory of the 'Captation' of Publics: Understanding the Market with Little Red Riding Hood," trans. Couze Venn, *Theory, Culture and Society* 24.7–8 (2007), 203–23. Cochoy argues that in the situation of consumerist publics, captation has the task of controlling a fleeting target and thus must devise strategies that suggest possibilities of exit, flight, and freedom. For scholars who have studied the phenomena of commodified literature (including pulp fiction and television soap operas), Cochoy's analysis may not come across as groundbreaking, but what is noteworthy is the fact that when he needs to explain the intricacy of captation, he turns specifically to narrative fiction—in this case the story of Little Red Riding Hood (see 212 and following)—both in terms of what narrative actions can signify within the story, and in terms of fiction itself as a device adopted by the literary author for purposes of captivating the reader.

aggressive move and an affective state, and carries within it the force of the trap in both active and reactive senses, without their being organized necessarily in a hierarchical fashion and collapsed into a single discursive plane.[34] As an experience formed through a collaboration of intensities, sensuous and imaginary as well as rationalist, captivation seems—or so it can be proposed—to have a privileged relationship to art and literature, in ways that are irreducible to other frames of interpretation.

In this light, Rancière's reading of *Madame Bovary* begins to assume an interestingly opaque quality. The ingenuity of Rancière's analysis lies in his endeavor to restore to the degenerate (adulterous, frivolous, selfish, irresponsible, immoral . . .) character of Emma a kind of agency. Indeed, reading with Rancière, we may say that Emma's scandalous behavior is a kind of muted speech or silent witnessing, which is symptomatic of an indifference "to the system of social differentiations defining what the daughter of a peasant can feel, think and do,"[35] an indifference that should be given its share and place in history. Such a reading would be consistent with Rancière's formulations of "emancipation": "a set of practices guided by the supposition that everyone is equal and by the attempt to verify this supposition." Rancière names the politics of emancipation a "heterology": "The politics of emancipation is the politics of the self as an other, or, in Greek terms, a *heteron*. The logic of emancipation is a heterology."[36] While Rancière's reasoning is persuasive, a disagreement

34. Although he offers very sensitive formulations of captivation, Gell tends to preserve the hierarchy between the active and the reactive senses, as for instance in the relation between the artist and the spectator. This is evident in the rather negative terminology he uses to describe the spectator's condition of being trapped (or awestruck) when confronted by the artist's virtuosity: "fundamental inequality," "demoralization," "inability," "'blockage' in cognition," "defeat," and so forth (*Art and Agency*, 68–72). And, while he introduces themes of paradoxical recursion and exchange of places between captive and captor, with artworks attaining a certain universality in their function as "thought-traps," "impeding passage" ("Vogel's Net," 213) and becoming agents in a distribution of personhood (a distribution whereby agents may be as entangled as patients or recipients), Gell nonetheless retains the notion of a "primary agency" (as the source of intentional action), which he only indirectly, and perhaps incompletely, deconstructs in his analysis of the extended mind (*Art and Agency*, 221–58). What seems missing from his otherwise extraordinary work is a theorization of the *state* of being trapped (or awestruck)—that is to say, of captivation as an experience that exceeds an ex post facto analysis of power relations, and that exceeds the type of formalization that is based strictly on cognition or mind.

35. Rancière, "A Few Remarks on the Method of Jacques Rancière," 122.

36. Jacques Rancière, "Politics, Identification, and Subjectivization," *October* 61 (Summer 1992), 58–64. The two quotations are from 58 and 59.

with him needs to be voiced over the nature of otherness and heterology in regard to Emma's behavior. By referring to Emma as a peasant's daughter and a poor country doctor's wife, Rancière implies that such otherness and heterology should, ultimately, be articulated to class, and yet his class-oriented assessment seems rather ambiguous. If what Emma personifies is indeed class emancipation as such, why does Rancière need to devote so much space to rationalizing how she *has to* die for Flaubert's art to succeed, as though such emancipation contains in it a surplus of signification that has to be reabsorbed (either accounted for or wiped away)? What is it about Emma's emancipatory trajectory that seems so unsettling that it is not enough to accept her death as suicide, as the novel has presented it, but necessary to reframe it with a categorical imperative—as something that demands a violent solution, an *act* of killing by her author, as though the latter recognized in her something of a dangerous equal or rival, who must be cautiously warded off?[37]

Whereas for Flaubert, the indistinction of art and life means that even the most lowly aspects of life may be turned into—that is, refined and purified as—Art, Emma's "problem" is that she readily yields, physically and mentally, to pleasures of the unproductive and nonpurifiable kind: romance novels, fleeting sensations, and idle aspirations. Much as their difference is amply registered by Rancière, it is also what constitutes the opacity of his analysis: Flaubert might have been as much a captive as Emma is to the menacing new social condition of the indiscriminate equivalence of things, but, like a good, hard worker from the ranks of (what Rancière calls) the reactionary bourgeoisie, he (re)directed his captivity to a new purpose, the purpose of an exquisite art, whereas Emma's response to this new social condition is that of a steadily intensified madness until her life is completely ruined.[38] In living in such a manner as to dramatize the border or threshold between fantasy and reality, Emma is much less the conventional proletarian seeking class

37. For an interesting discussion of *Madame Bovary* in terms of mimetic desire, see René Girard, *Deceit, Desire, and the Novel: Self and Other in Literary Structure*, trans. Yvonne Freccero (Baltimore: Johns Hopkins University Press, 1965), 63–64, 148–49.

38. Foucault's essay "Madness, the Absence of Work," trans. Peter Stastny and Deniz Sengel (*Foucault and His Interlocutors*, 97–104), would be a relevant intertext to read alongside Emma's lack of productivity. Toward the end of his essay on *Madame Bovary*, Rancière briefly invokes "hysteria" as a possible key to the literature (by authors such as Flaubert, Marcel Proust, and Virginia Woolf) in which human bodies suffer from a disease provoked by the "excess" of thought (see "Emma Bovary," 246 and following).

emancipation than a proto–mass culture consumer who abandons herself to the lure of inanimate, fictional objects, which are her vital sources of happiness.[39]

Emma's emancipation, if it can be so called, is not only a matter of her wanting to convert fantasies into life (as Rancière suggests); rather, it is also that she prefers daydreaming to life itself, and that she wants to live continuously *entertained*, even at the expense of her own and her family's well-being, by those spectral objects, those absent presences that are part fantasy, part sensation, and part reality. (To "entertain" is, etymologically, to hold between, in a manner that resonates with the phenomenon of captivation.) Having endless desires; having desires in endlessly repeated and serialized forms: *this* is Emma's heterology and project of self-transformation and self-invention. In a manner that anticipates the behaviors of both the perpetrators and the victims of the global financial crisis of the early twenty-first century (the unregulated investment bankers, subprime mortgage lenders, and home purchasers with zero down payments), Emma plunges headlong into disaster because, we might say, of her overimaginative claims—claims that are based exclusively on the imagination and increasingly detached from and independent of material reality—so much so that suicide becomes her only viable form of debt repudiation (the only way she can declare bankruptcy). But suicide is also a form of intransitive speech: like Flaubert's Art, it is about severing the ties to the sentiments, to the messiness of life itself, by drawing an absolute line between the imaginary world and the social world. If Flaubert drew the line with self-discipline and hard work, Emma draws the line with her own life. She too is an artist, and perhaps not only a kitsch artist (as Rancière writes) but also a hunger artist; her Art too is crafted with precision and exactitude, though not of words but of death.[40]

Much as Rancière's discussions prompt an understanding of Emma's story as one about class, therefore, something about the story does not quite fit such a reading, which somehow cannot account for the exces-

39. Rancière's definition of the proletarian, it should be noted, is etymologically specific: "a certain way of being at one and the same time inside and outside the symbolic order of the distribution of social identities" ("Politics, Identification, and Subjectivization," 80). See also his elaboration of the links between "proletarian" and processes of subjectivization and identification on 60 and following.

40. The reference here is, of course, to Franz Kafka's remarkable short story "A Hunger Artist," in which what the artist, who lives in a cage, keeps performing (or putting on display) until death is, arguably and allegorically speaking, his craving—an insatiable metaphysical demand, a bottomless existential abyss that can never be filled.

siveness of captivation—with its combination of pleasure and unfreedom—except, perhaps, by reducing it to false consciousness. Obviously, Rancière recognizes the unsatisfactory nature of that language of an anachronistic, orthodox Marxist analysis,[41] but even as he is invested in being affirmative of Emma's transgressive behavior, he seems to have stopped short of probing the significance of her experience of being captivated to its logical conclusion. By reinscribing Emma's perverse solutions to ennui in a kind of heterology that is, nonetheless, rooted in class, and by reverting the agency of her final self-performance to her author and creator, Rancière is, of course, not mistaken; it is simply that he has not gone far enough. Borrowing his concept, might not we see in Emma's final self-performance precisely a redistribution of the sensible—in the extreme form of a cessation of the senses, of non-sense?[42] In not granting Emma authorship or ownership of her suicide, and in transferring that authorship or ownership—that deed, as it were—to Flaubert and recoding it as an act of *his* artistic resistance, has not Rancière inadvertently further muted Emma's muted speech?

But Rancière should probably not be held responsible for what is a much larger problematic about art in modernity. Unlike other types of social transformation that bear clear, progressive designations such as "class struggle," "decolonization," "women's lib," "gay rights," and "transgender," the state of being captivated has no such collective name recognition based in identity politics, even though it is a situation in which an undeniable relation to alterity unfolds. How to describe a form of solidarity that is not with other members of one's class, race, nation, or gender but—in what may be the real scandal of Flaubert's tale—with the specters of thought, abstraction, fiction, and illusion? Like a virulent parasite that has gradually overtaken its host,[43] Emma's state of captivation—and the pleasure and unfreedom that accompany it—brings into play the entire supplementary discursive domain that tangles up the open/shut determinism of the trap with its own creative-cum-destructive momentum. As the *imbalance* between the claims and demands made

41. See, for instance, his remarks on the worker, as cited in note 6.

42. Rancière is in fact quite sympathetic to this line of thinking, which he associates with the theme of the self-destructive will and a race toward nothingness in some examples of nineteenth-century literature; see his remarks in "Aesthetics and Politics," 208.

43. For a philosophical discussion of parasitism as a type of origination, see Michel Serres, *The Parasite*, trans., with notes, by Lawrence R. Schehr (Baltimore: Johns Hopkins University Press, 1982).

by those specters, on the one hand, and so-called reality, on the other, accrues to the point of no return, captivation spirals into catastrophe. Captivation, then, is the deranged remainder that is unassimilable to the metanarratives of freedom that underlie both capitalist consumerism (in which a supposedly autonomous subject makes choices from an endless proliferation of material goods) and socialist revolution (in which a supposedly autonomous subject emancipates herself from the constraints imposed by class, race, colonialism, gender, and so forth). Even while inextricably enmeshed with these two dominant discourse networks, captivation poses the question of art and politics not in the form of an integration with such networks but in the form of a disjunction, an encounter—and interrogation—of an insistently ontological import.

That is to say, the state of captivation brings to the fore questions of being—of origination, freedom, finitude, and infinitude: Where do I come from, where am I heading toward, when and where will I end? By whose script and design do I exist? What does it mean to have a life of my own? Is there more to I than I? As they confront us with the abyss of existence, these open-ended, because ultimately unresolvable, questions have conventionally lent themselves to purposes of mass rationalization and indoctrination, purposes that, as Louis Althusser has shown, are readily appropriated and abducted by, and sutured with, ideological state apparatuses such as the church, the state, the family, the police, the school, the military, and so forth. For Althusser, the ontological as well as sociopolitical reward for accepting the interpellation by such apparatuses is the shelter of coherent identification, which shields and protects one from the openness of the abyss. When realized on a collective scale, identification ensures the indefinite reproducibility of a particular type of society (as for instance, the modern, postindustrial, secular, bourgeois society of Western Europe) and its infrastructure.[44] Is captivation simply a variant of interpellation? A response to this question may be offered by way of a brief discussion of a contemporary film. (For reasons of space, the discussion will have to be limited to those aspects of the film that are most salient to the present topic.)

44. See Louis Althusser, "Ideology and Ideological State Apparatuses (Notes towards an Investigation)," *Lenin and Philosophy and Other Essays*, trans. Ben Brewster (New York: Monthly Review Press, 1971), 127–86.

Capturing the Lives of Others . . .

Like *Madame Bovary*, the film *Das Leben der Anderen* (*The Lives of Others*, 2006; directed by Florian Henckel von Donnersmarck) offers a provocative staging of captivation, in a social context quite distinct from the nineteenth-century French countryside. The story takes place in East Germany during the period before the fall of the Berlin Wall and German reunification. Wiesler, an ambitious Stasi interrogator with expertise in coercing confessions, is ordered by his superiors to eavesdrop on the writer Georg Dreyman and his lover, Christa Maria Sieland, a well-known stage actress, in whom a high-ranking Stasi official, Hempf, has a sexual interest. At the level of the plot, then, the trap appears readily in two closely linked and by no means subtle manners: first, as the secret police state itself, which imprisons its citizens in a universal network of surveillance; second, as the particular eavesdropping operation installed in Dreyman's apartment building to capture the details of his and his lover's lives. By today's media standards, the eavesdropping operation is a rather simple setup, which "bugs" the apartment and transmits the sounds to a tape recorder, while the recorded contents are interpreted and reported by typewriter onto paper documents to be filed in the Stasi bureaucracy. (These documents will become available to the public after German reunification, which is how Dreyman eventually discovers the truth.) Insofar as it serves to objectify the seamless, pervasive, and omniscient workings of the police state, the figure of the trap can be thought of as the most crucial, albeit silent, mediator in this story.

Dramatically, in the minimalist, audial medium in which the lovers are taken captive, another scene begins to unfold. The poetry reading, music, intimate conversations, lovemaking, social gatherings, and other happenings in Dreyman's apartment, received by Wiesler in the form of intermittent sounds, gradually exert a magical hold on him. Instead of monitoring his prey with the sadistic detachment of an all-knowing captor, Wiesler undergoes a transformation in which his victims begin to assume a new kind of significance, affecting him as though they were the fictional characters in a radio play. Drawn *beside himself* into this other, imaginary world, Wiesler tries participating in it vicariously, by gestures of appropriation and mimicry: he reenters Dreyman's apartment, looks around, touches Dreyman's bed, and steals Dreyman's copy of Brecht's poems for his own reading. Such attachment to this other world culminates at the critical juncture when Dreyman's clandestine activity of writing articles for the West is about to be exposed. The Stasi, having been alerted by Sieland (through a coerced confession) to a doorsill where Dreyman hides his typewriter, plans to break into his apartment and arrest him on charges of treason. At great peril to himself, Wiesler preempts this planned exposure by removing the typewriter just in time. With the Stasi unable to arrest him, Dreyman survives as a writer. Eventually, upon learning the truth by reading his own file in the former East German government archives, Dreyman dedicates a new book to Wiesler, identifying the latter simply by his former Stasi work number, HGW XX17. By then, Wiesler has become a low-level postal worker.

Wiesler's transformation easily lends itself to an anticommunist reading, according to which this film would be laudable on account of its reaffirmation of a kind of universal humanism: by daring to abandon his sinister assignment and to rescue a writer who courageously criticizes the secret police state, Wiesler regains his humanity, vindicates good morals, makes the world a better place, and so forth. The logic of this anticommunist reading would be consistent with the celebration of the fall of the Berlin Wall as a triumph of Western enlightenment in the barbarous East, the celebration of the reunification of the German nation, and other such teleological narratives. The details of the film, meanwhile, tell a different story, especially if we approach it from the perspective of the trap.

Trapping in this instance is, significantly, enacted in a series of mimetic efforts. Like Wiesler's attempt to appropriate and mimic bits of Dreyman's life, the injunction to tape-record and transcribe by typewriter amounts to a methodical process of copying. But once the activity of copying begins—that is, once the state-sanctioned, instrumentalist trapping procedure is in force—a different discursive plane begins to assume existence *side by side* with the oppressive agenda of the state, in such a way as to bring about a reversal of the positions of captor and captives, a reversal that coincides with a mutation of the very medium of surveillance and capture. Sound, intended officially for the purpose of recording and copying, now breaks off from itself into an alternative audial pathway: in the process of being heard by Wiesler in a reduced form, with most of the accompanying empirical "reality" subtracted, sound becomes instead an aperture for interventional creativity.

Like a musical conductor or stage director, Wiesler proceeds to reassemble and rewrite the official score, script, and plot. Not only does he intercept Sieland's plan to continue to meet with her abuser, Hempf, and not only does he hide what Dreyman is writing—an article about artists and suicides in East Germany, which eventually appears in *Der Spiegel*—by fabricating details of a nonexistent, politically uncontroversial play; he also alters the position and role of one little prop: Dreyman's typewriter. From its original status as the incriminating piece of evidence sought by the Stasi, this writing tool has now turned into a false lead, *a new object whose significance lies in the fact that it is missing*. This gesture of alteration, by which the thing that is at once the good writer's means of protest and the evil state's means of persecution vanishes into a useless deception, unveils itself as a void, successfully obstructs the Stasi's procedure in an innovative politics, one that erupts simultaneously as an artwork, in the midst of the most oppressive of political situations.

This, then, is how captivation may be distinguished from Althusser's formulation of interpellation: rather than putting its stresses on a coherent and overdetermined process of identification with the ideological state apparatuses, captivation, as a type of receptivity, is at once involved and devolved—and separate. Its reciprocation of the hailing of alterity, in other words, takes the form not of an obedient conformity with an absolute structure of domination, which allows one to find and anchor oneself in a rewarding relation to such a structure (as in Althusser's argument), but rather in the form of a loosening, and losing, of that self, often in "nonproductive" processes such as daydreaming and art.[45] In the slipping away of the shelter that is identification emerges that heteronomous affective assemblage, as mentioned in the foregoing discussion, whereby politics returns not to government but (possibly through the voiding of a particular political agenda, as in this film) to anarchy, the condition of having no *arche*.[46]

This loosening or loss of the self, moreover, is not the result of crossing an external border or overcoming a constraint; rather it occurs from within the limits imposed by the situation, which ambiguates between Wiesler's role as audience and his role as actor. Wiesler's isolation—

45. A helpful text here is Alain Badiou's Althusserian reading of the apostle Paul's interpellation by the event of Christ's resurrection. Instead of losing himself in the experience, Paul found and anchored himself successfully by establishing the institution of the Christian church and empire; his subjective upsurge thus became a coherent part of a biopolitics of government through religious conviction. See Badiou, *Saint Paul: The Foundation of Universalism*, trans. Ray Brassier (Stanford: Stanford University Press, 2003).

46. See Rancière, "Politics, Identification, and Subjectivization": "Politics is not the enactment of the principle, the law, or the self of a community. Put in other words, politics has no arche, it is anarchical" (59).

staged in his opaque looks, his lonely movements, and his restricted access to the world which he is to oversee—blocks the possibility of a total overview. Yet it is precisely in the midst of such a blockage that Wiesler metamorphoses into the dreamer-artist of an unanticipated political situation, in which his captives and victims are given a new existence as the imaginary objects he seeks to set free. In this entanglement of politics and art, captivation brings with it a terrifying kind of freedom. Stripped of the identification that is the protection of the state, the bureaucracy, and the hierarchy of officialdom, Wiesler ends up living the life of a modest, now nameless messenger, a "nobody."

Insofar as Wiesler is neither the intellectual and writer nor the professional actor (the conventional agents of literature and art, even in a communist state, as represented by Dreyman and Sieland), his captivation may ultimately be seen as a form of self-distraction-cum-self-destruction. Whereas Emma Bovary commits suicide, Wiesler annihilates himself by enmeshment in a foreign universe, a universe in which he is the other, in which he has no speech of his own except that of being captivated. Interestingly, this speechlessness of the other is exactly the place where *Das Leben der Anderen* becomes a rejoinder to Rancière's compelling notions of equality and democracy. As Rancière writes, such notions are not so much about the liberation of thought per se as about the restoration to the world around us of a collective agency, a common "speech" that is otherwise mute, anonymous, and unacknowledged.[47] As history is typically a record composed by the victors, the challenge to us is to be able to hear, to listen for such common speech.

The present analysis could have ended at this point, but it is of relevance to introduce one more complication, even though a full discussion of it will have to be deferred. The trap also functions in an important manner in relation to the actress Sieland, Dreyman's lover, who throughout the film is referred to as an artist. In focusing attention on Wiesler's transformation by captivation, the film has simultaneously cast Sieland in the position of an abject female, who, despite her artistic talent, is held captive to her body, which serves both to inaugurate and to conclude the plot that revolves around the male characters (Hempf, who desires her and forces her into an affair with him; Grubitz, who supervises the eavesdropping operation; Dreyman, who loves her, is aware of the affair, but somehow continues to believe that he himself is an exception to the state's surveillance; Wiesler, whose captivation changes his own life).

47. See in particular Rancière's comments in "Aesthetics and Politics."

Of all the male characters, Wiesler is closest to Sieland in his capacity for self-sacrifice and self-annihilation; at the same time, if Wiesler's ingenious removal of the typewriter saves Dreyman, it also seals Sieland's tragic fate. As the Stasi officers arrive to make their planned arrest of Dreyman, Sieland flees the apartment in guilt (we may surmise) as she believes that her betrayal of her lover is about to be revealed, only then to be fatally hit by a truck rushing by. If she had stayed behind, the fact that the typewriter is missing would have meant that the Stasi would return to punish her for lying and step up its harassment. In Sieland's case, all exits have been blocked, and her death is in effect a suicide.

In a disturbing parallel to Emma Bovary and Flaubert, therefore, here is a situation in which, to paraphrase Rancière, a woman artist "has to be killed" as the sociohistorical conditions of her life world become entangled with the makings of the male author's creative work, which in this case applies both to Dreyman's article about artists in East Germany who commit suicide and to Wiesler's dream-art rescue of his characters from the persecution of the state. Furthermore, it applies to the plot of the film (that is to say, director von Donnersmarck's story), for which the killing is arguably an easy escape, conserving the narrative center of gravity in the male protagonists.

Traversed by the multiplicities of homosocial (in particular, male homosocial) as well as heterosexual bonding, the discursive planes rotating around the trap are potentially endless—and often incommensurate. Whose captivation *counts* in the end, and whose captivation counts *as art*? That of a male, a female, or . . . ? Are not group identities as such, including sexual identities and their many variants, ultimately also traps? These questions of agency may never be fully answered, but the implications of their unfolding should be part of any in-depth consideration of the indistinction of art and nonart.

3

Fateful Attachments

On Collecting, Fidelity, and Lao She

Collectors are among the most suggestive characters in literary histories East and West. What is intriguing about them is often not only what they collect but also the paradoxical movement, inscribed in their collecting behavior, from the frivolous to the serious, from the casual pleasures of accumulating gratuitous objects to the most perverse kinds of addiction. In this movement lies a type of personality disorder that can be aesthetically fascinating. But aesthetic observations alone have far from exhausted the interpretative possibilities of the collector's captivation; other libidinal ramifications, albeit less frequently observed and explored, lurk behind what seems at first to be a matter of an eccentric, individualistic obsession. This is especially the case if a collector is faced not only with his or her collected objects but simultaneously with the forces of socialization, such as the moral imperative of self-sacrifice to a collective. At the juncture between the love for the inanimate and the demands of group identity, what might the act of collecting signify? What might an intimacy with inanimate objects do to one's sense of belonging, of being part of, say, a national community?

These questions are unveiled by the remarkable, little known short story "Lian" ("Attachment") by the modern Chinese author Lao She, the pen name of Shu Qingchun or Shu Sheyu (1899–1966).[1] In the discussion

1. See Lao She, "Lian," *Pinxue ji* (Chongqing: Wenjin chubanshe, 1944), 110–21; Lao She, "Attachment," trans. Sarah Wei-ming Chen, *Blades of Grass: The Short Stories of Lao She*, trans. William A. Lyell and Sarah Wei-ming Chen (Honolulu: University of Hawaii Press, 1999), 211–25. The story was first published in the journal *Shi yu chao wenyi*, 15 March 1943, 37–43.

to follow, I shall suggest that inscribed in this narrative of an ordinary man's idiosyncratic absorption in collectibles is nothing short of an alternative way of thinking about what we nowadays call identity politics. Accordingly, the far-reaching implications of social identification are illuminated not so much through the familiar light of human subjectivity as through the obscure allure of material objects, an allure that in turn tells us something about the convictions with which such love for objects has characteristically been denounced in certain types of modern theory.

Often characterized as a humorous realist novelist, Lao She is, among modern Chinese writers, second perhaps only to Lu Xun in international renown, with works translated into some twenty languages.[2] Lao She had a prolific writing career, which spanned four decades, from the 1920s (when he was a lecturer in Chinese at what was then known as the School of Oriental Studies at the University of London) to the 1960s, and which included numerous novels, short story collections, essays, plays, and poems.[3] In the West, he is best known for his novel *Luotuo xiangzi* (*Rickshaw*, 1936–37), which features a lower-class laborer, a rickshaw puller. It is notable that Lao She had authored the first significant proletarian novel in China even as the Chinese Communist Party was gathering momentum and beginning to make propagandist declarations about writing for the people.[4] In "Attachment," we find a very different kind of story, one that returns us by an alternative route to the problematic of collective purpose and struggle in a modern political state.

First published in 1943 during China's War of Resistance against Japan, this story tells of the events that take place in the life of an unremarkable art collector, Zhuang Yiya. Lao She begins by observing that there are two kinds of collectors. The first are those who collect as a distraction. Typically, these collectors "have some learning that enables them to make an honest living" and, "whenever they have spare money, they will spend it on things that delight their hearts and enhance their sense of refinement." The second kind of collector is different: "They collect, but they

2. For an account of the foreign translations of Lao She's works, see Lao She, *Lao She shenghuo yuchuangzuo zishu*, ed. Hu Jieqing (Hong Kong: Sanlian shudian, Joint Publishing, 1981), 527–28.

3. For a list of Lao She's works, see *Lao She* (Zhongguo xiandai zuojia xuanji), ed. Shu Ji (Hong Kong: Sanlian shudian, Joint Publishing, 1988), 266–95.

4. "While the rest of the Chinese literary world debated hotly, and for years, the value of proletarian literature, Lao She wrote the novel that the left wing insisted on but failed to produce." Quoted from the dust jacket of Lao She, *Rickshaw: The Novel Lo-t'o Hsiang Tzu*, trans. Jean M. James (Honolulu: University of Hawaii Press, 1979).

also peddle. They appear to be refined, but at the core they are no different from merchants." These other collectors' collecting "is equivalent to hoarding" ("Attachment," 211–12).

Among theorists of modernity, Walter Benjamin's account of the book collector serves as a relevant intertext here because of its unapologetic acknowledgment of the importance, in collecting, of ownership. For Benjamin's book collector, to acquire an old book is to give it rebirth, and collecting is thus part of an endeavor to renew the world by tearing things out of their original contexts and inserting them in the novel one of the collection. Ownership, Benjamin writes, "is the most intimate relationship that one can have to objects. Not that they come alive in him [the collector]; it is he who lives in them."[5] Approaching his topic at the historical juncture when the high bourgeois values of European society came face to face with the disposable mass culture of global modernity, Benjamin saw in collecting an intellectual practice that allows one to remain in touch with the past in intense, because subjectivized, ways. What are being assembled through collecting are not just the things themselves but also memories: "Every passion borders on the chaotic, but the collector's passion borders on the chaos of memories" ("Unpacking," 60). Together, the twin obsessions with ownership and with memory suggest that collecting carries with it a desire for possessing history, even if such a possession can only come in fragmented, incomplete forms. At the same time, because of the often accidental nature of the encounter with objects—one can never be sure what may come one's way, when and where—the nostalgia for owning the past that is embedded in collecting is, arguably, inseparable from a utopian sense of anticipation, of looking forward to a future that is not entirely known or knowable.

Benjamin's stance on collecting is thought-provoking because it offers a significant shift from the stern criticism of commodity fetishism that, since Marx's *Capital*, has been a predominant way of viewing material things in capitalist culture. In his analysis, Marx points out that commodities are artificial objects that hide the human labor that has gone into their making. To underscore his point that such commodities are false representations of the real relations of production, Marx mobilizes a series of terms—such as "mist-enveloped," "secret," "disguised," "hid-

5. Walter Benjamin, "Unpacking My Library: A Talk about Book Collecting," *Illuminations*, trans. Harry Zohn, ed. Hannah Arendt (New York: Schocken, 1969), 67. For another interesting account of collecting, see Susan Stewart, *On Longing: Narratives of the Miniature, the Gigantic, the Souvenir, the Collection* (Baltimore: Johns Hopkins University Press, 1984), 151–69.

den," "absurd"—that foregrounds the fabulous, beguiling nature of their appeal. "The whole mystery of commodities, all the magic and necromancy that surrounds the products of labour as long as they take the form of commodities," he writes, "vanishes . . . so soon as we come to other forms of production."[6] Despite the ambiguities that may be detected in Marx's memorable portrayal, this portrayal has nonetheless given rise to a prevalent modernist intellectual tendency to regard things as superficial and conducive to spiritual pollution. Writing in the 1920s, Georg Lukács, for instance, extended the implications of Marx's argument for his own theory of the reification of human consciousness in capitalist society. For Lukács, the thing-dominated relation between man and the world is what gives rise to ideology, an inverted, distorted understanding of history that can only be corrected through the proletarian revolution.[7] A few decades later, armed with the fashionable tool of semiology, Roland Barthes recast this classic critique of false consciousness yet another way by putting examples of petit-bourgeois French mass culture—from advertisements of soap powders and detergents, to ornamental cooking, to toys and plastic—through a chic "scientific" analysis based on staggered levels of the linguistic sign.[8] The novelty of his analysis (at the time he wrote) notwithstanding, Barthes was by and large still participating in a neo-Marxist tradition of suspicion and distrust of the objects that saturate the commercial cultural environment of the industrialized modern world.

In view of this persistent sense of misgiving about things even within late capitalist Western society, it is not surprising that things were also among the evils that had to be purged in a self-consciously revolutionary political state such as communist China. Among popular representations of the happenings of the Chinese Cultural Revolution during the 1960s and 1970s, for instance, is the burning of books and artifacts, the shameful reminders of bygone eras of spiritual corruption. Such burning was characteristic of the class struggle that was officially launched against both China's feudalist tradition and Western imperialism. As such, the demolition of incorrect things became communist China's way

6. Karl Marx, *Capital: A Critique o Political Economy*, trans. Samuel Moore and Edward Aveling, ed. Frederick Engels, 3 vols. (New York: Modern Library, 1906), 1:7.

7. See Georg Lukács, *History and Class Consciousness: Studies in Marxist Dialectics*, trans. Rodney Livingstone (Cambridge: MIT Press, 1971).

8. See Roland Barthes, *Mythologies*, trans. Annette Lavers (London: Paladin, 1973).

of honoring, in a literal manner, the critical revolutionary ethos of thing phobia that arguably began with Marx. Ironically, in the retrospective assessments of the Cultural Revolution, scholars and writers have tended overwhelmingly to interpret such destruction of things as part of a larger violence against humanity, when such destruction was, strictly speaking, genealogically consistent with the Marxist criticism of *de*humanization as made manifest in the processes of reification and commodification. In the midst of this theoretical confusion dominated by humanism (what is human and what is inhuman—preserving things or destroying them?), an interesting question is elided: If these remnants of the past are indeed so objectionable, why not simply confiscate and dispose of them in secret? Why the visual, almost celebratory, public display of the act of destruction?

One possible answer, of course, is: So as to teach everyone a lesson. This displacement onto an altruistic purpose is perhaps the most readily available—and respectable—antidote to any fascination with things in themselves, a fascination that is usually considered a symptom of selfishness. One reason Benjamin's work is so powerful, it follows, is that he managed to turn around this entrenched stereotyping of love-of-things-as-index-of-selfishness by arguing that collecting, however private and selfish it may seem, can also be understood as a form of historical-materialist practice.[9] He thus made it possible to lavish attention on the "mist-enveloped" objects of bourgeois modernity while holding on to Marx's emphasis on a radical critique of history. Indeed, by combining that emphasis with a sympathetic or empathetic reading of the inorganic, Benjamin paved the way for a distinctly different type of theoretical attitude to materialize toward the universe of objects. At the same time, his modes of inquiry, because they stemmed concretely from a historical materialism that specializes in the cultural sediments of high capitalist bourgeois Europe, do not necessarily provide answers for every kind of question that arises with the act of collecting and its existential implications, especially when such questions pertain to a non-Western culture in the throes of modernization and nationalist revolution. To return to the example of China, what kind of historical lesson may be gleaned from the Cultural Revolution practice of setting piles of things on fire? In the demonstrative spectacle of burning that is supposed to teach every-

9. See, for instance, Walter Benjamin, "Edward Fuchs, Collector and Historian," *The Essential Frankfurt School Reader*, ed. Andrew Arato and Eike Gebhardt (New York: Urizen, 1978), 225–53.

one a lesson, there seems to be something in excess of the rationale of the attributed pedagogical function and, for that matter, in excess of any attempt to define the handling of things within a strictly historical-materialist framework. It is in this light—that is, the possible theoretical inadequacy of even an unusually sensitive historical materialist reader of things, such as Benjamin—that the work of a writer such as Lao She may, I believe, prove to be provocative.

In Lao She's protagonist Zhuang Yiya we see a good example of the Benjaminian passion for owning bits and pieces of history. History here appears in the form of culture—the cherished collectibles that, supposedly, enhance people's sense of their own refinement. Remarkably, Lao She depicts changing attitudes toward history by way of the changing attitudes toward collecting and thereby incidentally introduces the issue of *class understood in cultural rather than economic terms*.[10] The first kind of collector, his story tells us, includes those who may be described as members of the new middle class in early twentieth-century urban China: "In terms of profession, these people are perhaps government employees, or perhaps middle school teachers. Sometimes we also find lawyers or doctors" ("Attachment," 211). But in terms of the enjoyment of leisure, these people are members of an older society in which culture still means something pleasurable, something to be enjoyed for itself. Their behavior toward objects, the scraps and ruins of bygone years, contains a lingeringly indulgent quality that is fast becoming out of step with their times. By contrast, the second kind of collector is merely opportunistic. Though these collectors may appear to be refined, they are not collecting for the sake of the pleasure given by the objects but rather in order to make money. Accumulating bits and pieces of the past is for them simply a means to an end, the end of generating capital. To this extent, they belong to a newer order of society, a newer class whose ties with the past are strictly through the external relation of exchange and trade. Apart from the past's commodified forms, which offer themselves to be raided,

10. Among modern Chinese writers, Xu Dishan has made use of the figure of a lower-class woman collector, an urban ragpicker, to point a moral about the hypocrisy of patriarchal society's investment in cultural refinement; see his short story "Chuntao" ("Big Sister Liu" [1934]), trans. Sidney Shapiro, *Stories from the Thirties*, 2 vols. (Beijing: Panda Books, 1982), volume 1, 111–41. I have offered a discussion of this story in *Woman and Chinese Modernity: The Politics of Reading between West and East* (Minneapolis: University of Minnesota Press, 1991), 145–50. According to Lao She, Xu was the friend who encouraged him to become a writer; see his essay mourning Xu, "Jingdao Xu Dishan Xiansheng," *Lao She* (Zhongguo xiandai zuojia xuanji), 184–90.

these people have little or no use for history, which they consider readily discardable in their march toward the future.

Its brevity notwithstanding, "Attachment" is carefully organized into three distinct narrative segments, each bearing a progressively different significance. The first of these segments concentrates on establishing Zhuang as a character with his eccentric habits of collecting. A member of the Jinan gentry, Zhuang is a college graduate and has worked as an administrator and middle school teacher. He began collecting by buying numerous inexpensive items, on which he bestows rapt, ritualistic attention. Under his gaze, these items become personified with human features; at the same time, he loves putting them through an impersonal, methodical process of sorting and classifying before they can be safely tucked away:

> He will take home a couple of such eighty-cent treasures, full of insect holes, smudgy, smeared, and crinkled up like an old woman's face. Only at night, after locking the door to his room, will he savor the pleasures of his modest purchases, handling them over and over again. After numbering them, he will carefully press his seal on them, then put them in a large cedar chest. This bit of exertion will send him to bed, happily weary and satisfied. Even his world of dreams will be quaintly ancient. ("Attachment," 213)

As time goes by, Zhuang acquires the reputation—given in jest and with sarcasm by fellow collectors and shop owners—of being a "connoisseur of Shandong's minor artists" ("Attachment," 215). Although he would like to earn more in order to buy better pieces of calligraphy and painting, Zhuang never considers using his collection to make money: "Selling his calligraphy and paintings to make some money is something he will not do. For better or for worse, this is *his* collection, and it will follow him to his grave. He will never sell it. He is not a merchant" ("Attachment," 216, translators' emphasis).

The second segment of the narrative begins as Zhuang turns forty. It is 1937, the year China was invaded by the Japanese. By this time, Zhuang has fully internalized the idea that he is an expert; he understands the conventions that accompany the activity of collecting and wants to leave a name: "He has made no contribution to the world, but becoming a collector by a fluke isn't too bad an achievement. He hasn't lived in vain. After all, as the saying goes, When people die they leave behind their name; when wild geese fly away, they leave behind their cries!" ("Attachment," 218). Zhuang decides that he will purchase something that is truly worth money. By luck and circumstance, he comes into possession of a painting by the master Shi Qi. Because the authenticity of the piece is at first dubious, many collectors are unwilling to bid, and rumors are soon spread by Yang Kechang, a rival bidder, that Zhuang is a fool for having purchased it. The tables are turned, however, when a connoisseur of international reputation, Mr. Lu, certifies that the Shi Qi is indeed a bona fide work by the master. Since Mr. Lu's seal of approval enjoys credibility even among "European and American" collectors, Zhuang is completely vindicated ("Attachment," 221).

It is important to remember that Lao She places this crowning achievement of collecting in the midst of a national catastrophe, Japan's invasion of China. In terms of symbolic significance, the acquisition and authentication of the painting by Shi Qi are simultaneously the acquisition and authentication of Zhuang's social identity; he is no longer simply fantasizing about being an expert collector but has become one. He has taken on the identity that was previously awarded to him only in jest. The second segment ends at the point when even Yang Kechang, the person who once mocked Zhuang's credibility, wants to mend fences with him. Precisely at this point, however, Lao She inserts the historical reminder "July seventh—war breaks out with Japan" ("Attachment," 221). The third and final segment brings the entire narrative to a crux with the imminent arrival of the Japanese. We are now offered a shocking observation about Zhuang: "It isn't that he lacks patriotic feelings. . . . However, for the sake of his beloved objects, it seems to him that surrender is not necessarily impermissible" ("Attachment," 222–23). During a time of national crisis, Zhuang continues to be unswervingly faithful to his collection of strange old objects. Unlike everyone else, he has not fled and is not exactly sorry for not having done so: "Every day he waits for the Japanese, holding the Shi Qi in his arms and saying to himself, 'Come on then! The Shi Qi and I will die together!'" ("Attachment," 223).

One day, Yang comes to inform Zhuang that the Japanese have arrived in town and would like to appoint him as the head of the education bureau. Zhuang's first reaction is that he can't work for the Japanese ("Attachment," 224). Then Yang explains the conditions: should Zhuang agree, he would save his collection and the Japanese would shower him with gifts. Should he refuse, his things would be confiscated and he would be punished, perhaps even killed. With tears in his eyes, Zhuang looks at the two chests of his collection and nods his head. The story ends with the statement "To be attached to something is to die with it" ("Attachment," 225).

By the end of this story, the Benjaminian themes of ownership and remembrance, which foreground the collector's relationship with the past, have given way to another theme, fidelity. What makes Lao She's story perplexing is not simply the collector's fetishization of his objects or even the historical-materialist implications of such fetishization; it is, ultimately, the exclusiveness of his attachment, in comparison with which other kinds of attachment do not seem to have any weight. If history is present, it is present by way of an antagonism at the core of the process of social identification, and by way of a seeming irreconcilability between the personal collection and the political collective as such.

Interestingly, Lao She took a diametrically opposite attitude toward attachment to things in the autobiographical essay "Si da jia kong" (An empty house), also written in 1943 and on the similar topic of personal possessions. Lao She describes how, having been forced since 1937 to move from place to place and often in a state of emergency, he has lost all his books, furniture, utensils, and savings, as well as precious gifts of calligraphy and paintings from friends. Despite such losses, his conclusion is upbeat. In sharp contrast to the fictional tale, the autobiographical essay ends with a morally unambiguous call to arms: "Let's not be sad over the loss of these books. To save [our] culture, we must [first] defeat the Japanese soldiers!"[11] The remarkable divergence in tone between these two pieces of work from the same period suggests that Lao She was profoundly ambivalent about this topic, and that he found in the medium of fiction a way of handling this ambivalence that was impermissible in other types of discourses.

Whereas for Benjamin the critical interest of collecting lies in the impossibility of disentangling it from *re*collection, from the chaos that comes with memory, for Lao She it is less a question of remembrance and nostalgia than a question of incommensurable loyalties, a question he stages explicitly through the confrontation between Zhuang's attachment to his collection and the impulse toward patriotism when one's homeland is under siege.[12] Rather than the temporal and historical transition emphasized by Benjamin, therefore, the boundary highlighted by Lao She is an existential one, replete with the tensions between submitting to one's native culture and submitting to foreigners (in this case, when the foreigners are the enemies invading and looting one's coun-

11. Lao She, "Si da jia kong," *Lao She shenghuo yu chuangzuo zishu*, 421–24.

12. Even in real life, Lao She's nostalgia for the calligraphy and paintings he had lost was due primarily to the fact that they had been personal gifts from friends and elders. See Lao She, "Si da jia kong."

try). Lao She, who was Manchurian rather than Han Chinese, but who served as the secretary general for the All China Resistance League of Writers and Artists during the eight-year war with Japan, could not not have been sensitized to this fraught, indeed ironic complex of ethnic and national identification in modern China.[13]

If what the collector in Benjamin refuses to give up is an intimate, albeit outmoded, relationship with the past through its remnants, what is it that a character such as Zhuang refuses to give up?

To respond to this question, it would be necessary to discern the crude Lacanian theoretical implications of the story's narrative movements.[14] In the first segment, it is possible to see Zhuang as rummaging around in the realm of the Imaginary: he is obviously attracted to the bric-a-brac; he is even neglecting his obligations to his wife because of his penchant for collecting, but he has not really grasped the meaning of what he is doing. It is as though what he is rummaging around for are not only the objects but also his self-knowledge. In this regard, the objects may be seen to provide a kind of mirroring function, an external reflection of his groping (and as yet uncoordinated) efforts. This initial phase gives way next to Zhuang's determination, as he reaches middle age, to make something of his life by acquiring at least one worthy item. The purchase and possession of the Shi Qi, together with the expert recognition that fol-

13. Lao She's interest in his own ethnic background is best seen in the unfinished, semiautobiographical novel *Zheng hong qi xia* (first published in 1979), which can be found in *Lao She shenghuo yu chuangzuo zishu*, 179–350; for an English translation, see Lao She, *Beneath the Red Banner*, trans. Don J. Cohn (Beijing: Panda Books, 1982). For a discussion of Lao She's use of his Manchu heritage in some of his works, see Peter Li, "Identity and Nationhood in Lao She's *Teahouse*," *Chinese Studies* 13.2 (1995), 275–97. One of the incidents that saddened him throughout his life was the manner in which his father was killed. A lowly paid palace guard during the last days of the Manchu Dynasty, Lao She's father was carrying gunpowder during the Boxer Rebellion (1900), when the international Eight-Nation Allied Army invaded Beijing. Ignited by an incendiary bomb, the gunpowder exploded; with severe burns, Lao She's father crawled into a grain shop to await death. When his nephew discovered him by chance, his body had turned black and he was unable to speak. He handed the nephew a pair of socks he had removed from his swollen feet; these socks were later buried with some other possessions in his empty tomb. For an account of Lao She's involvement in the resistance against Japan, see *Lao She*, 255–56; see also his own account of his activities during the war in "Bafang fengyu," *Lao She shenghuo yu chuangzuo zishu*, 430–77.

14. I emphasize "crude" because, as the rest of my discussion shows, the recognizable Lacanian features in the story are seldom a precise match with Lacan's theories, which are best regarded as handy explanatory tools rather than as perfect decoding solutions.

lows, stands in effect as an entry into the Symbolic. If in the initial phase Zhuang is merely collecting curiosities for idle pleasure, by the time the Shi Qi is bought and authenticated he has found a definite purpose—a confirmed social status—for himself.

The difficult and traumatic question emerges in the third segment with the demand made by the Japanese, in what may be considered an encounter with the Real. The scenario around Zhuang at this point is a curious reminder of the well-known forced choice cited by Lacan, "Your money or your life!" In terms of logic, the interest of this threat inheres in the impossibility of choice set up by the word *or*, for although the word gives the impression of a choice between two things, the choice is illusory: one cannot hold on to money without holding on to life itself. The moral is that one can in reality only "choose" life, that in fact this is not a real choice between equal alternatives because one of the terms is the precondition for the other.

In Lao She's story the logic is quite different. The choice presented to Zhuang by the Japanese is an inclusionary one: You can have your collection *and* your life! Holding on to the material object and holding on to life belong in this command on the same plane rather than being separated by the dividing line *or*. The dividing line that matters in this case lies *outside* the choice proposed: *from the perspective of being Chinese*, what would be lost, should one choose this generous offer, is a crucial kind of value or possession, namely, one's place in the national community, for which a specific act of negation—the banning of the enemy—defines the terms of belonging. The dilemma faced by Zhuang is thus more akin to the Confucian teaching of *she sheng qu yi*, "to surrender one's physical life for moral righteousness."[15] If we translate this teaching into a form such as "Moral righteousness or your life!" the choice advocated by the ancients is clear: moral righteousness has to be more valuable than life, and life itself should not be viewed as the ultimate possession, as something of which we cannot let go. The ancients were in effect saying: Be morally righteous or be dead. The person who holds on to his own life rather than to moral righteousness, so their logic goes, is a coward unworthy of the respect of his fellow human community.

During a national crisis when there is a clearly identifiable enemy, patriotism often occupies precisely the elevated place of "moral righteousness" in the above imperative. Yet patriotism itself—and moral

15. *Yi* can also be translated as "a just cause" or "brotherhood." Its chief emphasis is that of fidelity of a social or communal nature.

righteousness by implication—can function so resolutely only because it represses the ideological mechanism that gives it its momentum. This ideological mechanism works by polarizing external reality into an antagonism between "us" and "them," offering those who subscribe to patriotism an unambiguous purpose in which to anchor themselves. As Slavoj Žižek suggests, the reason ideology works is never simply because it tells lies ("*Ideology has nothing to do with 'illusion,'* with a mistaken, distorted representation of its social content") but rather because it serves a protective function: the polarities, the antagonisms on which ideology depends for its persuasion in fact help to shield us from the terror of a free field of significatory possibilities and thus from complete identificatory chaos.[16] Adhering to the ideology of patriotism during war, for instance, would allow one the security of an epistemic closure (we are good, the enemy evil), which in turn would make it possible to act without self-restraint or compunction. Take the character Yang Kechang in Lao She's story. He is not at all virtuous or likable, but he has internalized the imperative of patriotism sufficiently to know how to act appropriately under the historical circumstances. While he is obviously working for the Japanese (who send him to talk to Zhuang) and is hence a national traitor (*hanjian*), he can act with a clear conscience because he believes that he is only superficially subservient to the enemy. This is evident when he is contemplating buying the Shi Qi. Even though he doubts the authenticity of the painting, Yang rationalizes his wish by way of a patriotic reflex, namely, that it is all right to take advantage of the Japanese:

> He wants to secure the painting at the price of a fake painting, then turn around and sell it to the Japanese as genuine. There is no question that the painting is a fine piece. Moreover, even if it should be a fake, the Japanese will pay a hefty price for it, because in Japan Shi Qi pieces are highly marketable. ("Attachment," 219)

When Zhuang declines to act in accordance with patriotism, he is declining a socially endorsed ideological anchoring and the moral protection it allows him. His declination brings to the fore the inarticulate fact that there is perhaps something *else* at stake, and that the closure and security offered by national chauvinism, with its polarization of us and

16. Slavoj Žižek, "Introduction: The Spectre of Ideology," *Mapping Ideology*, ed. Slavoj Žižek (London: Verso, 1994), 7. See also Žižek, "How Did Marx Invent the Symptom?," *Mapping Ideology*, 296–331.

the enemy, are not necessarily final. But it is lethal to dare forsake such closure and security. Hence, even though by his decision Zhuang gets to live, the concluding line suggests the opposite to be the case; his surrender to the Japanese is in effect a kind of suicide, the annihilation of an existence that has been socially and culturally derived. When he was brutalized and humiliated by the Red Guards at the onset of the Cultural Revolution, Lao She too chose to commit suicide. (He thus became one of relatively few modern Chinese writers to do so, in contrast to the significant number of suicides among, say, modern Japanese writers.) In retrospect, the narrative of "Attachment" seems to stand as an uncanny kind of foreboding.[17]

As a collector, what exactly is it that Zhuang refuses to give up? Is it the love of art itself? Lao She seemed, according to at least one critic, to have intended such a reading.[18] Consider again the manner in which he begins his tale, when he offers what appears to be a straightforward categorization of collectors into two types. Accordingly, Zhuang can be read as the artistic collector who, unlike his mercenary counterpart, refuses to give up his dedication to art. On closer examination, in fact, what Lao She has established is a familiar binary opposition between intrinsic and extrinsic relations, a binary opposition that recalls none other than the classical Marxist analysis of commodities in terms of use and exchange values (an analysis that, as I mentioned earlier, is inscribed in a deep-rooted suspicion of commodities as mendacious objects). The problems inherent in such an opposition have been effectively clarified by poststructuralist analysis, which has demonstrated that there can be no object of use- or intrinsic value which does not at some point come into relation with what is other than itself or outside itself.[19] Use or intrinsic value, in

17. For a discussion of the clear sense of skepticism toward patriotism that runs throughout Lao She's writings, a skepticism that is accompanied by a recurrent fascination with self-destruction, see David Der-wei Wang, *Fictional Realism in Twentieth-Century China: Mao Dun, Lao She, Shen Congwen* (New York: Columbia University Press, 1992), 157–200.

18. Wei-ming Chen, "Pen or Sword: The Wen-Wu Conflict in the Short Stories of Lao She (1899–1966)," Ph.D. dissertation, Stanford University, 1985; see in particular 89–98: "As a story about art, 'Attachment' is Lao She's strongest affirmation of art as the seed as well as the fruit of love; art gives meaning to man's existence. The war years seem to have consolidated Lao She's view of himself as a man of the pen and to have confirmed in his mind the validity and importance of art." Chen continues, "The last line in 'Attachment' provides a possible reason why Lao She may have committed suicide at the beginning of the Cultural Revolution when he was attacked for his writings."

19. For a well-known and helpful example of such an analysis, see Jean Baudril-

other words, is always already an outcome—an aftereffect—of exchange and circulation. By extension, if art can only receive its value when it is inserted in a system of comparison, circulation, and exchange (however primitive), can there ever be a kind of collector who collects purely for the pleasure (use- or intrinsic value) of the objects themselves?

The untenable nature of this binary opposition between the two kinds of collectors is clearly something sensed by Lao She also, for the rest of his narrative performs nothing short of a problematization or deconstruction of the opposition. Consequently, we see Zhuang, despite his initial classification, actively building a social life around his collecting habit (befriending antique shop owners, exchanging views with and offering advice to fellow buyers), gradually acquiring a reputation, and finally achieving professional recognition for owning the painting by Shi Qi. Throughout the story we are made aware of the presence of *foreigners*. When Yang brings two Japanese to look at Zhuang's collection the first time, Zhuang thinks to himself afterward, "Even the Japanese have come for a viewing. Hm, so this little collection of his has already brought him international recognition!" ("Attachment," 218). There are also the "European and American" antique collectors who are said to give credit to the connoisseur Mr. Lu's endorsements. These narrative details, which foreground the interpersonal and transcultural import of Zhuang's activities, offer an alternative understanding of the collector to the binary categorization that is set up at the beginning. Such details suggest that, however pure and secluded an object may be in its owner's fantasy, it is virtually impossible to avoid its coming into contact with a system of evaluation that is external to and other than itself (such as

---

lard, *For a Critique of the Political Economy of the Sign*, trans. Charles Levin (St. Louis: Telos Press, 1981). This analysis of Marx enables Baudrillard to deconstruct, in a systematic manner, the hostility toward commodity fetishism that lies at the core of classical political economy. Unfortunately, in Baudrillard's case this perceptive understanding of the contradictions inherent in the traditional Marxist critique of "false consciousness" has led, in his subsequent writings, to the other theoretical extreme, an a priori cynical attitude that tends to scoff at any attempt at ideology critique because everything is always already ideological. Žižek puts it succinctly: "One should be careful to avoid the trap that makes us slide into ideology under the guise of stepping out of it. That is to say, when we denounce as ideological the very attempt to draw a clear line of demarcation between ideology and actual reality, this inevitably seems to impose the conclusion that the only non-ideological position is to renounce the very notion of extra-ideological reality and accept that all we are dealing with are symbolic fictions, the plurality of discursive universes, never 'reality'—*such a quick, slick 'postmodern' solution, however, is ideology par excellence*" ("Introduction," 17).

money, social recognition, or the professional approval of the connoisseur); the intrinsic or use-value of an object, that is, comes inevitably to be validated by what is foreign or extrinsic to it. By implication, the collector who only collects for the sake of the object (for the love of art) is at best a fantasy; in actual practice he is not entirely distinguishable from the peddling and hoarding kind.

The necessary bifurcation of the narrative into these two incongruent, indeed contradictory versions of Zhuang (who is said to belong to the first kind of collector, only then to behave in a manner not entirely distinguishable from the second) is further amplified by the enigmatic ending. Let us retrace again the narrative thread Lao She provides. According to the categorization at the beginning of the story, what distinguishes the two kinds of collectors is mercenariness, which is normally not considered a virtue. Unlike Yang, Zhuang is not interested in the money he can make from the Shi Qi or his collection. Yet precisely because of this—his lack of mercenariness—Zhuang turns out to be the more extreme traitor. This is the unnerving part of the story, but it would be insufficient to explain it by way of a collector's so-called love for art. (Such an explanation would validate a meticulous elaboration of art, things, and objects in the name of how history is inscribed in them, but it would also leave intact the binary opposition—between art and reality, between intrinsic and exchange value, between unworldly and worldly collectors—that I questioned earlier.)

What makes Zhuang's decision provocative or scandalous, it should be noted, is not simply that he surrenders (or pretends to surrender, as in the case of Yang) to the enemy for the sake of art, but that *he is faithfully (that is, positively) attached to something other than the national community*. If he lacks mercenariness, he nonetheless has not (as the more moralistically minded might expect) filled this lack with patriotism, but instead has filled it with devotion to his objects. Though unthinkable under the political circumstances at the time, his surrender to the national enemy, a traitorous act to be sure, is only symptomatic of a still deeper perversion—namely, that he does not desire to live without his objects. To him, the reward of life is only the incidental byproduct of this perversion, *this other fidelity*. To recall the terms of our discussion, not only has Zhuang overturned the assumption that physical life is the ultimate possession (as in the threat "Your money or your life!"), but he has also substituted dedication to a grand collective meaning such as moral righteousness (as in the imperative *she sheng qu yi*) or love for one's nation with an idiotic and narcissistic dedication to a set of objects.

As Benjamin writes, "Not that [the objects] come alive in [the collector]; it is he who lives in them." The disturbing nature of Zhuang's behavior has less to do with the fact that he gets to keep his life by becoming a national traitor or a moral coward than it has to do with his absurd feeling that life is worth nothing without his own collection of man-made things.[20] What Zhuang refuses to give up is therefore neither the pure pleasure provided by the objects nor the social recognition he has won through contacts with others; rather, it is the nonexchangeable, irreplaceable bond—and bondage—he has established with his collection as such. These inanimate things, which in one respect are mere baggage or garbage, have now been raised to a supreme status—not simply the status of physical life itself, which can still be destroyed, but indeed the status of that higher, indestructible sublime ideal, that *something to die for*. In the language of morals, these objects are now on a par and openly vying with *yi*, the intangible virtue of human fellowship and communal belonging for which—and only for which, it is thought—individual life should be sacrificed.

In an elegant narrative mode, thus, Lao She's story captures a kind of experience that borders on identificatory anarchy. Being Manchu in Han-dominated China and likely to be more alert than many around him to the artificial, that is, historically contingent nature of patriotic submission, he found in the tale of an apparent betrayal the occasion to dramatize something that goes much further than the ever-shifting polarities of patriotic ideology. This occasion emerges in the most unremarkable of situations, in the humdrum collecting habits of a middle-class citizen who thinks he is gathering bric-a-brac for entertainment. In the midst of the objects appears a void that the man refuses to fill with his fellow citizens' belief in the nation. Lao She, who actively championed the cause of resistive patriotism during the war, did not allow the impending nihilism

20. In the semiautobiographical short story "Xiaorenwu zishu" ("Autobiography of a Minor Character") Lao She writes of private property in similar, albeit not identical, terms: "People with brains may consider abolishing private ownership. Some intellectuals may advocate the destruction of the family system. But in my mind, if all private ownership were like our rickety old house and our two jujube trees, I would be happy to declare myself a conservative. Because even though what we possessed didn't relieve us from our poverty, it did provide us that stability that made each blade of grass and each tree come alive in our hearts. At the very least, it made me a small blade of grass always securely rooted to its own turf. All that I am began here. My character was molded and cast here" ("Autobiography of a Minor Character," trans. Chen, *Blades of Grass*, 244).

of such a revelation to disrupt the predominantly realist surface of his storytelling; rather, he relies on the old-fashioned method of letting his story's plot do the work, bringing the story to a stop at the moment when the obsessiveness of Zhuang's attachment transforms into the moral horror of surrendering to the Japanese. But *which is the greater horror: surrendering to the Japanese, or surrendering to objects?* The matter-of-fact style of his light, descriptive prose notwithstanding, by the end we are suddenly faced with the starkest of existential questions: What kinds of attachments make life worth living? What kinds of attachments are worth dying for? Can these questions still be answered with the old moral imperatives? Should Zhuang come to his senses, give up his objects, and die a resistive patriot in the hands of the Japanese? Is he not in some way redeemed by his captivation by the objects—while others go on to destroy themselves and other people in the name of patriotism? With the concluding line, a chasm has gaped open through the epistemically indeterminate behavior of this most ordinary of *xiaorenwu* (minor characters).[21]

The nuanced apprehension of such paradoxes of fidelity was obviously not admissible to the construction of national literature in the China of the mid-twentieth century. Instead, patriotism made great leaps forward in myriad performances of the polarizations of "us" and "them," coercively transforming old allies into new enemies in the years ahead, when communism forged its stronghold in the populace's imagination. Such polarizations fueled the Red Guards' torture and murder of writers and intellectuals such as Lao She in the name of class struggle. Yet Lao She's politically incorrect story from the 1940s teaches us something important about the frenzy of the Cultural Revolution. In Zhuang's faithfulness to his objects, in his belief that he would be nothing without them, don't we in fact witness a familiar kind of libidinal investment—*exactly the kind that the party and the nation want of its people*? A passage from Žižek helps explain my point here:

21. Again, the short story "Autobiography of a Minor Character" may be noted here for the similarly stark existential questions it poses. Consider a passage like the following: "Every time I saw a mangy dog . . . I had to ask, 'Why the heck are you living? How the devil do you manage to go *on* living?' This bit of concern did not rise from contempt but from the commiseration of 'One who pities another remembers himself.' In this pathetic creature I saw my own shadow. Why the heck was I living? How had *I* managed to go on living? Like this dog, I had no answer but felt lost, afraid, and indescribably sad. Yes, my past—what I remembered, what I heard, and what I seemed to remember and seemed to forget—was a stretch of darkness. I did not know how I had groped my way out" (234, emphases translator's).

> Why, precisely, does Marx choose the term *fetishism* in order to designate the "theological whimsy" of the universe of commodities? What one should bear in mind here is that "fetishism" is a *religious* term for (previous) false idolatry as opposed to (present) true belief: for the Jews, the fetish is the Golden Calf; for a partisan of pure spirituality, fetishism designates "primitive" superstition, the fear of ghosts and other spectral apparitions, and so on. And *the point of Marx is that the commodity universe provides the necessary fetishistic supplement to the "official" spirituality*: it may well be that the "official" ideology of our society is Christian spirituality, but its actual foundation is none the less the idolatry of the Golden Calf, money. ("Introduction," 20; first two emphases in the original, last emphasis mine)

Rather than being the moral opposite of the altruistic ideal of class struggle, the loyalty to things—what Žižek calls false idolatry—stands in fact as class struggle's "fetishistic supplement," a supplement which rivals the "official spirituality" of the Cultural Revolution in its demand for the love of the people. It is the danger posed by this rival spirituality, equally if not more capable of exerting a magical hold on the people, that is conjured in the perverse collecting behavior of a minor character like Zhuang. For the party, in other words, things are not realities in themselves but rather symbols: to destroy them is to destroy the evil idea, ideology, tradition, or history behind them; the condemnation of the material is in the end still part of idealist warfare. This, ultimately, is the reason it is imperative, in the process of class struggle, to *stage* demonstrations of destroying things. The burning of books and artifacts is tantamount to a form of exorcism, the point of which is not simply to dispense with objects but to combat—to tame by mimicry—a competing illusion in full potency. Nothing short of a deliberate display of violence, repeated at regular intervals for all to see, is deemed sufficient to ward off this competitor's fierce power. Only by such vehement gestures of a ritualized attack can an alibi of official ideology's difference from its enemy be safely established: "Since I (the Communist Party) denounce you (feudalist and imperialist objects), I must be completely different from what you stand for." And, once ritualized in this manner, violence and the loyalty it demands are turned into properties or possessions exclusive to the political state, which can henceforth legitimize, indeed normalize, the ruthless stamping out of an equal contender for popular submission in the name of the collective good. Class struggle, then, assumes in the Chinese Cultural Revolution exactly the function of that socially constructed antagonism, polarized between the purity of our own position and the culpability of an enemy who is not one of us simply because we are struggling against it. Such social antagonism is typically mobilized in such a manner as to allow one group (in this case the party and the state) the privilege of monopolizing violence and loyalty, thereby veiling the more fundamental, radical antagonism that surfaces in what Lacanians such as Žižek refer to as the encounter with the Real and in what Lao She depicts as a fidelity to objects.[22]

Writing books, Benjamin suggests, is the most praiseworthy method of acquiring them; the books written by an author are, accordingly, his most intimate possessions.[23] This subtle connection among collecting, ownership, and self-possession through writing—made by a German Jewish author who chose to end his own life in 1940, when persecution by the Nazis seemed imminent—was well understood by those in charge of the harassing agenda of the Cultural Revolution. For the latter, it was thus not enough only to demolish relics of the past and strip people of their collectibles; it was also peremptory to attack writers on the basis of their most cherished possessions—their writings—and to wrest from them the loyalty that, it was thought, could only belong to the party.

Lao She's story of the art collector offers a clue to the complex significance of his reported suicide by drowning in Beijing on 24 August 1966. According to the account by his son, Shu Yi, Lao She, who had been ill that summer, was subjected to the typical demeaning interrogations and physical torture and branded a counterrevolutionary by the Red Guards on 23 August. He was detained and abused until after midnight and ordered to report again to the authorities the next morning. When morning came, Lao She left home after saying goodbye to his wife, Hu Jieqing (who thought he was going to the authorities) and to their three-year old granddaughter. Apparently, he then headed for the small park around Taiping Lake, where, it was later reported by a gatekeeper, he sat motionless the entire day. It is believed that he drowned himself around midnight on 24 August. When his body was eventually collected by his wife and cremated, his family was not allowed to retain his

22. I have offered a more extended discussion of Žižek's distinction between these two kinds of antagonisms; see my chapter "Ethics after Idealism," in *Ethics after Idealism: Theory—Culture—Ethnicity—Reading* (Bloomington: Indiana University Press, 1998), 32–54.

23. "Of all the ways of acquiring books, writing them oneself is regarded as the most praiseworthy method" (Benjamin, "Unpacking My Library," 61).

ashes. More than a decade later, when blame for the terrors of the Cultural Revolution was officially laid on the so-called Gang of Four (the influential ultra-leftist clique spearheaded by Jiang Qing, Mao Zedong's fourth wife), Lao She was exonerated by party leaders as one of modern China's greatest writers. In the container that should have held his ashes, his family placed a pair of glasses, a pen, a brush, and some jasmine tea leaves—the very things that had accompanied him in his life as a writer.[24]

During his last moments by the lake, did Lao She come to the realization that his selfless devotion to his country and the party had come to nothing? For all his patriotism he had been branded an enemy of the people, someone who had to be eliminated. Was his suicide one last act of loyalty—of attachment—to the patriotic community, by proving his innocence with his own life? Or was it one last act of defiance and self-defense—against that very community which had betrayed him—by holding on to his ultimate collection and object, his self-possession as a writer and an intellectual? "To be attached to something is to die with it": the statement with which he had ended the story he wrote in the 1940s stands as a fateful, if forever cryptic, emblem of the manner in which he ended his own life narrative.

The things that are the most relentlessly condemned have a way of getting their retribution. In the ideologically chaotic aftermath of the Cultural Revolution, in the period of disillusionment, since the late 1970s to the present time, with the altruistic pronouncements of official ideology, what are some of the obsessions that have aggressively (re)surfaced in the People's Republic of China? Aside from the McDonalds, Rolexes,

24. In a tragic coincidence, then, Lao She's bodiless burial came to resemble his own father's; see note 13. For an account of the last couple of days of Lao She's life, see Shu Yi, *Lao She* (Beijing: Renmin chubanshe, 1986), 178–81; see also Hu's moving account of the circumstances of Lao She's death, including the manner in which she received notification to collect his body, as documented by Wang Xingzhi in *Lao She shenghuo yu chuangzuo zishu*, 535–62. A somewhat different account, also citing Shu Yi, is offered by William A. Lyell, "Translator's Postscript: The Man and the Stories," *Blades of Grass*, 279–81. Paul Bady has suggested that Lao She's suicide was most closely paralleled by the suicide of the character Qi Tianyou in *Si shi tong tang* (Four generations under one roof); see Bady, "Death and the Novel: On Lao She's Suicide," *Two Writers and the Cultural Revolution: Lao She and Chen Jo-hsi*, ed. George Gao (Hong Kong: Chinese University Press, 1980), 5–14. Bady's view is shared by Shu Yi and elaborated by Wang in *Fictional Realism*, 198–99. For a study of the historical circumstances around Lao She's suicide and the controversies it has generated, including attempts to track down Lao She's persecutors, see Fu Guangming, *Lao She zhi si ji qita* (On Lao She's death and the rest) (Taipei: Wenshizhe chubanshe, 2004), 72–195.

Mercedes Benzes, Hong Kong and Western lifestyles, it is, in elite and nonelite circles alike, the cosmopolitan culture of Shanghai of the 1920s, 1930s, and 1940s, the pinnacle of a decadent, commodities-studded materialist environment, that has returned to captivate the mainland populace with a vengeance, while the Golden Calf, money, has, to all appearances, replaced communism as the object of belief and idolatry. Such collective attachments to the "fetishistic supplements" to "official spirituality" are perhaps simply footnotes to the prophetic tale Lao She told nearly three quarters of a century ago.

4

Sacrifice, Mimesis, and the Theorizing of Victimhood

In his provocative study *Homo Sacer: Sovereign Power and Bare Life*, Giorgio Agamben brings attention to the notion of biopolitics as expounded by Michel Foucault in the first volume of *The History of Sexuality* and elsewhere, to argue an originarily juridicopolitical basis for the relationship between sovereign power and naked human existence, what Agamben refers to as "bare life."[1] This basis, understood by Agamben as the near indistinguishability or irreducible connection between law and violence, is also described by him as "the single real content of law."[2] Few readers, I suspect, would detect in Agamben's book any substantial link to the subject of mimesis. In the context of the twentieth century, it would certainly seem more logical to explore such a link in more well-known classics on art, literature, representation, and cultural politics—as for instance Walter Benjamin's discussion of technological reproducibility, which destroys auratic distance and enables the replica-

1. Giorgio Agamben, *Homo Sacer: Sovereign Power and Bare Life*, trans. Daniel Heller-Roazen (Stanford: Stanford University Press, 1998); see in particular part 2, chapters 1–3. For Foucault's discussions of biopolitics, see Michel Foucault, *The History of Sexuality: An Introduction*, vol. 1, trans. Robert Hurley (New York: Vintage, 1980); *"Society Must Be Defended": Lectures at the Collège de France 1975–1976*, trans. David Macey (New York: Picador, 2003); *Security, Territory, Population: Lectures at the Collège de France 1977–1978*, trans. Graham Burchell (New York: Palgrave Macmillan, 2007); *The Birth of Biopolitics: Lectures at the Collège de France 1978–1979*, trans. Graham Burchell (New York: Palgrave Macmillan, 2008).

2. Agamben, *Homo Sacer*, 65. He is discussing Walter Benjamin's essay "Critique of Violence," in Benjamin, *Reflections: Essays, Aphorisms, Autobiographical Writings*, ed. and with an introduction by Peter Demetz (New York: Schocken Books, 1986), 277–300.

tion of images on an unprecedented scale; Erich Auerbach's ruminations on the historically evolving relationship among narrative style, temporality, and humanity; Foucault's description of the decline of language's capacity for corresponding to the world's plenitude; or Edward W. Said's criticism of the ideologically suspect, fantastical caricatures of the East by Western scribes, artists, and imperialists alike.[3] My indebtedness to all these studies notwithstanding, what interests me about mimesis is a more specific problem, namely, the manner in which mimesis has figured in certain kinds of theorizing about victimhood and what may be loosely termed subordinated or stigmatized existence.[4] Given the massive unresolvable conflicts that shape the contemporary world, this problem is likely to remain topical in the twenty-first century. In order to follow the conceptual paths around it, it is necessary, I have noticed, to push against the limits of what is accepted as commonsensical thinking (humanistic, moral, or ethical). This essay is, essentially, an attempt at such "following" and "pushing"—hence its speculative, rather than conclusive, nature.

Since he has not discussed mimesis per se, the relevance of Agamben's book is, as I will go on to show, surprising and convoluted: it lies dormant in a part of his argument that, with a kind of suggestiveness that can only result from the kinship of ideas, alerts me to what I'd like to argue as mimesis's conceptual double or conjoined twin: sacrifice.

Sacrifice as a Mythologeme, or, the Aesthetics and Ethics of the Unrepresentable

Agamben's use of Foucault's work is intriguing in at least two respects. First, he sees sovereignty as residing in the relation of what he calls "ban": "He who has been banned is not, in fact, simply set outside the law and

3. See Walter Benjamin, "The Work of Art in the Age of Mechanical Reproduction" (1936), *Illuminations*, ed. and with an introduction by Hannah Arendt, trans. Harry Zohn (New York: Schocken, 1968), 217–51; Erich Auerbach, *Mimesis: The Representation of Reality in Western Literature*, trans. Willard R. Trask, 50th anniversary ed., with an introduction by Edward W. Said (1953; Princeton: Princeton University Press, 2003); Michel Foucault, *The Order of Things: An Archaeology of the Human Sciences*, trans. Alan Sheridan (London: Tavistock, 1970); Edward W. Said, *Orientalism* (New York: Vintage, 1978).

4. For an exploration of this problem in the contemporary politics of ethnicity, see my *The Protestant Ethnic and the Spirit of Capitalism* (New York: Columbia University Press, 2002), in particular chapters 2 and 3.

made indifferent to it but rather *abandoned* by it, that is, exposed and threatened on the threshold in which life and law, outside and inside, become indistinguishable. . . . *The originary relation of law to life is not application but Abandonment.* The matchless potentiality of the *nomos, its originary 'force of law,'* is that it holds life in its ban by abandoning it."[5] This emphasis on ban suggests that Agamben's understanding of power is, unlike Foucault's, essentially negative and prohibitive in orientation. Whereas Foucault's major intervention has been to shift this traditional understanding of power to the positive, indeed enabling and progressive capacities in which power thrives in modernity, for Agamben power remains the power to taboo, exclude, withhold, and annihilate (despite his nuanced articulation of the paradox between exception and rule).[6] Hence his pronouncement, on a universal scale:

> Everywhere on earth men live today in the ban of a law and a tradition that are maintained solely as the "zero point" of their own content, and that include men within them in the form of a pure relation of abandonment. All societies and all cultures today (it does not matter whether they are democratic or totalitarian, conservative or progressive) have entered into a legitimation crisis in which law (we mean by this term the entire text of tradition in its regulative form, whether the Jewish Torah or the Islamic Shariah, Christian dogma or the profane *nomos*) is in force as the pure "Nothing of Revelation." But this is precisely the structure of the sovereign relation, and *the nihilism in which we are living is, from this perspective, nothing other than the coming to light of this relation as such.*[7]

By its definitive tone—"Everywhere on earth," "All societies and all cultures today"—this passage not only reinforces the negative and prohibitive notion of power but also asserts that such power applies in all societies and all cultures regardless of their actual systems of government (and, by implication, regardless of their histories of political evolution). As is the case throughout his book, Agamben names this power "law" (in a move that goes in the opposite direction from Foucault's explicit warn-

5. Agamben, *Homo Sacer*, 29.

6. Agamben's elaboration of this notion of power, which is closely linked to Heidegger's notions of concealment, withholding, and the open, can be philosophically provocative and suggestive. See, for instance, his sensitive discussions of Kafka's "Before the Law" on 49–62 of *Homo Sacer* and of the status of the human in Western thought in *The Open: Man and Animal*, trans. Kevin Attell (Stanford: Stanford University Press, 2004).

7. Agamben, *Homo Sacer*, 51, my emphasis.

ing that law is an inadequate model with which to deal with questions of power).[8] Agamben holds that power-as-law is facing a legitimacy crisis because its basis is increasingly revealed to be "nothing." For him, however, this nothingness, which may be understood as the nonexistence of any concrete justification or grounding for whatever happens to rule, is, precisely, the heart of the matter, the truth about politics based on law. Accordingly, the "nihilism" we are experiencing everywhere today is simply, to return to our discussion in chapter 1, the *laying bare* or deconstructive illumination (the "coming to light") of this fundamentally vacuous "structure of the sovereign relation."

Second, in keeping with his formulation of power as ban, Agamben's argument also seems to overlook, inevitably perhaps, the attempt Foucault made at historicizing. For Foucault, biopolitics, with its dedication to the proliferation of apparatuses for the management of bodies, took shape as the older notion of sovereignty premised on the power to kill evolved into more lenient and gentle forms of governance in the modern period. As in the case of his other studies of the institutionalization and socialization of the modern subject, Foucault's overall intellectual interest in biopolitics was directed, to invoke his memorable phrase, at "the entry of life into history."[9] Agamben's emphasis is quite different, and contrary: he is interested rather in articulating the meanings of a modern and contemporary Western world in which "bare life," even when reduced to seemingly mere biological existence, is nonetheless entirely enmeshed in sovereign power—a world in which, in other words, biological survival itself must be recognized as always already political, as defined in the aforementioned terms of a definitive nihilism. (He therefore holds that there is no outside to the law.) In order to argue this absolute—and thus timeless—relationship between sovereign power and bare life, Agamben must of necessity sidestep the historicity of the transition (from premodern to modern times) that Foucault clearly introduced into his argument. And, because sovereignty (power as ban) remains the only viable form of agency Agamben envisages, bare life itself, instead of being historicized, is implicitly *eroticized* by him in the form

8. These remarks by Foucault sound like a point-by-point refutation of Agamben's project: "In order to make a concrete analysis of power relations, we must abandon the juridical model of sovereignty. That model in effect presupposes that the individual is a subject with natural rights or primitive powers; it sets itself the task of accounting for the ideal genesis of the State; and finally, it makes the law the basic manifestation of power" (*"Society Must Be Defended,"* 265).

9. Foucault, *The History of Sexuality*, 1:141.

of an obscene spectacle, in which the subject that matters is not only one that has been totally crossed out (annihilated) but also one that has been crossed out (violated) by denudation, by being *stripped* bare.

Even if Foucault's mode of historicizing is questionable (a point that can certainly be made), it seems evident that Agamben's argument of a continuous biopolitics that runs, conceptually, from European antiquity to European modernity, culminating in the catastrophe of the Nazi concentration camps of the 1930s and 1940s, has still fundamentally neglected the critical dimension of Foucault's work that foregrounds the supremacy of *life* as the biopolitical imperative in the modern age. It is in this sense of a coercive imperative to live and stay alive that Foucault's work resonates most readily with the high-tech, biomedical, pharmaceutical, and political manipulations of contemporary human existence, from the ostracization and incarceration of the insane and the criminal, to the surveillance of sexual practices, to the ever-generative forms of discipline and production of docile subjects in our civil institutions. In the twenty-first century, as such manipulations of human existence are brought to unprecedented levels of sophistication and efficiency through intersecting global networks of communications and commercial trafficking, Foucault's point that biopolitics is a matter of governing the living, of regulating and normativizing how populations should live, remains incontrovertibly on the mark. For Agamben, on the other hand, the coercive imperative at stake is a matter of extermination: his transformation of Foucault's biopolitics into a thanatopolitics in this regard is justified by his primary example of the Nazi camps. In the finality of the slaughter of the Jews, the Gypsies, the communists, and the homosexuals, as well as the euthanasia imposed on those who were mentally deficient or physically handicapped, there is, he suggests, little leeway for considering life other than as bare—that is, stripped of all supplemental attributes that would have rendered it "more" human. His real point, however, is that even such bare, reduced life, life shorn of all human decency, needs to be returned and restored to its due human connection, a connection that he reiterates as fundamentally juridicopolitical, in the double sense of law-cum-violence and law-cum-nothingness.[10]

10. Numerous scholars have discussed the distinctions and tensions between Foucault's and Agamben's views on biopolitics and sovereignty. For a sampling of these lively and stimulating debates, see Mika Ojakangas, "Impossible Dialogue on Biopower: Agamben and Foucault," *Foucault Studies* 2 (2005), 5–28; Lee Medevoi, "Global Society Must Be Defended: Biopolitics without Boundaries," *Social Text* 25.2 91 (2007), 53–79; Didier Fassin, "Humanitarianism as a Politics of Life," *Public*

Being aware of the fact that his subject of study can easily be—indeed has often been—approached through the notion of sacrifice, Agamben takes pains to distance his own argument from such sacrificial logic. Referring to the sacred as a "mythologeme" that originated from William Robertson Smith's *Lectures on the Religion of the Semites* (1889) and passed quickly into French sociology, Agamben rejects the sacrificial logic on account of its imputed ambivalence—that is, its capacity for holding together and making interchangeable two opposed categories, the holy and the profane. This is a capacity that fascinated thinkers from Émile Durkheim and Marcel Mauss to Sigmund Freud, Émile Benveniste, and Claude Lévi-Strauss. Precisely what these thinkers considered to be the attractive conceptual resilience of the sacred—its potential for a certain duplicity, for shuttling back and forth between the polarities of high and low, consecrated and filthy—becomes for Agamben a kind of "veil," an "aura" whose spell needs to be broken: "The wish to lend a *sacrificial aura* to the extermination of the Jews by means of the term 'Holocaust' was, from this perspective, an irresponsible historiographical blindness. . . . The truth—which is difficult for the victims to face, but which we must have the courage *not to cover with sacrificial veils*—is that the Jews were exterminated not in a mad and giant holocaust but exactly as Hitler had announced, 'as lice,' which is to say, as bare life."[11]

Its morally austere nature notwithstanding, this argument leaves open an important question: What if the notion of sacrifice is subscribed and adhered to by the victims and their community, as an inalienable part of their memory and belief? In other words, what if sacrifice is part of an effort to (re)imagine and (re)narrativize an otherwise lost, because inaccessible, past—part of a collective, retrospective striving for coherence? True, such striving often leads to the (problematic) monumentalization of catastrophes, but on the basis of what or whose moral authority should such striving be repudiated and invalidated? Another well-known example from Judeo-Christian history may help clarify the problem at stake: to the Roman officials in occupied Judea, the execution of a political dissenter such as Jesus, too, probably meant little more than the routine extermination of "lice," but for the followers of Christianity, that execution (together with its iconic instrument, the cross) has carried a definitive symbolic significance of sacrifice over the centuries.[12]

Culture 19 (2007), 499–520; Malcolm Bull, "Vectors of the Biopolitical," *New Left Review* 45 (2007), 7–25.

11. Agamben, *Homo Sacer*, 114, my emphases.

12. For this interesting point, I am indebted to Yuan-horng Chu, "Dusk or Dawn:

For these followers, it is the subject that bears the cross, rather than the subject that has been crossed out, that remains noteworthy.

Agamben's critique of the sacrificial logic can, of course, be seen as an eminently post-Enlightenment, secularist gesture. To this extent, his question "In what, then, does the sacredness of the sacred man consist?" is a rhetorical one.[13] The answer is obvious: such sacredness consists not in any (residual) religious sense of the sacred but rather in the inextricable link between sovereign power and human existence. Just as this link manifests itself in bare life—the "life that may be killed but not sacrificed" (a phrase Agamben repeats numerous times in his book)—so too would sovereignty become groundless were it not for the existence of such bare life and its potential to be killed.[14] At the same time, as more and more people get killed in our contemporary world without reason, justification, or representation—as the lives of the innocent pile up like wreckage against the precarious grounds of sovereignty—the sovereign relation itself is increasingly exposed for what it is: an arbitrary configuration of power that has immense potential for abuse and that has, indeed, been thoroughly abused.

The ambivalence of sacrifice is unacceptable in Agamben's analysis because for him, ultimately, there can be no room to imagine—to imagine, for instance, that the victims of the death camps were sacrificed for some transcendent purpose or meaning. Nor is there room to imagine a kind of politics that would involve a struggle for hegemony in the form of a resistant or antagonistic confrontation with tyrannical dominance. All relations of substitution and exchange—and by implication all possibilities of redemption understood in a broad sense—came to a halt with the acts of cruelty (and exercise of sovereign power) in the camps, rendering the ambivalence inherent to the sacrificial logic an illusion and a lie.

This said, there is a further dimension embedded in Agamben's rejection of sacrifice that is worth considering, perhaps less for the reasons he offers (on secularist moral grounds) than for the affinity that sacri-

---

On Agamben Painted Exceptional Rule" [*sic*], *Wenhua yanjiu/Router: A Journal of Cultural Studies* 1 (September 2005), 197–219; see in particular 211–12. I should add that I am aware of the fact that the historical circumstances surrounding Jesus' disappearance and death are a subject of great dispute among scholars; the point here is simply that being killed may hold very different—yet perhaps equally valid—meanings for the victims (and their community) from the intentions harbored by the perpetrators of killing. However, this possible difference does not seem to matter in Agamben's argument.

13. Agamben, *Homo Sacer*, 72.

14. See the cited phrase in Agamben, *Homo Sacer*, 114.

fice shares with another order of thinking: mimesis. In this light, Agamben's emphasis on the absolute finality of the Nazis' thanatopolitics may be seen to have its precedents in a well-known (though debatable) *aesthetic and ethical* approach to the Holocaust, whereby, notwithstanding the representational materialities and mimetic effects involved, the artist or critic insists that the Holocaust is unrepresentable. One thinks, for instance, of documentary film classics such as Alain Resnais's *Nuit et Brouillard* (*Night and Fog*) and Claude Lanzman's *Shoah*, in which the historical weight of the catastrophe is shown or given to us through the muteness of the most ordinary of scenes, such as a lush green landscape or a decrepit empty building, even as the directors emphasize how difficult or impossible it is to represent the enormity of what happened. In this kind of aesthetic and ethical approach, the most natural or unadorned sight (much like Agamben's bare life) is understood not only as that which has been divested of all cultural accoutrements but also as that which, in its so-called nothingness, reveals the basic, yet utterly ruthless and nihilistic, reality of a juridicopolitical relation.[15] It is in this connection, what may be termed an antimimetic aesthetics and ethics, that I believe Agamben's stringent critique of the notion of sacrifice with regard to the Holocaust should finally be grasped: recast in terms of mimesis-as-representation, this critique would seem akin to none other than the familiar assertion that the Holocaust is an unrepresentable—that is to say, inimitable, irreproducible, and untranslatable—experience.[16]

Ironically, such a critique of sacrifice is, in the end, operating fully within the bounds of sacrificial logic, the logic that something must be forfeited or cast off. This sacrificial logic is, of course, also a version of the notion of ban that Agamben stresses as essential to the way juridical power functions. By prohibiting the sacrificial logic, therefore, Agamben has in effect taken on the capacity for banning (a particular form of ban), and put himself in the place of the (arbitrary?) sovereign and judge,

15. I should make clear that I do not find this aesthetic and ethical approach (which insists on the unrepresentability of the Holocaust) persuasive, especially when the medium in question is a visual one such as film. For an informed critique of this approach, see Naomi Mandel, *Against the Unspeakable: Complicity, the Holocaust, and Slavery in America* (Charlottesville: University of Virginia Press, 2006).

16. Agamben's reflections on the testimonies about Auschwitz are similar: he holds that survivors bore witness to something to which it is impossible to bear witness. See *Remnants of Auschwitz: The Witness and the Archive*, trans. Daniel Heller-Roazen (New York: Zone Books, 1999).

ruling against the nobody who wants to hold on to the myth of sacrifice in his or her history.

What Follows (or Remains after) Sacrifice: Mimesis as Substitute

Appearing as it does in the context of contemporary political philosophy debates, Agamben's antisacrificial, antimimetic aesthetics and ethics resonate with certain strands of what may be schematically called poststructuralist theoretical thinking. For some time now, since the arrival of poststructuralism in the mid-twentieth century, mimesis has been viewed in some contemporary theoretical sectors with suspicion and disdain, as the legacy of a rigid and conservative representational politics with its demand for realist verisimilitude—that is, for the production, in art or literature, of a replica of what supposedly exists beforehand. As Martin Jay writes, "For . . . theorists normally labeled, for better or worse, poststructuralist, a conventional aesthetic privileging of mimesis or what is taken to be its synonym, imitation, is an ideologically suspect recirculation of the ready-made, a false belief in the fixity of meaning and the possibility of achieving full presence, a language game that fails to see itself as such."[17] This antimimetic stance notwithstanding, one notices, on reflection, a curious paradox embedded in poststructuralist maneuvers in general: even as the mimetic is distrusted as an ideology of mechanical duplication, copying, and re-presentation (one that assumes the presence of some original determinant), poststructuralist theory nonetheless tends to depend for its deconstructive work on acts of substitution, alternation, and differentiation—acts that, in the terms of our present discussion, may in fact be seen as part and parcel of the entwined logics of sacrifice and mimesis.

This close kinship between sacrifice and mimesis informs the arguments of some of the authors who have had the strongest influences on poststructuralist writing. In his well-known theory of the gift, for instance, Marcel Mauss dispels the idea of the free, innocent gift by shifting

17. Martin Jay, *Cultural Semantics: Keywords of Our Time* (Amherst: University of Massachusetts Press, 1998), 120. For examples of French writings that elaborate the theatrical dimensions of mimesis in complex manners, see the collection *Mimesis, Masochism, and Mime: The Politics of Theatricality in Contemporary French Thought*, ed. Timothy Murray (Ann Arbor: University of Michigan Press, 1997).

attention to relations of exchange and reciprocity as the rationale behind gift-giving: understood precisely, the giving of a gift, as Mauss argues, always carries with it the significance of a gesture of retaliation—of a return of something. Similarly, by introducing the distinction between the penis and the phallus in his semiotic rewriting of Freud's discussions of anatomical differences, Jacques Lacan clarifies the indispensable exchange principle that underpins Freud's argument about sociality: in order to be socially acceptable, an individual must learn to give up, to trade in, as it were, his own solipsistic or narcissistic pleasures. Closer to our time, in her theory about the social origins of gender, Judith Butler too confirms the function of exchange in the construction of an intimate part of our identity: the way we go about picking our objects of desire. Butler argues that gendered identities, in particular for those who are or who think of themselves as heterosexual, are a matter of learning to relinquish the type of love object that is socially prohibited (as for instance a person of the same sex as oneself). Gender is haunted by melancholy because, whether or not one is conscious of it, it is a matter of negotiating and performing the effects of a premandated and internalized loss.

I have brought up these few examples of influential frames of thought as a quick reminder of the indispensability in representational politics of the mutuality of loss and gain, and of surrender and redemption—a mutuality that, I contend, may be reconceptualized as the twin logics of sacrifice and mimesis. To this extent, I'd like to speculate that mimesis has retained its relevance to this day less because of its persistence as imitative representation (even though this undoubtedly remains the case in many circles) than because of its potency as part of an inescapable structural relation—the relation of exchange and substitution, absence and presence, disappearance and appearance, and so forth, without which the acts of thinking and writing would be impossible. Understood in these terms (and not merely in terms of a secondary duplication of a primary event), the mimetic-as-representation, even when it assumes the positivistic form of appearing as or like something else, should be described more precisely as the accessible portion of a certain foregone *transaction*, a transaction, moreover, during which something was for one reason or another lost, given up, or surrendered—in other words, sacrificed. Rather than being a static replication or re-presentation of a preexisting plenitude, mimesis, one may argue, is the sign that *remains*—in the form of a literal being-there, an externalization and an exhibition—in the aftermath of a process of sacrifice, whether or not the sacrifice has been witnessed or apprehended as such. Mimesis is the (visibly or sensorially accessible) substitute that follows, that bears the effects of (an often invisible or illegible) sacrifice.

Reformulated in this manner, sacrifice and mimesis would seem a double epistemic passage underlying all acts of signification, a passage that tends to become acute in contexts of dominance and subordination, in which loss and gain are existentially palpable phenomena impinging on individual and group identity formation. Is this perhaps the reason mimesis has figured so prominently in scenarios which carry the charge of victimization (and by implication, the charge of voluntary or involuntary sacrifice)? I am thinking, for instance, of the scenarios of patriarchy and colonialism, in which the status of those whose lives are compromised and demeaned has been explored, often, via the tropes of mimesis.

As I mentioned, biopolitics, as Foucault discusses it, is not necessarily or exclusively about the mandating of death but more often than not takes the coercive form of an imperative to stay alive. Would adhering to Foucault's conceptualization (with its emphasis on life) bring about an alternative understanding of the implications of Agamben's discussion, by allowing us to *localize* the latter as simply one possible method of theorizing victimhood—a method in which the antimimetic resistance to sacrifice (and with it, representation) amounts to a particular aesthetics or ethics, based implicitly on a specific way of (re)distributing the sensible?[18] Conversely, in other scenarios of violence, such as patriarchy and colonialism, in which the goal has not been extermination tout court but rather the multifaceted governance and subjection of live bodies, what would happen to the logic of sacrifice—discredited in no uncertain terms by Agamben—and with it the mimetic?

Mimesis as a Coping Mechanism and Survival Tactic

Luce Irigaray, for instance, has offered a well-known reappraisal of femininity by distinguishing between two forms of mimesis: the productive

18. I borrow the notion of the distribution of the sensible from Jacques Rancière; see *The Politics of Aesthetics: the Distribution of the Sensible*, trans. and with an introduction by Gabriel Rockhill (London: Continuum, 2004), 12–34. For Rancière's very different perspective on the politics of representability in the contemporary world (in contradistinction to those who hold that certain things are unrepresentable), see his essay "Are Some Things Unrepresentable?" in Rancière, *The Future of the Image*, trans. Gregory Elliott (London: Verso, 2007), 109–38; see also the related discussions in chapters 2 and 7 of this book.

and the recuperative. Putting it in deliberately simple terms, she writes, "There is *mimesis* as production, which would lie more in the realm of music, and there is the *mimesis* that would be already caught up in a process of *imitation*, *specularization*, *adequation*, and *reproduction*."[19] Referring to the latter kind of mimesis as "masquerade," Irigaray allows for the recognition of femininity as a type of social sacrifice, whereupon women must imitate or reproduce—at their own peril—the norms of femininity that have been prescribed in advance by patriarchal mores:

> I think the masquerade has to be understood as what women do in order to recuperate some element of desire, to participate in men's desire, but at the price of renouncing their own. In the masquerade, they submit to the dominant economy of desire in an attempt to remain "on the market" in spite of everything. But they are there as objects for sexual enjoyment, not as those who enjoy.
>
> What do I mean by masquerade? In particular, what Freud calls "femininity." The belief, for example, that it is necessary to *become* a woman, a "normal" one at that, whereas a man is a man from the outset.[20]

At the same time, Irigaray asserts that the mimetic also contains the possibility of a different relation, one in which women, precisely because they understand what has been prescribed for them, may set out consciously to perform these prescriptions in such ways as to turn them into subversive acts. She calls this kind of mimesis

> *mimicry*. One must assume the feminine role deliberately. Which means already to convert a form of subordination into an affirmation, and thus to begin to thwart it. . . .
>
> To play with mimesis is thus, for a woman, to try to recover the place of her exploitation by discourse, without allowing herself to be simply reduced to it. It means to resubmit herself . . . to ideas about herself, that are elaborated in/by a masculine logic, but so as to make "visible," by an effect of playful repetition, what was supposed to remain invisible . . . "to unveil" the fact that, if women are such good mimics, it is because they are not simply resorbed in this function. *They also remain elsewhere.*[21]

This association of the mimetic with feminist cunning and, in particular, with a playful, self-conscious repetition, made to resemble and

19. Luce Irigaray, *This Sex Which Is Not One*, trans. Catherine Porter with Carolyn Burke (Ithaca: Cornell University Press, 1985), 131.

20. Irigaray, *This Sex Which Is Not One*, 133–34.

21. Irigaray, *This Sex Which Is Not One*, 76.

conjure the normative image of femininity yet simultaneously undermining this image from within, is perhaps one of the most important instances in contemporary thought in which mimesis is credited with the potential to exceed, rather than simply to compensate for, the sacrifice which precedes it. This potential enables mimesis to take on the value of a type of behavior—a camouflage conformism—which, even if it does not exactly set women free, allows them (to imagine) a utopian space-time of alterity from within the bounds of patriarchal subordination. In ways that resonate with the high-modernist conceptualization of reflexivity as performance (see chapter 1), the overtones of Irigaray's method are recognizably Brechtian: mimicry is, for her, *sexual politics as gestus*, a radical way of defamiliarizing (the pose and posture of) femininity, making it strange to its bearer and audience alike.

In the discussions of colonized existence, mimesis has likewise played a significant role in theorists' attempts to configure a breathing space for those who have been subjected to injustice. In the contexts in which cross-cultural encounters entail the imposition and enforcement of one group's (typically, Westerners') superiority over another (typically, the "natives" of African, Asian, American, Australian, and New Zealand cultures), mimesis is a routine rite of initiation: those from the so-called inferior group, the colonized or semicolonized, are bound to want to imitate their supposedly superior aggressors as part of their strategy for social survival and advancement. Under these circumstances, the question is how agency can be assessed: Must agency be understood to lie only with the so-called original (the superior group, the one being imitated), or can it also be understood to reside in the act of imitation—in those who imitate? What kind of agency?

As I have discussed elsewhere, various levels of mimesis traverse this kind of situation.[22] I will concentrate on two here. The first level, probably the most obvious, is a direct legacy of Western imperialism and colonialism of the past few hundred years: the mimesis with the white man as the original. The logistics involved are time-proven: the white colonizer, his language, and his culture stand as the model against which the colonized is judged; the colonized must try her best to become like her master even when knowing full well that her efforts at emulation will be deemed less than satisfactory. The values involved—superior and inferior—are hierarchically determined and tend to work in one direc-

22. See the extended discussion in Chow, *The Protestant Ethnic and the Spirit of Capitalism*, 95–127.

tion only: the original, so to speak, exists as the authentic standard by which the imitator is judged, but not vice versa. The colonized subject, condemned to a permanent inferiority complex, must nonetheless try, in vain, to become that from which she has been excluded in an a priori manner. Try as she may, she will always remain a poor copy; yet even as she continues to be debased, she has no choice but to continue to mimic and replicate.

At a second level, as theorists no longer feel comfortable dismissing the colonized as merely inadequate, mimesis takes on a more complex set of connotations. As exemplified by the work of a scholar such as Homi Bhabha, who pursues the rationale of Frantz Fanon's impassioned arguments about black subjectivity in works such as *The Wretched of the Earth* and *Black Skin, White Masks*, one important feature of the colonized's subjectivity that was previously ignored—the ambivalent, contradictory emotions embedded in her identitarian plight—now assumes center stage. As Fanon writes, for the person of color (in his case, the black man) "there is only one destiny. And that is white." With insight and foresight, he also suggests that "only *a psychological interpretation* of the black problem can lay bare the anomalies of affect that are responsible for the structure of the complex."[23] Fanon's incisive dissection of colonized subjectivity is summarized by Bhabha in this manner: "The ambivalent identification of the racist world . . . turns on the idea of man as his alienated image; not Self and Other but the otherness of the Self inscribed in the perverse palimpsest of colonial identity."[24]

In psychological terms, what Bhabha, taking the lead from Fanon, introduces to the colonial scenario is desire (and its irrational, often unconscious modes of working). As in the case of Irigaray's endeavor to reclaim femininity (as performativity) for women, desire in this instance serves as the very grounds on which to reappraise the value of dominated subjecthood. Instead of being written off as the inferior partner in an asymmetrical historical encounter with the West, the colonized is now understood, with much more suppleness and sympathy, in terms of a desire to be white that exists concurrently with the shame and resentment accompanying the inferior position to which she has been socially, culturally, and racially consigned. Between the (positive) condition of wanting to imitate the white man and the (negative) condition of self-

23. Frantz Fanon, *Black Skin, White Masks*, trans. Charles Lam Markmann (New York: Grove Weidenfeld, 1967), 10, my emphasis.

24. Homi K. Bhabha, *The Location of Culture* (New York: Routledge, 1994), 40, 44.

loathing and abatement, lies a dynamic range of epistemic and representational possibilities, possibilities that infinitely enrich the theorization of postcolonial subjectivities. Whereas at the first level of mimesis, relations between the colonizer and the colonized remain immobilized in a static hierarchy, the introduction of desire transforms the entire question of mimesis into a fluid, because vacillating, structure, in which the thoroughly entangled feelings of wanting at once to imitate the colonizer and to eliminate him become the basis for a new kind of analysis, with the tormented psychic interiority of the colonized as its theatrical nerve center. Much like Irigaray's mimicry, the colonized's desire here makes way for a flexible, because mobile, framework for imagining alterity from within subordination.

By focusing on the colonized person as an indeterminate, internally divided subject, a subject that is not self-identical, Bhabha and the critics influenced by him thus enable what may be called a poststructuralist redemption of colonial victimhood that is reassuringly humanistic: it is the failure, the incompleteness or incompletability of the mimetic attempt (a point on which the second level of mimesis in fact concurs with the first) that makes the nonwhite subject theoretically interesting—indeed salvageable (one might say, in the aftermath of colonial sacrifice). Consciously or unbeknown to herself, and oscillating between black and white, the subjectivity of the colonized is now dispersed, pluralized, and multiplied across the many possible circuits of desire. No longer rigidly polarized or dichotomized against each other, black and white can now be considered mutually constituted and mutually constituting. The question remains as to how this neoliberal rendering of victimhood can ultimately distinguish itself from the productivity of colonial power. In both cases, it would seem, it is the ambivalences, the contradictions, and the fissures, always already inherent in the act of articulation, that are considered to contain the potential for opening things up, so to speak. How to draw the line in between? Or—to push Bhabha's reasoning to its limit—is that not so important?

Concomitant with the issue of mimesis in these gendered and racial scenarios of violence, then, reemerges in a different guise exactly the problematic of sacrifice at which Agamben has directed his skepticism. Recast in sacrificial terms, the paradigm shift that poststructuralist feminist and postcolonial criticism has brought about is none other than a suspension, and thus a revaluation, of the substantiality and nonnegotiability of victimhood through behavioral and psychic buoyancy—playful mimicry and fluctuating desire—so that, even if it seems degrading and

CARDIFF UNIVERSITY ★ PRIFYSGOL CAERDYDD ★

humiliating (involving the sacrificing of one's autonomy and dignity), the very act of imitating one's victimizer may yet turn out to be an aperture to a different kind of future. Mimesis amounts in these cases to a creative repackaging and repurposing of the givens of dominated existence for survival in a situation that is not about to improve any time soon.

On balance, much as this survival kit of mimetic tricks (with mimesis either as subversive performativity or as ambivalent desiring) has been greatly influential in contemporary cultural criticism, as a coping mechanism it still by and large leaves in place the inequities of the situation—which remains governed by man or the white man as the original—with the important proviso that the playful imitation by women or the not-quite-right imitation by colonized subjects is now deemed, at least by some, to be equally deserving of critical attention. Insofar as it is a coping mechanism, moreover, mimesis seems to have retained the quality of a secondary phenomenon whose raison d'être is derived from something external to itself. Although what is at issue is no longer so-called art's imitation of life, the fact that mimetic behavior and psychology are construed as a response, a reaction to fraught ideological conditions suggests that mimesis continues to be accorded a subaltern and instrumentalist status. Obviously, this conclusion is not very satisfying.

Mimesis as Originary Force, and a Different Hypothesis about Victimhood

A useful, if controversial, interlocutor at this juncture is René Girard, whose work offers many remarkable insights into the bondage between sacrifice and mimesis.[25] Given that Girard has explicitly referred to the double meanings of the Latin word *sacer*, which, as he points out, has been translated alternately as "sacred" and as "accursed," and that he, like Agamben, is clearly skeptical of the ambivalence of the sacred as disseminated by French sociology, the absence of any reference to Girard's work in Agamben's book is conspicuous.[26] Can this be because, as I have

25. René Girard, *Violence and the Sacred*, trans. Patrick Gregory (Baltimore: Johns Hopkins University Press, 1977). For related interest, see also Girard, *Deceit, Desire, and the Novel: Self and Other in Literary Structure*, trans. Yvonne Freccero (Baltimore: Johns Hopkins University Press, 1976), and *"To Double Business Bound": Essays on Literature, Mimesis, and Anthropology* (Baltimore: Johns Hopkins University Press, 1978).

26. See Girard on the word *sacer* in *Violence and the Sacred*, 257; see also his dis-

been suggesting, a rejection of sacrifice (as in Agamben's case) is not only a rejection of sacrifice but in essence amounts to a rejection also of mimesis, the very basis of Girard's theory?

Like many mid- to late twentieth-century thinkers, Girard has been influenced by Freud, and the psychological vocabulary of desire is eminently present in his readings. His understanding of desire is, however, quite unique. For Girard, desire is not some kind of original human nature which for historical or cultural reasons (such as patriarchy or colonialism) adapts itself into a desire *for* something (such as a desire to imitate). Instead, desire is always learned, and can be borrowed and transferred. Rather than the commonsensical question "What does x want?," then, Girard asks: How does x come to want this or that? As he has famously argued, the answer to this latter question is mimesis: to desire means not simply to desire an object but also to imitate a model's way of desiring. In this manner, the model one tries to imitate inevitably becomes a rival:

> Rivalry does not arise because of the fortuitous convergence of two desires on a single object; rather, *the subject desires the object because the rival desires it.* In desiring an object the rival alerts the subject to the desirability of the object. The rival, then, serves as a model for the subject, not only in regard to such secondary matters as style and opinions but also, and more essentially, in regard to desires.[27]

In his classic *Violence and the Sacred*, Girard illustrates his bold argument by providing readings of numerous texts, often from myths, classical Greek tragedies, psychoanalysis, and anthropological studies of tribal beliefs and practices, but his reading of Freud's Oedipus complex offers perhaps the most eloquent demonstration of his logic. Girard traces the shadowy presence of a mimetic understanding in Freud's description of the little boy's desire for his mother. As Freud points out, this desire has something to do with the boy's special interest in his father, to grow

---

cussions on 263–65, 298. Regarding the ambivalence of the sacred, Girard puts it in this manner at the very beginning of his book: "Because the victim is sacred, it is criminal to kill him—but the victim is sacred only because he is to be killed. Here is a circular line of reasoning that at a somewhat later date would be dignified by the sonorous term *ambivalence.* Persuasive and authoritative as that term still appears, it has been so extraordinarily abused in our century that perhaps we may now recognize how little light it sheds on the subject of sacrifice. Certainly it provides no real explanation. When we speak of ambivalence, we are only pointing out a problem that remains to be solved" (1).

27. Girard, *Violence and the Sacred*, 145.

like and be like him and take his place everywhere. His cathexis to his mother, then, can be seen as an outcome of a primarily mimetic impulse to identify with his father; only thus, Girard writes, does it make sense to see the father, who is the boy's model, become a rival, a hindrance, and a nuisance standing in the way of the boy's gratification. However, notwithstanding his intuition of the potential held open by mimetic desire, Freud, according to Girard, turned aside and erased the effects of mimetic desire from his construction of the Oedipus complex so as to preserve the complex's purity and validity:

> Although traces of the mimetic conception are scattered through Freud's work, this conception never assumes a dominant role. It runs counter to the Freudian insistence on a desire that is fundamentally directed toward an object; that is, sexual desire for the mother. When the tension between these opposing tendencies becomes too great, both Freud and his disciples seem to resolve it in favor of the object-desire.[28]

What sets Girard's conception of mimesis apart from many of his contemporaries', therefore, is the epistemic status he grants it: mimesis is an originary force rather than a secondary phenomenon whose rationale or justification comes from somewhere else.[29] This conception has the advantage of freeing us from the common tendency to fixate on a predetermined object as the source of desire (as is the case, arguably, of Fanon's and Bhabha's ruminations, in which whiteness exists as the object to which the black man becomes cathected in imitation).[30] By making mimesis the first term, Girard shifts the emphasis away from the conventional assumption of desire as natural, autonomous, or originating: instead, desire is now understood as the outcome of human social interaction. Mimesis, in turn, is no longer simply a derivative or instru-

28. Girard, *Violence and the Sacred*, 169. Girard goes on to show how Freud, once he succeeded in establishing the Oedipus complex, allowed the mimetic to return in his formulation of the superego.

29. For this reason, Girard's thesis has been critiqued by Philippe Lacoue-Labarthe as a type of foundationalist or essentialist thinking (that seeks to reveal the foundational or essential violence of sociality); see Lacoue-Labarthe, *Typography: Mimesis, Philosophy, Politics*, introduction by Jacques Derrida, ed. Christopher Fynsk, editorial consultant Linda M. Brooks (Cambridge: Harvard University Press, 1989), 101–30. Unlike Girard, however, Lacoue-Labarthe does not simultaneously deal with sacrifice.

30. Girard writes, "A radically mimetic conception of desire offers a novel approach to psychiatric theory, one as far removed from the Freudian unconscious as it is from any philosophy of consciousness camouflaged as an existential psychoanalysis" (*Violence and the Sacred*, 177).

mental act in response to a situation in which those who are underprivileged, envious, or malcontent find themselves obligated to copy whatever preexists them as normal and superior. With desire detached from all predetermined objects, the mimetic process is here allowed to stand as a power dynamic, one that fuels, to return to Foucault's term, the biopolitics of intersubjective relations. Following Girard, one may go so far as to claim that mimesis is what activates the act of desiring; it is what gives desire its direction and trajectory as well as its objects.

This all-pervasive, mediating presence of mimesis means that to desire is, behaviorally speaking, to *compete* with a rival in a vicious circle of reciprocal violence, in which the antagonists become increasingly indistinguishable from each other—become what Girard calls "monstrous doubles." The only way the circle can be broken is through sacrifice—that is, through an artificial process in which someone who is a member of the community like everyone else becomes chosen as a scapegoat and expelled as a surrogate victim. Herein lies the crucial aspect of Girard's theory: "Social coexistence," he writes, "would be impossible if no surrogate victim existed, if violence persisted beyond a certain threshold and failed to be transmuted into culture. It is only at this point that the vicious circle of reciprocal violence, wholly destructive in nature, is replaced by the vicious circle of ritual violence, creative and protective in nature."[31] This point, very much resonant with Freud's arguments about human group behavior in works such as *Totem and Taboo* and *Civilization and Its Discontents* (and to some extent *Moses and Monotheism*), is reiterated by Girard in a succinct recapitulation of mimetic desire:

> *Mimetic desire* is simply a term more comprehensive than *violence* for religious pollution. As the catalyst for the sacrificial crisis, it would eventually destroy the entire community if the surrogate victim were not at hand to halt the process and the ritualized mimesis were not at hand to keep the conflictual mimesis from beginning afresh. . . . By channeling its energies into ritual forms and activities sanctioned by ritual, the cultural order prevents multiple desires from converging on the same object.[32]

For Girard, the sacrifice that is collectively ordained and practiced is thus (the violence of) mimetic desire *ritualized*. Practices of culture such as art, literature, and religion are all instances of such "ritualized mimesis"—that is, a substitute violence—designed to enable human society

31. Girard, *Violence and the Sacred*, 144.
32. Girard, *Violence and the Sacred*, 148–49.

to proceed against the blind destructiveness of the primal "conflictual mimesis." Girard speaks often of "a fundamental truth about violence": "If left unappeased, violence will accumulate until it overflows its confines and floods the surrounding area. The role of sacrifice is to stem this rising tide of indiscriminate substitutions and redirect violence into 'proper' channels."[33]

Girard's two-pronged formulation of mimesis—as both nature (constant, primal antagonism among human beings) and culture (collective, artificial ritual) and thus irreducible to either—whose violence must be understood dialectically, as both internal and external, both pernicious and beneficial, may be one reason his thesis has not exactly been taken up with enthusiasm in the left-leaning varieties of contemporary cultural criticism. For those who prefer to adhere to the more fashionable habit of denouncing universalist claims, Girard's assertion of mimesis as an absolute and universal condition—an assertion that is accompanied by a refusal to explain violence by confining it to domains of cultural difference or particularism such as religious fanaticism, nationalism, communism, patriarchy, Eurocentricity, U.S. imperialism, and so forth—can be disturbing. And since Girard's frame of reference is literary, mythological, and religious rather than empirical or scientific, the validity held by his conception of mimesis in various disciplines, even those with obvious social and historical import, will likely have to remain a matter of conjecture and debate.[34]

Nevertheless, because it recognizes the unavoidability and universality of violence, Girard's hypothesis ironically implies a basic, incontrovertible evenness and equality among human beings that tends to be absent in other formulations. In the feminist and postcolonial writings discussed earlier, for instance, in which it is typically the disparity between those who have power and those who are deprived of it that provokes theorization, mimesis tends to be pursued, more or less, as a means of addressing—that is, compensating for, displacing, complexifying, and,

33. Girard, *Violence and the Sacred*, 10.

34. He puts it this way: "The apparition of the monstrous double cannot be verified empirically; nor for that matter can the body of phenomena that forms the basis for any primitive religion. Despite the texts cited . . . the monstrous double remains a hypothetical creation, as do the other phenomena associated with the mechanism that determines the choice of surrogate victim. The validity of the hypothesis is confirmed, however, by the vast number of mythological, ritualistic, philosophical, and literary motifs that it is able to explain, as well as by the quality of the explanations, by the coherence it imposes on phenomena that until now appeared isolated and obscure" (*Violence and the Sacred*, 164).

it is hoped, transforming—such a disparity (and the sacrifices it exacts). Girard's emphasis is decidedly different—and clearly un-Rousseauian and nonutopian at that. In his hands, mimesis (in the raw, primal form) involves rather the possibility, through an act of doubling, of *leveling with* the rival, in a world in which the "self" as such is never alone (or sui generis) but always defined socially and antagonistically in relation to others, in a generalized state of competition. Hence the key to this form of mimesis is reciprocity—the "gift" of an eye for the returned "gift" of an eye, ad infinitum—in a kind of undifferentiated repetition that may go on indefinitely. If the violence thus generated is circular, it is also a violence that renders the antagonists structurally on a par with, indeed resembling and becoming indistinguishable from one another. But this situation of equality, in which every person is like or becoming just like another, is in fact a lethal situation to which human society cannot afford to return (or so it has convinced itself). Such equality, Girard implies, is the source of our greatest terror because anyone at any moment can find himself or herself the target of irrational violence and persecution.

Meanwhile, when mimesis is (re)enacted as cultural ritual, Girard, by highlighting the indispensable role played by the victim—be it the surrogate victim who is sacrificed on behalf (or in substitution) of the entire group or the ritual victim who is sacrificed in imitation (or in substitution) of the surrogate victim—also offers a distinctly divergent way of thinking about victimhood.[35] To put it bluntly, for Girard victimhood is more a matter of structural and social necessity—for the purification of pollution and the restoration of peace and order—than one of humanistic moral concern. The victim is the means with which a community interrupts the otherwise unstoppable circle of (mimetic) violence through a representative act of exclusion and expulsion. Often selected randomly, the victim is sacrificed not because he is weak or inferior (or strong and superior), but paradoxically because he is like us, because he resembles the community of those who would otherwise be engaged in an endless frenzy of retaliations. His (lone) alienation and expulsion are thus the substitute offered in exchange for the preservation of the group as a whole—a substitute that serves in effect as a protective shield against the threat of immolation posed by the group's own propensity toward mimetic contagion and annihilation.

35. See his interesting explanations in chapters 3 and 4, especially 101–2, of *The Violence and the Sacred.*

Questions

In an age in which the phenomenon of *homo sacer*, of which Agamben has so solemnly reminded us, seems to multiply daily across the globe with the glaringly unconstrained proliferation of state violence and abuse of power, a consideration of sacrifice and mimesis—what I have been suggesting as a conjoined epistemic passage—would seem more than timely. The ramifications involved are immense and clearly beyond the scope of a dozen or so pages. In lieu of a conclusion, let me offer a brief summary of the issues raised so far, in the form of questions.

Whereas Agamben (implicitly) argues victimhood in terms of bare life, which is the residue or remainder of an inequitable juridicopolitical relation between sovereign power and those it kills (in an increasingly arbitrary fashion), a relation that renders mimesis altogether irrelevant because there is no room for confrontation and resistance, and whereas Irigaray, Fanon, and Bhabha alert us to the depths of ambiguity, neurosis, and perversion that define the mimetic acts of disadvantaged victims, Girard challenges us instead to think of victims not simply as victims but rather as the bearers of a systemic function. And rather than speaking against violence as the unfortunate moral outcome of human social interaction, Girard gives us a dialectics of violence, one that understands violence (or mimetic desire) both as a fundamental antagonism that defines every confrontation among human individuals and as what constitutes cultural processes of reenactment that are aimed at warding off the original violence. As a result, he has also offered what might be called a dialectics of victimhood, wherein victimhood has no intrinsic quality to it but can be both horrendous and redemptive. Like sacrificial violence, sacrificial victims are surrogates, substitutes, or stand-ins whose destruction helps save others (like them) from some larger horror.

If, for the sake of speculative discussion, we were to disregard Agamben's dismissal of the sacrificial logic and rethink the Nazi camps in terms of Girard's interpretation of sacrifice and mimesis, two very hard—and for some undoubtedly scandalous—sets of questions would arise.

First: Could the extremism of the Nazi state apparatus be understood as a form of originary violence, a primal mimetic desire that had somehow been allowed to run amok? (Did the Germans not, in a mimetic manner, consider the Jews their competitors, their rivals? Did they not, against their own denunciatory proclamations, actually want to become (like) the Jews—take the Jews' place everywhere—by appropriating all that the Jews possessed?[36] Could their violence have been reciprocated?) Second: Alternatively, could such extremism be seen as a cultural process of ritualized violence or mimesis wherein those who were reduced to bare life in the camps could be considered surrogate or ritual victims? To follow Girard's logic to its deeply unsettling conclusions, if the Jews, the Gypsies, and other exterminated groups were surrogate or ritual victims, does that mean that genocide, however reprehensible it is on ethical grounds, should nonetheless be understood as a sacrificial ritual, a cultural process—not unlike an extreme form of performance art, a theater of cruelty, or an obscene reality show—the purpose of which is to forestall a worse form of disaster?

But what could possibly have been a worse form of disaster than the Nazis' willful murderous efforts, and what larger horror could they be preventing?—the disaster and horror of being victimized *themselves*, of being reduced to bare life, of having their own group unity disintegrate in the potentially unstoppable spread of mimetic violence: in other words, the disaster and horror of losing *their* monopoly on violence and with it their claim to (the Aryan) difference. *It would be unthinkable for "the Germans" to become like everyone else.* The status of the victim, structurally indispensable in Girard's formulations, must thus be further specified as the externalization—the *banishment* (to use a term that recalls Agamben's notion of ban) to the outside, in the form of a guilty adversary—of a group's capacity for self-destruction. As a crowd whose members imitate one another's behavior, the group derives an important benefit from the unanimous—that is, mimetically induced—hatred for the victim: this hatred unifies the members and creates the community. As surrogate, therefore, the victim is simultaneously the symptom of a group's fundamental lack of cohesion, its fundamental nonidentity with itself. As Girard writes in his study of the Book of Job, "In a world controlled by mimetic desire . . . the appetite for violence may grow and may be ultimately satisfied at that moment when the global tendency to uniformity focuses the mimetic substitutions and polarizations on some victim or other, or perhaps not so randomly but on a victim who is more vulnerable because of his visibility, one who is somehow predestined by the exceptional position he holds in the community—someone like Job."[37]

36. "They cannot stand the Jews, yet imitate them." Max Horkheimer and Theodor W. Adorno, "Elements of Anti-Semitism: Limits of Enlightenment," *Dialectic of Enlightenment*, trans. John Cumming (New York: Continuum, 1987), 183.

37. René Girard, *Job the Victim of His People*, trans. Yvonne Freccerro (Stanford: Stanford University Press, 1987), 65. See also his essay "Job as Failed Scapegoat" in

On the other hand, if, in light of the atrocities committed by the Nazis, any rationalization of victimhood as such must be deemed outrageous regardless of how sympathetic the critic might be with the victims—and this is certainly the point of Agamben's fundamental expulsion (sacrifice) of the sacrificial logic—does it mean that mimesis, whether imagined as nature, as culture, or as both, must also be thoroughly expunged (banned, banished, abandoned) as a concept because it is simply too perilous to think with, because it is bound to lead to conclusions that are without or outside of moral compunctions? Yet what is the defense of moral compunctions, to return again to Girard's logic, if not precisely a collectively ordained exercise of violence aimed at preserving *our* social order from crumbling—a ritualized mimesis, no less? Would not the expunging of mimesis turn it precisely into a symptom about us as a community, in the aforementioned terms?

Interestingly, this is also the point at which Girard's seemingly amoral, religion-oriented argument of mimetic violence comes closest to Agamben's nihilistic, atheist understanding of law and power. As the fundamental vacuity of the sovereign relation is exposed by the increasingly arbitrary abuses by those in power, what is so-called law is revealing itself—and here is the logical transition from Agamben into Girard—to be nothing more than a collectively ordained exercise of violence, intended once upon a time to preserve the social equilibrium, perhaps, but now functioning as nothing more than a frenzied killing machine. Despite his adherence to the need for moral compunctions in his (antisacrificial and antimimetic) approach to the concentration camps, Agamben's bleak depictions of political-power-gone-berserk the world over suggest that his grasp of the unmitigated, and perhaps intractable actuality of human violence (defined by Girard as mimetic) is, in the end, not that distant from Girard's.

The Voice from the Whirlwind: Interpreting The Book of Job, ed. Leo G. Perdue and W. Clark Gilpin (Nashville: Abingdon Press, 1992), 185–207. Girard's analysis of the problem of evil, the problem that has preoccupied generations of interpreters of the Book of Job, parallels his critique of the object-centered understanding of desire. In discussing the enigma, the "why" of Job's unjust suffering, he shifts the emphasis from the canonical hermeneutics about divine providence to a reading of the mimetic contagion of collective human behavior. Because, rather than simply accepting his persecution by his community, Job fervently protests against the absurdity of such persecution, Girard sees his story as a text that consciously reveals or demythologizes the scapegoat or victimage mechanism. He also suggests that Job is a prefiguration of Jesus.

One final question and speculation: Insofar as any discussion of them seems ineluctably to arrive at these formidable, and terrifying, questions of freedom, violence, moral constraints, community, and boundaries-setting, are not sacrifice and mimesis perhaps the surrogate victims and ritual victims par excellence in the domain of representational politics today?

5

"I insist on the Christian dimension"

On Forgiveness . . . and the Outside of the Human

The questions I would like to explore in this essay pertain to the type of action specific to human relations we call forgiveness. Hannah Arendt's erudite reflections in *The Human Condition* provide a powerful justification for the necessity of forgiveness as a moral virtue: "Without being forgiven, released from the consequences of what we have done, our capacity to act would, as it were, be confined to one single deed from which we could never recover; we would remain the victims of its consequences forever, not unlike the sorcerer's apprentice who lacks the magic formula to break the spell."[1] Arendt's language of release, confinement, recovery, and victimhood suggests that the absence of forgiveness in human relations would be tantamount to a perpetual condition of captivity and enslavement; her metaphor of the sorcerer's spell, which can only be broken with a magic formula, further analogizes forgiveness to a miracle. As the harbinger of a welcome interruption, forgiveness is thus the remedy that restores social order by redeeming us from being held hostage to an irreversible past.

Her persuasive reasoning notwithstanding, the imperative tone of Arendt's comments gives one pause: From where does the urgency come? Since forgiveness has, arguably, been known to exist in practice (that is, in a variety of forms) in different cultures across the centuries, what are the historical forces that motivate and advance the specific thinking that forgiveness is *a rescue mission*, one that liberates us from bondage to

1. Hannah Arendt, *The Human Condition* (Chicago: University of Chicago Press, 1958), 237.

something wretchedly unshakable, like the albatross around the neck of the Ancient Mariner? In her discussion, Arendt attributes the discovery of forgiveness to the figure of Jesus, adding that his teaching, although religious, ought to be taken just as seriously in a secular setting: "The discoverer of the role of forgiveness in the realm of human affairs was Jesus of Nazareth. The fact that he made this discovery in a religious context and articulated it in religious language is no reason to take it any less seriously in a strictly secular sense."[2]

The controversial relation between religion (in this context, Judaism and Christianity) and secularity aside, a basic question seems ineluctable: Without an implicit concept of the sovereign individual anchored in (arguably modern) Western psychosocial models such as action versus passivity, rationality versus irrationality, ownership versus privation, emancipation versus incarceration, and so forth, would the imperative to forgive and be forgiven, as cast in the terms presented by Arendt, carry the same import?[3] And might there be other ways of thinking about forgiveness—for instance, by juxtaposing it with cultural phenomena that bear an unexpected and as yet unexamined kinship—that challenge some of these categories underpinning the continuum of the autonomous liberal subject and his capacity for action?

To respond to these questions, I shall begin with a reference to a striking key episode at the heart of the South Korean film *Miryang* (*Secret Sunshine*, 2007, directed by Lee Chang-dong), which stages forgiveness in a local situation of twenty-first-century, globalized Christian evangelism. As I will go on to show, the connotations of forgiveness do, in fact, extend beyond a strictly religious setting (albeit not in the way Arendt suggests), going so far as to bear on more contemporary theoretical issues of translation and the secularization of representation.

2. Arendt, *The Human Condition*, 238.

3. David Konstan, for instance, has argued that forgiveness and the cluster of emotions associated with it (such as remorse and repentance) were unknown to Greco-Roman antiquity. See his "Assuaging Rage: Remorse, Repentance and Forgiveness in the Classical World," *Phoenix* 62 (2008), 243–54. For an extended study, see David Konstan, *Before Forgiveness: The Origins of a Moral Idea* (Cambridge: Cambridge University Press, 2010).

A Secret Sunshine Unveiled

At the beginning of *Secret Sunshine*, Shin-ae Lee, a young widow, is on her way from Seoul to Miryang with her young son, Jun.[4] Miryang, which in Chinese characters means "secret sunshine," is her husband's hometown. By relocating there, Shin-ae tells people, she is trying to honor her husband's wish that the boy know something about the place. After they arrive and establish their daily routine (with the help of an enthusiastic admirer), including setting up a studio where Shin-ae teaches the piano and finding a school for Jun, disaster strikes: Jun has been kidnapped. On her cell phone, Shin-ae is instructed by the kidnapper to empty her savings account and deposit the money in a bag, to be put inside a garbage bin in a remote area. She complies with all the instructions, only to discover that the ransom has been paid in vain. Jun's dead body is soon found by the police. The murderer, it turns out, is Jun's schoolteacher, Park Do-Seob, who developed his extortion plan after hearing Shin-ae talk about buying a plot of land and inferring (incorrectly) that she has money.

In her grief-stricken state, Shin-ae chances upon a Christian fellowship gathering where believers are engaged in various poses of emotionally intense worship. (Earlier in the film, a neighbor, a pharmacist and deaconess, attempted to proselytize to Shin-ae but without success.) As Shin-ae follows suit and lets out screams of pain, the pastor comes to her side, laying his hand on her head to calm her. In the next scenes we see Shin-ae transformed: composed, smiling, and sociable, she tells her friends she has found inner peace through God. The heaviness that was weighing on her heart has been lifted, she says, and the feeling is like being in love, when one knows that someone else is always watching and caring for one. Some time later, at her birthday celebration, Shin-ae expresses the wish to visit the prison and confront her son's murderer. When asked why this is necessary, she explains that since she has, through religious conversion, forgiven him, she needs to tell him personally so as to "spread God's love."

The visit to the prison, then, brings us to the key episode mentioned earlier. Face to face with the criminal, Shin-ae informs him of her reason for being there. As translated in the English subtitles, an excerpt of their dialogue goes as follows:

4. Jeon Do-yeon, who played the role of Shin-ae, was the recipient of various awards, including the Best Actress Award at the Cannes Film Festival in 2007.

Shin-ae: The reason I've come here . . . is to spread God's grace and love. I never knew such things. I couldn't believe in God. I couldn't see Him, so I didn't believe. But . . . through my Jun, I learnt of God's love. I found peace and a new life. I'm so thankful . . . so happy to feel God's love and grace. That's why I came. To spread His love.

Park: Thank you. I truly thank you. Hearing from you about our Lord makes me truly thankful. I too have gained faith. Since I came here, I have accepted God in my heart. The Lord has reached out to this sinner.

Shin-ae: Is that so? It's good that you have found God.

Park: Yes, I'm so grateful. God reached out to a sinner like me. He made me kneel to repent my sins. And God has absolved me of them.

Shin-ae: God . . . has forgiven your sins?

Park: Yes, after I repented in tears. . . . And I have found inner peace. I pray as soon as I wake. I am so thankful every day. My repentance and absolution have brought me peace. Now I start and end each day with prayer. I always pray for you, Mrs. Lee. I'll pray for you until I die. Seeing you here today tells me that God has heard my prayers.

This brief exchange offers a provocatively refreshing way of posing the question of forgiveness. Much more than the loss of her husband and even the loss of her son, the murderer's words devastate Shin-ae. Indeed, the rest of the film after this scene may be seen as a portrayal of the stark aftermath of this devastation—of a person who has become, ontologically speaking, destitute: Shin-ae is temporarily institutionalized and, even after she is discharged, is considered by her neighbors to be a mad woman. Just why is this exchange so traumatic? What kind of blow has the murderer dealt our heroine?

When Shin-ae was "born again," she traded in her grief, as it were. This spiritual rebirth parallels her relocation to Miryang at the beginning. As in the physical move to Miryang, she plans to settle in the new location, her newfound inner peace, by holding on to a new life routine. What empowers her in this new life routine is her belief that she has forgiven her enemy. Forgiveness, at this juncture, is precisely the "secret sunshine" or mysterious *potency* (as connoted by the Chinese character *yang*) of which Shin-ae has come into possession. However, just as she made the fatal mistake of revealing her (apparent) wealth in public (by talking about her plans to buy land), so again does she err by visiting the murderer and displaying her forgiveness to him. This demonstrative act—deliberately performed in order to spread the love of God, she says—accomplishes exactly what it purports to do (communicating pardon to the murderer), only to unveil the fundamental antagonism that constitutes the truth and desire of Shin-ae's act of benevolence: she really wants to know that her enemy too has been suffering. She wants his eye for her eye, his tooth for her tooth. Only if he has been in that tormented state would *her* act of forgiveness have meaning as an act of absolute kindness, an act of which, moreover, she alone, because she has labored so hard (suffered so singularly), should be capable.

Instead, what does she hear?—that the murderer has already found forgiveness! Well before she came, he says, he had been praying and God had already absolved him; moreover, he has been praying for her every day, and her appearance in the prison is the sign that God has answered his prayers.

At one level, this is, of course, the logic that drives criminals in general: a criminal has always already forgiven himself by allowing himself the freedom to commit a crime. But more disturbingly, the murderer's composure (even as he refers to himself as a sinner) suggests that forgiveness is perhaps not at all the outcome of hard work and suffering that Shin-ae so desperately wants it to be. Rather, forgiveness is something readily available; anyone is eligible to seek it: just as she can find it, so too can he. If anything, God is unfair: while she has had to go through so much personal pain before attaining this peaceful state of mind, the murderer has, to all appearances, arrived at the same place with ease, even though he has deprived her of her child and is behind bars. If forgiveness is a kind of destination, the murderer has managed to cross the finish line before Shin-ae is aware of it. *How dare God have already absolved him before she does?* she demands afterward, in a fit. Does not that mean she is not at all powerful, that the secret she thinks she uniquely possesses—forgiveness—is just a trifle, is nothing, whereas the murderer, in addition to killing her son, has now beaten her a second time, this time with the help of a new accomplice: God? Does this mean she must work harder still and try to forgive God too?

As the name "secret sunshine" intimates, therefore, this story brings to the fore a series of unresolvable aporias about forgiveness. As the pardoning of a debt that redeems without imposing a further debt, forgiveness is, supposedly, a free and absolute gift, an index to the morally elevated or superior status of those who have the power to bestow it. But what happens when forgiveness becomes an act of display, when the potency of benevolence (the secret sunshine, that is) is no longer silently understood but consciously performed? (If God loves us and forgives us, why does he also have to send his beloved son, Jesus, to the world to be sacrificed? Why do we need this extra advertisement, this publicity?)

Does not the very act of showing forgiveness transform the essence of forgiveness, turn it into hypocrisy? Instead of simply adopting the cynical stance implied by these questions, which would easily lead to a debunking of the Christian doctrine as a mere lie (as Shin-ae herself now believes it is), *Secret Sunshine* pursues the ingenious design of stripping forgiveness of its supposedly absolute status and finality.

It does this by (re)inserting forgiveness in the circuit of social exchange, thus displacing it from its supposedly secret potency back into a mundane, matter-of-fact realm. This is clearest in the murderer's delivery of his news. Whereas Shin-ae's desire, we surmise, is for him to show remorse on seeing and hearing how magnanimous she is (for only then would the primal necessity for revenge be gratified and her own ontological equilibrium restored), his relaxed, self-assured demeanor signals rather the successful functioning of progressivist Christian evangelism. In the latter system, God's secret is to be found in the open, flexible networks of circulation—of spreading, verbalizing, and physically performing to and by all and sundry. This is a system in which no one is considered too lowly or inferior because everyone is God's beloved lamb. In making the decision to *talk* to him face to face in prison, therefore, Shin-ae has already placed herself unwittingly within the logic of this system and defeated her own purpose from the start. Once this system is in play, forgiveness is de facto rendered nonabsolute and reconfigured discursively as part of an unending series of human transactions in which one-upmanship is always possible but never permanent. Thus, Shin-ae's evangelical act of transmitting forgiveness leads not to a peaceful ending but rather to a revelation of the vindictiveness that rages unappeased in her heart. This time, though, with God himself becoming an adversary, the ransom is considerably higher: to be released from this increased burden, Shin-ae must pay with her own sanity.

When Mercy Seasons Justice

The understanding that forgiveness, as an act of (interpersonal) transmission, may involve the potentially destructive revelation of an unmitigated antagonism underlying human social relations also informs Jacques Derrida's reading of Shakespeare's play *The Merchant of Venice*.[5]

5. Jacques Derrida, "What Is a 'Relevant' Translation?," trans. Lawrence Venuti, *Critical Inquiry* 27. 2 (2001), 174–200; hereafter references to this essay will be included in parentheses in the text.

As readers well know, this is the story about a dispute over a debt. Shylock and Antonio have an agreement, namely, that if Antonio fails to return the money he owes, Shylock, the moneylender, will cut off a pound of flesh near his borrower's heart as payment. What has enabled the play to achieve international renown over the centuries, however, is perhaps less a matter of Shylock's intransigence than the antidote of "wisdom" supplied to defeat it. The punitive Jew who insists on the letter of his contract and comes close to executing it, we recall, is trumped by Portia, the wealthy heiress and wife of Antonio's friend Bassanio, who arrives on the scene disguised as a young and learned doctor (a man of law) to help settle the dispute. Portia succeeds, in the end, by going Shylock one better: if he is to get his pound of flesh from Antonio, as he insists he must, it will, she says, have to be a pound of flesh without a drop of Christian blood.

As pointed out by Lawrence Venuti, the translator of Derrida's essay "What Is a 'Relevant' Translation?," Shakespeare's text had served as the basis of a seminar on forgiveness and perjury that Derrida taught in 1998, the same year that he delivered the lecture on the intimate links between forgiveness and translation.[6] For my purposes, what is of interest is not simply Derrida's inimitably insightful commentary on a canonical text. It is also Derrida's manner of articulating the notion of mercy—as invoked in Portia's pronouncement "when mercy seasons justice"—to what he argues as *relevant* translation.[7]

The intricacy of Derrida's articulation is twofold. First, he brings to Shakespeare's text his signature attentiveness to the workings of language, workings whose slippery or unstable nature is often amplified in the course of translation. Hence, Derrida writes, the notion of the relevant translation is both essential and questionable, as it emphasizes the legitimate need for a translation to convey the original with accuracy at the same time that the translation, being an act of transfer, must of necessity participate in an economy of in-betweenness. How, then, can a translation be relevant (in the sense of being a correct or faithful rendering of the original) when aberrances and infidelities seem unavoidable in the trafficking back and forth between languages?[8] Second, in this by

6. Venuti, "Introduction," *Critical Inquiry* 27.2 (2001), 170.

7. Although mercy and forgiveness are not identical phenomena, in this essay I follow Derrida's lead in not insisting on their distinction.

8. According to Venuti, relevance is a concept that dominates translation theory and practice in the twentieth century. See Lawrence Venuti, "Translating Derrida on Translation: Relevance and Disciplinary Resistance," *Yale Journal of Criticism* 16.2 (2003), 237–62.

now well-understood scene of the impossibility of translation, Derrida stages a further, explicitly ethical level of interrogation, foremost among which is the question of forgiveness. He introduces this question in a vocabulary of indebtedness, beginning his essay by declaring his own (and by implication our) "insolvency before translation," going so far as to announce that translators "are the only ones who know how to read and write," that "a summons to translation [stands] at the very threshold of all reading-writing," and that what we owe to translation and translators is "much like what is owed to Shylock, insolvency itself" ("What Is a 'Relevant' Translation?," 174–75).

Proceeding with his characteristic sensitivity to how the significance of words often resides between languages, Derrida writes that such significance tends to reveal itself most readily through acts of linguistic transfer, as, for instance, in the word "relevant," which "carries in its body an ongoing process of translation" ("What Is a 'Relevant' Translation?," 177). For this reason, whereas the standard French translation of Portia's pronouncement "when mercy seasons justice" uses the French word *tempère* for the English word "seasons," Derrida translates the phrase instead as "quand le pardon relève la justice." Recalling that it was he himself who had proposed the French word *relève* for the Hegelian term *Aufhebung* in 1967 ("What Is a 'Relevant' Translation?," 196), Derrida argues that, in translation, the notion "relevant" (which is etymologically linked to "relève") signifies not exactly equivalency or transparency but rather the process of seasoning, sublimation, and (as in Hegelian dialectics) elevation and interiorization—a process, in short, that preserves and enhances (the flavors of) what it negates or destroys. Having moved thus from the English word "seasons" to its possible translation in French (relève), to the affinity of the French word to German philosophy (Aufhebung), and finally back to the English original, Derrida offers what may be termed a thoroughly translational elaboration of *mercy*, in which commonsensical connotations (of seasoning and preservation in cooking) and philosophical connotations (relève and Aufhebung) converge with and reinforce one another.

As Venuti indicates, Derrida's analysis sheds light on the important cultural politics traditionally attached to translation strategies. In the history of Western translation, Venuti reminds us, Christianity is believed to favor strategies that more freely capture the sense or spirit of the foreign text, while Judaism is said to favor strategies that render literally by adhering to the word or letter. The implications of the tensions between the Christian and Jewish practices are described by Derrida as follows:

> This impossible translation, this conversion (and all translation is a conversion: *vertere, transvertere, convertere*, as Cicero said) between the original, literal flesh and the monetary sign is not unrelated to the Jew Shylock's forced conversion to Christianity, since the traditional figure of the Jew is often and conventionally situated on the side of the body and the letter (from bodily circumcision or [*sic*; to?] Pharisaism, from ritual compliance to literal exteriority), whereas St. Paul the Christian is on the side of the spirit or sense, of interiority, of spiritual circumcision. This relation of the letter to the spirit, of the body of literalness to the ideal interiority of sense is also the site of the passage of translation, of this conversion that is called translation. ("What Is a 'Relevant' Translation?," 184)

With this history in mind, Venuti recapitulates the ironic twist posed by Shakespeare's play:

> True to the stereotype, Shylock insists on a literal translation of the contract, demanding a pound of flesh for the unpaid debt while refusing the free "merciful" translation that would absolve his debtor. Yet the Christians adopt an even more rigorous literalism when Portia insists that, according to the wording of the contract, Shylock can't shed one drop of blood in carving out the pound of flesh. It is this unexpected Christian rendering of the letter that compels the Jew to submit to the translation of the hegemonic discourse, Christianity itself.[9]

In the end, as we know, Shylock refuses both to grant forgiveness (to Antonio) and to ask for forgiveness (for himself). In rejecting the roles of gracious giver and grateful recipient in the grand tale of forgiveness, he loses everything: not only must he agree to a complete remission of the debt, but he must also undergo a forced conversion to Christianity. As Derrida writes, Shylock understands only too well the odds that are stacked discriminately against him:

> There is a pretense of elevating him above everything, with this tale of divine and sublime forgiveness, but it is a ruse to empty his pockets while distracting him, to make him forget what he is owed and to punish him cruelly. . . . In the name of this sublime panegyric of forgiveness, an economic ruse, a calculation, a stratagem is being plotted, the upshot of which . . . will be that Shylock loses everything in this translation of transaction, the monetary signs of his money as well as the literal pound of flesh—and even his religion since when the situation takes a bad turn at his expense

9. Venuti, "Introduction," 172.

he will have to convert to Christianity. ("What Is a 'Relevant' Translation?," 188–89)

Is Portia's triumph really one of benevolent thinking and practice, then? Following Derrida's emphasis on translation, it would seem pertinent to see this triumph first and foremost as a translation or conversion—specifically, of an "ethnic" (read: primitive) code of justice into a "universal" (read: "evolved") code of mercy. Furthermore, in this translation and conversion, one party's idiom or language is upheld as the rationale for the verdict while the other party's idiom or language is made *irrelevant* because it has been divested of its means of argument.[10] Portia's success, therefore, leaves us, modern readers, with this question: What kind of advocacy of mercy is it that, in settling a dispute, has the effect of rendering one side (in this case the Jew) destitute? Adhering to Derrida's poly- and interlingual reading of the word "seasons," we may put this question in yet another way: If the effect of Portia's translation is that of negating and destroying Shylock's (inflexible) language, does this translation really "season" (as Derrida's logic implies) that language in the sense of preserving it and making it more flavorful, or does it not have the more brutal outcome of annexing and annulling it altogether? Is not Shylock's destitution caused not only by the technical denial of the contractual pound of flesh or by total financial loss but also by a fundamental forfeiting of his humanity (together with its code of fidelity) as detritus? Is not this, *some* human beings' condition of being abjected from the *socius* on account of their insistence on speaking or conducting social relations in a certain way (in Shylock's case, on abiding by the original oath so as not to perjure his soul in heaven), the most troubling consequence of Portia's translation and transmission of mercy?[11]

10. This situation is what Jean-François Lyotard means by a *différend*: "I would like to call a *differend* [*différend*] the case where the plaintiff is divested of the means to argue and becomes for that reason a victim. . . . A case of differend between two parties takes place when the 'regulation' of the conflict that opposes them is done in the idiom of one of the parties while the wrong suffered by the other is not signified in that idiom." *The Differend: Phrases in Dispute*, trans. Georges Van Den Abbeele (Minneapolis: University of Minnesota Press, 1988), 9.

11. These questions are clearly behind Michael Radford's compelling film production of *The Merchant of Venice* (2004), which foregrounds the historically inequitable, anti-Semitic social conditions under which Shakespeare's story takes place.

When Divinity Turns Self-Serve

As in *Secret Sunshine*, what *The Merchant of Venice* dramatizes is, we might say, a process of social, cultural, and ontological struggle at the very intersection of Christian mercy and (its) translation. Venuti summarizes Derrida's provocation succinctly:

> Derrida goes further than simply demystifying relevant translation: he also exposes its cultural and social implications through his interpretation of Shakespeare's play. Portia's translation of Shylock's demand for justice seeks an optimal relevance to Christian doctrine which ultimately leads to his total expropriation as well as his forced conversion to Christianity. Derrida thus shows that when relevant translation occurs within an institution like the state, it can become the instrument of legal interdiction, economic sanction, and political repression, motivated here by racism.[12]

Significantly, notwithstanding his knowledge of the historical hegemony of Christianity as state power and the documented anti-Semitic biases that evidently informed the construction of a character such as Shylock, Derrida's conclusion to his reading of Shakespeare's play is, as cited in the title of the present essay, "I insist on the Christian dimension" ("What Is a 'Relevant' Translation?," 199). The unequivocal nature of Derrida's moral position[13]—one that, as we know from his late work, favors the cluster of positive, humanistic (and humanitarian) attitudes such as mercy, gratitude, grace, friendship, hospitality, compassion, and forgiveness—could be rationalized, perhaps, by the advice from Arendt quoted at the beginning. Alluded to in Arendt's terms, "the Christian dimension" on which Derrida insists would amount to a complete pardoning, an unconditional giving that is the "magic formula to break the spell." As I have mentioned also, this conceptualization of forgiveness depends for its rhetorical effectiveness on a metanarrative of captivity and liberation: forgiveness is a kind of rescue mission that salvages us from the hold of something exotic and foreign, like magic.

12. Venuti, "Translating Derrida on Translation," 252.

13. Derrida: "In expressing all the evil that can be thought of the Christian ruse as a discourse of mercy, I am not about to praise Shylock when he raises a hue and cry for his pound of flesh and insists on the literalness of the *bond*. I analyze only the historical and allegorical cards that have been dealt in this situation and all the discursive, logical, theological, political, and economic resources of the concept of mercy, the legacy (our legacy) of this semantics of mercy—precisely inasmuch as it is indissociable from a certain European interpretation of translation" ("What Is a 'Relevant' Translation?," 198).

At the same time, by not only treating forgiveness on its own but also juxtaposing it with translation (which tends these days to conjure neoliberal associations of travel, traffic, diversification, negotiation, and so forth), Derrida has made things much more complex and, in effect, brought about a reconceptualization of each of the two terms. Accordingly, in his reading, the initial premise of a transactional process—the transfer of meanings from one language into another, back and forth; the forgoing of a specific debt from one human party to another—has given way to a broader epistemic frame in which the rationalist economy of mutuality, reciprocity, and incessant circulation, pertinent as it clearly is, is no longer the key. In the case of forgiveness, newly emerging into visibility is the potentiality of what may be called *fore-giving*, "a power above power, a sovereignty above sovereignty" ("What Is a 'Relevant' Translation?," 187), for which the traces (the aftereffects) of aversion are to be *fore-gotten*.[14] In the last part of his essay, Derrida reminds us precisely of this transcendent overtone of mercy not only in Shakespeare's play but also in Hegelian dialectics: "The movement toward philosophy and absolute knowledge as the truth of the Christian religion passes through the experience of mercy. . . . Mercy is a *relève*, it is in its essence an *Aufhebung*. It is translation as well. In the horizon of expiation, redemption, reconciliation, and salvation" ("What Is a 'Relevant' Translation?," 197).

When such transcendent fore-giving is cast in terms of translation, translation too would need to be understood anew, not simply technically but also philosophically, as *trans*-linguistic—that is, not only in the sense of being between languages but also in the sense of crossing over (language) to a *beyond*. Hence Derrida writes, following Portia's Christian logic, of the affinity between forgiveness or translation and prayer: "And what is, finally, a discourse on translation (possible/impossible) is also a discourse of *prayer on prayer*. Forgiveness is prayer; it belongs to the order of benediction and prayer on two sides: that of the person who requests it and that of the person who grants it" ("What Is a 'Relevant' Translation?," 188).

In this last sentence, Derrida is paraphrasing Portia, who announces that mercy is what "droppeth as the gentle rain from heaven / Upon the

14. For related interest, see Derrida's discussion of pure or unconditional forgiveness—that is, the forgiveness of what is unforgivable—as opposed to conditional forgiveness, which is based on an exchange economy regulating guilt and punishment, in *On Cosmopolitanism and Forgiveness*, trans. Mark Dooley and Michael Hughes, preface by Simon Critchley and Richard Kearney (London: Routledge, 2001).

place beneath: it is twice blest, / It blesseth him that gives, and him that takes."[15] As Derrida notes, Portia's words suggest that forgiveness is "a vertical descending movement . . . given from above to below" ("What Is a 'Relevant' Translation?," 192). By referring to the hierarchy involved, Derrida means to emphasize the super- or transhuman quality of forgiveness: "If in fact there is any [mercy], the so-called human experience reaches a zone of divinity: mercy is the genesis of the divine, of the holy or the sacred, but also the site of pure translation" ("What Is a 'Relevant' Translation?," 197).

As we know from *Secret Sunshine*, however, precisely the moral hierarchy involved in this Christian understanding of forgiveness—"given from above to below"—is a possible source of trouble. By granting forgiveness to the murderer, Shin-ae assumes that she has reached that "zone of divinity," which in the context of the film is also compared to nature (sunshine, rather than gentle rain), only to discover that the murderer *has already helped himself to it*, so to speak, without her benediction. Indeed, by dramatizing the moral hierarchy involved in forgiveness as nothing more than a psychological supposition premised on the desire for empowerment and superiority over the adversary—in a nutshell, the desire to win—*Secret Sunshine* has put its finger on what is perhaps the most ideologically charged aspect of the Christian enterprise. If the moral hierarchy involved in forgiveness is not really about the human becoming divine or the divine speaking, acting, and passing through the human, as Derrida advocates, but simply another variety of human competition for power and domination over others, then the harmony, mutuality, and spirit of sharing that is said to connect "him that gives" and "him that takes" forgiveness would also seem overstated.[16] For on what basis can it be supposed that the giving and the taking of forgiveness belong to the same plane or the same order (of benediction and prayer)?

As Shin-ae realizes to her shock, even without her giving, the murderer has already been granted and taken mercy. The two of them are not the

15. William Shakespeare, *The Merchant of Venice* (New York: Penguin, 2000), 4.1.181–83.

16. This is probably why Derrida also writes, "What I dream of, what I try to think as the 'purity' of a forgiveness worthy of its name, would be a forgiveness without power: *unconditional but without sovereignty*. The most difficult task, at once necessary and apparently impossible, would be to dissociate *unconditionality* and *sovereignty*. Will that be done one day? It is not around the corner, as is said. But since the hypothesis of this unpresentable task announces itself, be it as a dream for thought, this madness is perhaps not so mad" (*On Cosmopolitanism and Forgiveness*, 59–60).

two sides of a self-same order of benediction and prayer but simply consumers of a worldwide web of evangelically disseminated Christian messages. If anything, the murderer has a considerably more dynamic relationship with God, who has given him positive feedback (by answering his prayer for Shin-ae and making her appear in prison). No longer available only in a vertical movement from above to below, "as the gentle rain from heaven / Upon the place beneath," mercy is now readily downloadable on demand, without the necessary intercession of another human being who grants it (and who, in doing so, may be regarded as superhuman). Like everything that can be acquired through the conduits of global mass circulation, forgiveness has become self-serve fare. Is not this the secret of "sunshine" in the twenty-first century?

Forgiveness and the Secularizing of Representation

The ramifications of this displacement of forgiveness from its conventionally imagined, vertically downward (that is, hierarchical) axis are far-reaching and exceed the boundaries of religion. As an analytic experiment, I would like to propose that it is such a displacement that constitutes the rationale of a classic such as Erich Auerbach's *Mimesis: The Representation of Reality in Western Literature*,[17] which for many readers remains an authoritative founding text in the academic discipline of comparative literature after the Second World War (and largely in North America). Auerbach's book is inexhaustible in its learning and skillful attention to minutiae, and no attempt at recapitulation can ever do it justice. My focus here, propelled by questions raised in the discussion, has rather to do with one prominent aspect of the book, namely, the historical shifts in Western conceptions of the human that inform Auerbach's analysis. Let me venture that these historical shifts, which according to Auerbach manifest themselves in the secularizing of literary style, may also be articulated to forgiveness.

Consider the famous comparative reading with which Auerbach begins his study. With an explicit interest in style, Auerbach establishes the differences between the Hellenic and Hebraic ways of writing—specifically, the contrasts between Homer's picturesque depiction of

17. Erich Auerbach, *Mimesis: The Representation of Reality in Western Literature*, 50th anniversary ed., with a new introduction by Edward W. Said (1953; Princeton: Princeton University Press, 2003). Hereafter references to Auerbach's book will be taken from the 2003 edition and included in parentheses in the text.

Odysseus's homecoming in *The Odyssey* and the Bible's reticent account of the near-sacrifice of Isaac (*Mimesis*, chapter 1). There is a strong sense of purpose on Auerbach's part, as may be glimpsed in remarks he made in response to the early critics of *Mimesis* who faulted him for being unfair in his treatment of the Hellenic tradition: "I considered for a moment letting the Homer chapter fall entirely by the wayside. For my purposes it would have sufficed to begin with the time around the birth of Christ. . . . It is quite clear to me with what great justification, for example, early Christianity can be regarded as the product of late antiquity. . . . But the task that my theme imposed on me was a different one: I had to show not the transition but rather the complete change" (*Mimesis*, 560, 562).

With this emphasis on the Judeo-Christian tradition,[18] in other words, Auerbach intended not merely to argue a cultural difference or carryover but rather a definitively alternative inception of the Western canon. For this reason, although I do not dispute the common assessment that Auerbach favors the Judeo-Christian tradition over the Hellenic in the literary history he delineates, what needs to be stressed, I think, is the spiritual and ethical significance of his choices. For while literary scholars (including myself) are typically drawn to Auerbach's contagiously enthusiastic readings of his texts, few (including Auerbach himself) have paid attention to the fact that the biblical scene he picked (Genesis 22:1–19) for the negotiation of another beginning to Western literature is a scene about divine mercy: God spares Isaac's life just as Abraham is about to kill him.

As Auerbach painstakingly shows, the nature of divine mercy remains mysterious to the human characters involved and, by implication, to the reader. Repeatedly, Auerbach writes that "we are not told" of certain important details: God is without bodily form or local habitation; characters such as Abraham and Isaac are presented with no indication of their exact physical location, their specific features, or the purposes of their gestures; speech, instead of being used to manifest or externalize thought, serves to indicate thoughts which remain unexpressed. A sample passage of his reading goes as follows:

> The genius of the Homeric style becomes even more apparent when it is compared with an equally ancient and equally epic style from a different

18. It should be noted at the outset that Auerbach consistently contrasted the Christian origins of Western literature with the Hellenic, and that, perhaps for this reason, he did not highlight the differences between Judaism and Christianity. In the parameters he set up, "Judeo-Christian" and "Christian" seem interchangeable.

> world of forms. I shall attempt this comparison with the account of the sacrifice of Isaac, a homogeneous narrative produced by the so-called Elohist. The King James version translates the opening as follows (Genesis 22.1): "And it came to pass after these things, that God did tempt Abraham, and said to him, Abraham! And he said, Behold, here I am." Even this opening startles us when we come to it from Homer. *Where are the two speakers? We are not told.* The reader, however, knows that they are not normally to be found together in one place on earth, that one of them, *God, in order to speak to Abraham, must come from somewhere, must enter the earthly realm from some unknown heights or depths. Whence does he come, whence does he call to Abraham? We are not told.* He does not come, like Zeus or Poseidon, from the Aethiopians, where he has been enjoying a sacrificial feast. Nor are we told anything of his reasons for tempting Abraham so terribly. He has not, like Zeus, discussed them in set speeches with other gods gathered in council; nor have the deliberations in his own heart been presented to us. . . . It will at once be said that this is to be explained by the particular concept of God which the Jews held and which was wholly different from that of the Greeks. . . . *The concept of God held by the Jews is less a cause than a symptom* of their manner of comprehending and representing things.
>
> This becomes still clearer if we now turn to the other person in the dialogue, to *Abraham. Where is he? We do not know.* (*Mimesis*, 7–8, my emphases)

For Auerbach, the Hebraic narrative style lays claim to a powerful kind of truth—the sacred—that cannot be conflated with historical realism. This claim to truth is absolute or "tyrannical—it excludes all other claims. . . . All other scenes, issues, and ordinances have no right to appear independently of it, and it is promised that all of them, the history of all mankind, will be given their due place within its frame, will be subordinated to it" (*Mimesis*, 14–15). Furthermore, this sacred sense of truth is ineffable—in Auerbach's terms, symptomatic rather than causalist—and it is such ineffability that distinguishes the Judeo-Christian mimetic style from the pagans'. Thus, whereas an author such as Homer tends (for Auerbach at least) to domesticate signification in the form of endlessly digressive picturesque details, which can keep proliferating but ultimately hold no suspense, the biblical narrative specializes rather in the withholding of details and thus in the production of depth, which in turn necessitates interpretation.

When recast in the terms of our discussion, this ineffable sense of truth means that the movement of the axis of mercy is not always certain. From where does mercy come? Is it from above? Although Auerbach does speak about a "vertical connection" between God and various biblical characters, each of whom embodies a moment of the connection (*Mimesis*, 17), he also tends, carefully, to bracket a strictly unidirectional verticality in his reading of the story of Abraham:

> the two speakers [Abraham and God] are not on the same level: if we conceive of Abraham in the foreground, where it might be possible to picture him as prostrate or kneeling or bowing with outspread arms or gazing upward, God is not there too: Abraham's words and gestures are directed toward the depths of the picture or upward, but in any case the undetermined, dark place from which the voice comes to him is not in the foreground. (*Mimesis*, 9)

In other words, a human being (Abraham) may speak or gesture to God *as though* God were up there, but the source or location of mercy remains unspecified and unverifiable—or so, according to Auerbach, the biblical narrative insists. (God's voice, Auerbach writes, can also be coming from some unknown depths.)

The logic of a spiritual progression or descent may therefore be inferred from Auerbach's organization of the Western literary canon. This logic goes something as follows: the Judeo-Christian style, with its hallmark emphases on humble, earthly, and everyday contents (rather than heroic, spectacular, and sublime ones), and its liberal mingling of genres and idioms, embodies a distinctive paradigm of what it means to experience alterity. Whereas that alterity is originally named God, God has, through the centuries, been representationally displaced onto (or increasingly configured in the form of) the rich plurality of the human world. (See, for instance, chapter 2 of *Mimesis*, comparing the narrative methods of Roman authors such as Petronius and Tacitus with those of the biblical rendering of Peter's denial of Jesus, as recorded in the Gospel of Saint Mark; or chapter 13, in Shakespeare's introduction of tragic heroism in "man" in early modern Europe.) By the time we reach Auerbach's final chapter on Virginia Woolf (chapter 20), the notion of God has become so thoroughly dethroned from its or his place "up there" that even the authority of a novelist or her narrator (who used to be a stand-in for God) must be understood to have given way to a linguistic or stylistic multiplicity, made up not only of different human characters' exchanges but also of a Babel of appropriated, imitated, interrupted, partially heard, or inarticulate voices, marked by techniques such as the stream of consciousness, free indirect speech, interior monologue, and so forth, as well as by direct speech. In a novel such as *To the Lighthouse*, "the writer as narrator of objective facts has almost completely vanished; almost everything stated appears by way of reflection in the consciousness of the dramatis personae" (*Mimesis*, 534). Although Auerbach is ostensibly concerned with representational style, representational style itself, it turns out, is nothing less than the historical symptom of a remake of God's voice in human language. This remake means that the inscription of alterity, originally understood as divinity, has been brought up to date: alterity is now experienced as human polyphonicity. (For this point, see especially chapters 8 and 11, on Dante and Rabelais, respectively.)

Returning to the story of Abraham and Isaac, we may now reiterate the point that God's alterity, its unfathomable quality notwithstanding, manifests itself specifically as an act of mercy, which, moreover, takes the form of a permission to substitute: just when Abraham is ready to slaughter Isaac, an "Angel of the Lord" speaks to him in such a way as to enable him to substitute a ram for the boy. In the context of our topic, it would be tempting to advance the view that, as (re)staged by Auerbach, this other beginning of the Western canon is exactly a scene of mercy-cum-translation (translation in the sense of substitution). But the more important aspect to Auerbach's undertaking is perhaps not so much the felicity of locating yet another instance of forgiveness (which, incidentally, is my doing and does not inform Auerbach's discussion) as the larger ethical-political implications that follow from such a reading.

That is to say, if my reading of Auerbach's interpretative trajectory of de-sacralizing and (re)humanizing alterity is at all tenable, his gesture of using a biblical story about mercy to inaugurate this interpretative trajectory would seem poignantly motivated. In the story Auerbach tells, it is the Judeo-Christian tradition that is credited, in a state of exceptionalism, with the agency of laying the foundation for modern Western (and by implication global) democratic thinking. Central to this democratic thinking is a benevolent gaze, one that includes everybody, especially the lower classes and common folk whose profane and impure voices, as Auerbach's various chapters demonstrate, have helped (authors) transform the stylistic genealogy of the Western canon. But such a gaze is also, and more critically, the place of a definitive epistemic shift, whereby instances of inclusion (in the form of mixed genres, polyphonicity, multilingualism, and so forth) become a new testament to *the idea of a common humanity*. As Auerbach stated, what he wanted to foreground is "a world which on the one hand is entirely real, average, identifiable as to place, time, and circumstances, but which on the other hand is shaken in its very foundations, is transforming and renewing itself before our eyes" (*Mimesis*, 43). Hence his intriguing statements toward the end of the book:

> The more numerous, varied, and simple the people are who appear as subjects of such random moments [as depicted by modern writers like Woolf], the more effectively must what they have in common shine forth. In this unprejudiced and exploratory type of representation we cannot but see to what an extent—below the surface conflicts—the differences between men's ways of life and forms of thought have already lessened. The strata of societies and their different ways of life have become inextricably mingled. *There are no longer even exotic peoples. A century ago (in Mérimée for example), Corsicans or Spaniards were still exotic; today the term would be quite unsuitable for Pearl Buck's Chinese peasants.* Beneath the conflicts, and also through them, an economic and cultural leveling process is taking place. It is still a long way to a common life of mankind on earth, but the goal begins to be visible. (*Mimesis*, 552, my emphasis)

In such a fundamental change in thinking about humanity—a change that might, to borrow from classical idiom, be itself considered a type of *translatio imperii*, a transferring of political regimes—Judeo-Christianity, notwithstanding its status as religion, is reborn as the origination site of a tolerant secularism. Secularism in this instance does not seem entirely different from the capacious majesty of Christian transcendence that Derrida insists is the truth of a relevant translation. Just as the relevant (that is, transcendent) translation is what elevates and preserves that which it negates and destroys, so would secularism mean, first and foremost, a surpassing or overcoming (that is, transcending) of the narrow boundaries imposed by one's own religion, culture, and language—in sum, of the boundaries of ethnocentrism.[19] Understood in these comparative, trans-

19. Using as his example the depiction (in the Gospel according to Saint Mark) of Peter's denial of Jesus, Auerbach describes how Christianity spread historically by gradually detaching itself from more ethnically specific (Judaic) elements: "To be sure, for a time its effectiveness was hampered by practical obstacles. For a time the language as well as the religious and social premises of the message restricted it to Jewish circles. Yet the negative reaction which it aroused in Jerusalem, both among the Jewish leaders and among the majority of the people, forced the movement to embark upon the tremendous venture of missionary work among the Gentiles, which was characteristically begun by a member of the Jewish diaspora, the Apostle Paul. With that, an adaptation of the message to the preconceptions of

lational terms, the point of secularism would be less a matter of doing away with God per se than a matter of endorsing an egalitarian, cosmopolitan approach to human languages and cultures—an approach that in turn became the basis of a modern Western discipline such as comparative literature. The discipline's efforts at self-reform in recent years, from its previous Europe-centered foci to thinking about "world," "global," or "planetary" literatures, are arguably the best corroborations of this spiritual lineage.[20]

Outsiders to Our Humanity

Well before the more recent disciplinary self-reform in comparative literature, a secularized representation, understood, in accordance with Auerbach's vision, as the representation of a polyphonic universal humanity, clearly already informed the intellectual basis of a work such as Edward Said's *Orientalism*, first published in 1978. Despite the latter's pronounced criticism of Western literary and cultural representation (as being in complicity with Western imperialist invasions of non-Western lands and peoples),[21] once we reclassify the objectionable features of Orientalism, as Said analyzes them, as examples of cultural bigotry and ethnocentric bias, Said's trenchant critique has to be recognized as a logical sequel to Auerbach's work. Not surprisingly, *Mimesis* was acknowledged by Said as a book that had a profound influence on his thinking.[22]

---

a far wider audience, its detachment from the special preconceptions of the Jewish world, became a necessity and was effected by a method rooted in Jewish tradition but now applied with incomparably greater boldness, the method of revisional interpretation. The Old Testament was played down as popular history and as the code of the Jewish people and assumed the appearance of a series of 'figures,' that is of prophetic announcements and anticipations of the coming of Jesus and the concomitant events" (*Mimesis*, 48). For a brief discussion of Auerbach's notion of the "figura," see Said's introductory comments (*Mimesis*, xx–xxii). An English translation of Auerbach's famous essay "Figura," translated by Ralph Manheim, can be found in Erich Auerbach, *Scenes from the Drama of European Literature: Six Essays* (1959; Gloucester, Mass.: Peter Smith, 1973), 11–76.

20. For a related discussion, see my "A Discipline of Tolerance," *A Companion to Comparative Literature*, 1st. ed., edited by Ali Behdad and Dominic Thomas (London: Wiley-Blackwell, 2011), 15–27.

21. Edward W. Said, *Orientalism* (New York: Pantheon, 1978).

22. See Said, "Introduction to the Fiftieth-Anniversary Edition," *Mimesis*, ix–xxxii. Hereafter references to Said's introduction will be included in parentheses in the text. Said's comments on Auerbach can also be found in his other works, such as *Beginnings: Intention and Method* (Baltimore: Johns Hopkins University Press,

In the introduction he provided for the fiftieth anniversary of the publication of Auerbach's book, Said calls it "the finest description we have of the millennial effects of Christianity on literary representation (*Mimesis*, xxii). In his magisterial appraisal, Said, understandably, empathizes with Auerbach's historical situation as a Prussian Jewish intellectual forced into exile by mid-twentieth-century German National Socialism. Rather than subjecting Auerbach's claims about literature to stern criticism, Said chose to interpret them imaginatively (and we might say, forgivingly), as the flaws of a tragic hero: "The triumph of *Mimesis*, as well as its inevitable tragic flaw, is that the human mind studying literary representations of the historical world can only do so as all authors do—from the limited perspective of their own time and their own work" (*Mimesis*, xxxii). The ingenuity of Said's generous reading also subjectivizes Auerbach's work, leaving open the question precisely of the collective historicality of Auerbach's undertaking.

That historicality may be broached, once again, through the problematic of forgiveness. As mentioned at the beginning of this essay, forgiveness tends, in modern discourse, to be viewed as a kind of ethical imperative in large part because it is understood as a rescue, a break that can deliver us from the condition of being perpetually spellbound to what is irreversible. Far more than the pardoning of a particular debt, forgiveness is considered the kind of transmission and exchange that brings about *a new beginning*. Whether it is from above to below, as in Christian transcendence (according to Shakespeare's Portia and to Derrida), or from a divine voice with no specified location, as in the Bible, to the multiple vulgar voices of a common humanity, as in modern Western literature (according to Auerbach), the lesson of forgiveness is about being able to start afresh, to inaugurate and imagine a new history of human collective life based on the transcendence or overcoming of (ethnic and linguistic) boundaries and conflicts.[23] Together with some of the seman-

---

1975), in particular 68–69, 72–73; *The World, the Text, and the Critic* (Cambridge: Harvard University Press, 1983), in particular 5–9; and *Culture and Imperialism* (New York: Vintage, 1994), 43–61.

23. Arendt elaborates it in the following way: "Only through this constant mutual release from what they do can men remain free agents, only by constant willingness to change their minds and start again can they be trusted with so great a power as that to begin something new. . . . Forgiving, in other words, is the only reaction which does not merely re-act but acts anew and unexpectedly, unconditioned by the act which provoked it and therefore freeing from its consequences both the one who forgives and the one who is forgiven. The freedom contained in Jesus' teachings of forgiveness is the freedom from vengeance, which incloses [*sic*]

tic affiliates explored in this essay, such as mercy, translation, polyphonicity, egalitarianism, and so forth, forgiveness belongs in a radicalized conception of human differences, a conception whose spirit, or so we are led to think, is that of reconciliation.

As Auerbach tells us in the epilogue, the composition of *Mimesis* took place in Istanbul. Said's incisive comments on this locale of Auerbach's exile are worth citing at length:

> To any European trained principally, as Auerbach was, in medieval and renaissance Roman literatures, Istanbul does not simply connote a place outside Europe. Istanbul represents the terrible Turk, as well as Islam, the scourge of Christendom, the great Oriental apostasy incarnate. Throughout the classical period of European culture Turkey was the Orient, Islam its most redoubtable and aggressive representative. . . . The Orient and Islam also stood for the ultimate *alienation* from and opposition to Europe, the European tradition of Christian Latinity, as well as to the putative authority of ecclesia, humanistic learning, and cultural community. For centuries Turkey and Islam hung over Europe like a gigantic composite monster, seeming to threaten Europe with destruction. To have been an exile in Istanbul at that time of fascism in Europe was a deeply resonating and intense form of exile from Europe.[24]

Insofar as the focus remains on Auerbach himself as the tragic hero, thus, Said is quite right to conclude that *Mimesis* is not only "a massive reaffirmation of the Western cultural tradition," as it has often been assumed to be, but also "a work built upon a critically important *alienation* from it, a work whose conditions and circumstances of existence are not immediately derived from the culture it describes with such extraordinary insight and brilliance but built rather on an agonizing distance from it."[25] Even so, Said's repeated use of the word "alienation" alerts us to considerations other than Auerbach's personal circumstances.

Said's own consistent interventions on behalf of the non-Western world, in particular, make it difficult to overlook another important aspect of alienation: for a (re)construction of the European literary canon of its scope and scale, *Mimesis*, despite being written in Istanbul,

---

both doer and sufferer in the relentless automatism of the action process, which by itself need never come to an end" (*The Human Condition*, 240, 241). Arendt also writes that "Jesus likened the power to forgive to the more general power of performing miracles" (247).

24. Said, *The World, the Text, and the Critic*, 6, my emphasis.

25. Said, *The World, the Text, and the Critic*, 8, my emphasis.

bears little trace of the legacies left by the Arabs, the Turks, and Islam *in Europe*. Should this omission or disregard be explained strictly in terms of professional competence (that is, that Auerbach was a specialist of Romance literatures and thus could not have been held responsible for not addressing Islamic literatures and cultures)?[26] Or should it be accepted as the limit to the modern Western metanarrative of secularizing representation, a metanarrative that is genealogically traceable to a religious notion of mercy and forgiveness, that aspires toward redeeming all of humanity as common, unified, and worthy of note, and that nonetheless must leave some humanity on the outside? *This* "tragically flawed" alienation—in the literal sense of rendering alien—of some peoples and cultures from Auerbach's monumental literary history resonates a bit too well with the anguish Auerbach expresses in the essay "Philology and *Weltliteratur*" (1952) at the superabundance of non-European literatures and languages emerging on the modern historical stage. "There is no more talk now . . . of a spiritual exchange between peoples, of the refinement of customs and of a reconciliation of races," Auerbach writes sadly of the postwar era. Advocating the Goethean ideal of *Weltliteratur* as "a conception of the diverse background of a common fate," he holds on to the hope of a positive effect (cohesion, mutual understanding, common purpose) resulting from this conception, adding that such an effect "might . . . help to make us accept our fate with more equanimity *so that we will not hate whoever opposes us*—even when we are forced into a posture of antagonism."[27] For him as a philologist steeped in the Euro-

26. Auerbach was candid about his choice of texts: "The great majority of the texts were chosen at random, on the basis of accidental acquaintance and personal preference rather than in view of a definite purpose. Studies of this kind do not deal with laws but with trends and tendencies, which cross and complement one another in the most varied ways" (*Mimesis*, 556). In response to the question about his book's relation to German literature, he wrote, "The preponderance of Romance material in *Mimesis* is to be explained not only because of the fact that I am a Romanist, but rather above all because in most periods the Romance literatures are more representative of Europe than are, for example, the German" (*Mimesis*, 570).

27. See Erich Auerbach, "Philology and *Weltliteratur*," trans. Maire and Edward W. Said, *Centennial Review* 13.1 (1969), 1–17; the two quotations are from 6 and 7 (my emphasis). As a philologist, Auerbach was preoccupied in this essay with the methodological problem of synthesis, but the overtones of alarm and pessimism at a changing world are clear. Said's critical comments on this essay can be found in *Beginnings*, 68–69; *Culture and Imperialism*, 45; and *Mimesis*, xvi. See also Aamir R. Mufti, "Auerbach in Istanbul: Edward Said, Secular Criticism, and the Question of Minority Culture," *Critical Inquiry* 25.1 (1998), 95–125. In this fine essay, Mufti argues for understanding Said's secular criticism as being rooted in a

pean Romance tradition, the masses of the non-European world clearly presented, at the dawn of the cold war, a threat rather than a source of comfort.

If Auerbach's democratizing story of world literature can be understood as an allegory of forgiveness (and reconciliation), his remarks just cited also bring home the intimate kinship between forgiveness and hatred. That kinship is one good way of explaining why fictional characters such as Shylock, a law-abiding Jew, and Shin-ae Lee, a failed born-again Christian, can be so compelling to some of us. As mercy, whether in religious or secular forms, becomes the global logic of an imagined new (and ever renewable) beginning or end of humanity, it is precisely the characters who are unable to get on with the program, as it were, who pose the greatest fascination. Despite the vast differences in time, place, and personal situation, Shylock's and Shin-ae's incommensurate relation to forgiveness assumes the import of a kind of alterity that remains outside the religious, philosophical, literary, and cultural-political trajectories charted by Arendt, Derrida, and Auerbach (and to a certain extent, Said) in their shared orientations toward Christian love and its secularist avatars.

Shylock's alterity is signified by his refusal to forgive even when he is offered twice the sum of money he is owed in exchange for the pound of flesh (hence his reputation as an unsympathetic diabolical figure). Shin-ae's case is more complex in that she has, supposedly, gone through a major conversion. In the light of our discussion, Shin-ae has in effect translated her own terms of grief and vindictiveness into the currency of mercy and forgiveness, or so she supposes at first. Whereas Shylock never for a moment considers accepting trading in his terms for the Christian currency, but throughout insists on the untranslatability of those terms (that is, on the bond or agreement specified in his original oath), Shin-ae has tried it only to discover that she has been tricked and outdone, which drives her to insanity. More than an attachment to money, kin, love, or sex, these two characters' stories tell of an inassimilable, melancholic, and self-destructive aggressivity, which may be equated with an unquenchable desire for retributive justice in the face of persecution and violation. In both cases, this aggressivity persists like a foreign mode of allegiance or a genetic trait from a "less evolved" time, which, despite

---

minority-exilic conception of culture—that is, that it is aimed not so much at religion per se as at forms of majoritarian thinking such as nationalism.

attempts at a Christian makeover, voluntary or imposed, cannot be improved.

Such anachronistic attachment to something other than personal liberation and redemption, the kinds of existential hopes held out by (modern) investments in autonomous individuality and tolerant collectivity (including the collectivity expressed in literary history),[28] points to a very different kind of social order from that created by Christian networks. What might a world look like in which outsiders such as Shylock and Shin-ae do not have to appear as diabolical or insane? What conceptions of forgiveness, translation, and secularizing (or humanizing) would be necessary for them to be able to coexist with us, other than through the familiar mechanism of *our* transcendent benevolence? Difficult and counterintuitive though they may sound, these questions should serve as reminders that the Christian dimension, whether in the guise of religion or secularity, has perhaps not yet exhausted the possibilities of the future of the human, whatever the human may become.

28. For a series of astute discussions about tolerance, see Wendy Brown, *Regulating Aversion: Tolerance in the Age of Identity and Empire* (Princeton: Princeton University Press, 2006), in particular chapters 6 and 7.

6

American Studies in Japan, Japan in American Studies

Challenges of the Heterolingual Address

In his book *Translation and Subjectivity: On "Japan" and Cultural Nationalism*, Naoki Sakai explores the question of the production of subjectivity in an intercultural environment, such as that between the West and the non-West, through the figure of translation. Like Derrida, who associates translation with forgiveness and with a form of transcendence that, ideally, does not seek to consolidate its own power or sovereignty (see chapter 5), Sakai advances translation in ethical terms, as an overcoming of the more commonsensical definitions and strictures of human communication. Especially noteworthy is Sakai's emphasis that translation is not simply an act of transfer between units of two self-contained languages which exist regardless of whether translation takes place. Rather, he sees translation as the a priori condition, the very ground that enables linguistic exchange to proceed *as though* languages were autonomous, individuated phenomena. For Sakai, that is to say, translation is the name for an ongoing state of interactivity, a transindividual relation that structures human signification by way of the relation's incessant, iterative occurrences.

In light of translation delineated in these terms, Sakai further proposes what he calls the practice of heterolingual address, a type of speech act in which the otherness of the audience—defined not only in terms of their languages but also in terms of their habits, histories, cultures, assumptions, and preferences—is never repressed but acknowledged and included or inscribed in the very process of information delivery and exchange. To explain what he means, Sakai refers to the simple convention of the pronoun "we," typically used by a speaker to designate a putative collectivity between himself and the audience:

> "We" comprise an essentially mixed audience among whom the addresser's relation to the addressee could hardly be imagined to be one of unruffled empathetic transference, and to address myself to such an audience by saying "we" was to reach out to the addressees without either an assurance of immediate apprehension or an expectation of uniform response from them. *"We" are rather a nonaggregate community; for the addressees would respond to my delivery with varying degrees of comprehension, including cases of the zero degree at which they would miss its signification completely.* I want to call this manner of relating the addresser to the addressees the heterolingual *address.*
>
> *In the heterolingual address, therefore, the act of inception or reception occurs as the act of translation, and translation takes place at every listening or reading.*[1]

Ultimately, the heterolingual address functions in Sakai's account of intercultural exchange as a kind of categorical imperative, the conscious adoption of an ethical attitude, the attitude of the widest possible inclusiveness. The reason for this is simple: it is only when we adopt such an attitude that we can be prepared to come to terms with the otherness that not only unexpectedly but also inevitably resides in our addressees, whoever they happen to be. The heterolingual address is what makes it possible for us to seriously confront rather than simply assimilate or neutralize "foreigners" in our act of enunciation, including especially those who may not be prepared to understand us or agree with us; those "cases of the zero degree at which they would miss [our] signification completely."

When I was first invited to address the summer seminar on American studies at Nanzan University in Japan some years ago,[2] my immediate reaction was one of professional unease: I am, strictly speaking, an outsider to the academic specialization called American studies and not exactly qualified to speak. What could I possibly offer the audience? Although I did, eventually, have something to say, it was with a mixture of naïveté

1. Naoki Sakai, *Translation and Subjectivity: On "Japan" and Cultural Nationalism*, foreword by Meaghan Morris (Minneapolis: University of Minnesota Press, 1997), 4, 9, first and third emphases mine.

2. This was the Nanzan American Studies Summer Seminar, held in Nagoya, Japan, July–August, 2008, under the auspices of the Center for American Studies at Nanzan University and the Fulbright-Japan Educational Commission.

and curiosity that I ventured into this territory. Sakai's discussion of the heterolingual address, in particular, helped me rethink foreignness itself: being an outsider, Sakai suggests, need not translate into an absolute inhibition about speaking; the more challenging task is rather to articulate (my "foreign" reception of) American studies in a form of address that does not presume any putative collectivity to be already existing between my audience and myself, and that instead takes the uncertainty thereof as a point of departure, with the goal of creating, in the process of speaking, a new kind of "we," a collectivity based on the ineluctability of heterolinguality. Pushed to its logical extreme, the heterolingual address would be a kind of speech act that acknowledges the presence of multiple, indeed infinite perspectives among our fellow interlocutors and strives to be as nonexclusionary as possible of the heterogeneity involved.

With the political and practical ubiquity of America's presence—the U.S. domination of world politics since the end of the Second World War, to be specific—the first question posed by American studies (to me as an outsider to the specialization) is the status of America: Is it a traditional object of study, to be accessed, defined, and elaborated with a kind of disinterested academic gaze, supported by the usual scholarly apparatus? Presumably, if the answer to this question is yes, there is already a history of this objectification, which can be readily examined. At what point did that history begin, and under what conditions of possibility? What events and paradigms have been made legitimate contents or constituents of that history?[3] At the same time, it seems to me, the sheer magnitude of America's world power since 1945 means that the study of America must somehow go beyond this more traditional trajectory in which it could simply have taken its place among a plurality of objects and enjoyed "disinterested" scholarly attention among a multitude of possible examples. Such magnitude of power compels us to approach America in ways that exceed a routine object of study with set boundaries. As William Spanos argues, for instance, it is American exceptionalism, definable as "the perennial belief in America's unique ameliorative global mission in the world" and upheld for so long by American studies scholars of an older generation, that necessitates historical, ontological, and linguistic scrutiny. Without such scrutiny, American studies

3. For an authoritative and informative discussion of the history and future potential of American studies as a field of study, see Donald E. Pease and Robyn Wiegman, "Futures," *The Futures of American Studies*, ed. Donald E. Pease and Robyn Wiegman (Durham: Duke University Press, 2002), 1–42.

as a field of inquiry will likely remain, "as the inordinate focus of its criticism on the literature and culture of the United States suggests, vestigially inscribed by the exceptionalist code" and continue in its "disciplinary parochialism."[4]

The second question that may be posed to, about, and by American studies is therefore a theoretical one, having to do with discursive politics: How should we speak about an object that, in effect, has become so stupendous and preemptive that it tends to set the terms and criteria for the way knowledge is produced, indeed negotiated, disseminated, and normativized around the contemporary world? America in this sense is really a force field, one whose geopolitical, linguistic, and technological reach keeps expanding, and which can thus not be reduced to an object with securely determinable characteristics or limits. Instead, insofar as it represents progress and advancement—to many, the pinnacle of human civilization—America stands in another kind of trajectory altogether, a teleological one, to be exact, in which it is supposedly the ultimate goal and final destination for all other cultures. Conversely, as this goal and destination, America has also become the condition of possibility for these other cultures, in the sense that it is against America that such cultures' successes or failures are now measured, most typically by the cultures themselves. (The best case in point, in recent times, of such an America-oriented self-assessment is the People's Republic of China.)

This sense of America as a force field which subsumes the relevance of others, and which, whether or not we like it, provides the very terms on which others tend to be judged, is what seems to me a more urgent, if also controversial, way to engage with American studies. In this instance, the status of America is no longer simply that of an object of study or even a field of scholarship with a local history. Much more prominently, that status has to do with an ever-shifting international dynamics of power transaction and possession: whether or not we consciously speak of America, it has, somehow, already spoken (of) us.[5]

4. William V. Spanos, "American Studies in the 'Age of the World Picture': Thinking the Question of Language," *The Futures of American Studies*, ed. Pease and Wiegman, 387, 400.

5. Spanos describes this situation as "the global colonization of thinking by American instrumentalism or rather by the Americanization of thinking, that sense of futility that comes over us when we realize that even our criticism of America must be carried out in—must be answerable to—the language of America, that sense, in other words, that we have been compelled into tacit, frustrating silence in the face of the triumph of a banal instrumental thinking that routinizes violence" ("American Studies in the 'Age of the World Picture,'" 402).

When American studies is the occasion for a gathering outside the United States, such as the one I attended in Nagoya, the opportunity that awaits us is that of probing what the categorical imperative of the heterolingual address would entail and can enable. I felt obligated to reflect on how such an address would include in it an articulation with Japan, not only because Nagoya happened to be the location of that meeting but also because of Japan's complicated, entangled history with the United States since the mid-nineteenth century. To suggest what some constituents of such a heterolingual address about America *and* Japan might be in a context in which the audience was bound to have different expectations and ideas about nationhood, culture, and globalization, I briefly discussed two films. If the point of the heterolingual address, as delineated by Sakai, is sensitivity and responsiveness to the foreign in our midst, can film be an occasion, indeed a medium, for such an address? If so, how might the specifics of film language be (re)conceptualized and articulated with a view to such foreignness, in ways that go beyond reification and exoticization?

No Regrets for Our Youth

On a previous visit to Japan, in the summer of 2005, when I spoke at an international conference on Japanese cinema, I discussed Akira Kurosawa's *No Regrets for Our Youth* (1946), a film based on the controversy of the dismissal, in 1933, of a Kyoto University law professor, Takigawa Yukitoki, on grounds of his pro-communist views by the Education Minister Hatoyama. Kurosawa's film interested me because its narrative structure provides a discursive opening for rethinking political issues such as fascism, imperialism, and militarism with a transnational awareness. Kurosawa achieved this by a noticeable transition in the story, whereby the main female character, Yukie, undergoes a personal transformation from being a Westernized, bourgeois university student to being a sympathizer with the peasants' and women's movements in Japan's postwar countryside.[6]

Despite what seems to be its realism, the narrative transition in *No Regrets for Our Youth* is, I argued, Kurosawa's means of articulating Japan

6. See Rey Chow, "A Filmic Staging of Postwar Geotemporal Politics: Kurosawa Akira's *No Regrets for Our Youth*, Sixty Years Later," *boundary 2* 34.1 (2007), 67–77. Some passages in this chapter have been adapted, with modifications, from this earlier essay.

to America in ways that would become increasingly acute in the postwar world. Although, because of censorship during the Occupation led by the U.S. (1945–52), there are no explicit representations of the Second World War in the diegesis (except for the announcement, in 1941, of Japan's attack on Pearl Harbor and then eventually of Japan's loss of the war), this narrative mechanism bridges the world of the 1930s and 1940s, in which Japan was dominated by the furor over war (both in the form of pro-war and antiwar sentiments), and the postwar world that apparently embraces the "peace-loving" ways of Japanese agrarian life. In her function as the narrative hinge, Yukie objectifies this transition by turning herself into a dutiful widow and daughter-in-law, a hardworking peasant woman who is determined to vindicate her husband's (misunderstood) patriotism in the eyes of the community. Yukie's feminine hands and fingers, which once produced the tunes of Western music on the piano, are now shown to labor steadily in the soil, cultivating rice for the village.

In this simple temporal movement—what appears to be a series of successive chronological happenings in a moral fable—emerges a stark sense of what I would call epistemic uncertainty. If narrative transition is not a natural order of things but an event in itself, I asked, what are we to make of the shift between the early and final parts of the story? As mentioned, the early part of the story takes place in contemporary, urban Japan in what might be called a progressive time (the 1930s): all the trappings of Westernization, including the activist, antifascist sentiments, are there, propelling Japan toward a future in which it can become not only a mimic of but also an equal to the West. The later part of the story (first near the end of the war and then after it, in the mid-1940s), by contrast, returns us to a rural environment in which the most important activity is the cultivation of rice. Rather than the progressive time already encountered in the earlier part, we find here a time that seems backward- and inward-looking, as though the process of national soul-searching in the aftermath of political and military defeat must involve a (re)turn, literally, to roots and working through those roots by hand. (At one point Yukie says, "I have found my roots in that village.") The politics of temporality set up in the narrative transition thus evokes the classic opposition between Westernized modernity and non-Western native tradition, with the paradox that the seemingly backward and inward, spiritual (re)turn to Japan's roots is at the same time shown as a forward advancement (including a proto-feminist awareness of women's liberation). That is to say, the rehabilitation of tradition is now given to us, the audience, as the viable way of moving on to the future.

Is the later part of the story really a logical follow-up to the earlier one, then? Who exactly is making this claim, and to whom is it directed? If the film is taken as a kind of heterolingual address in Sakai's terms, the perspectives being implicitly or explicitly invoked are mind-boggling. Was Kurosawa primarily addressing the national Japanese audience, who, to all appearances, belonged to the same community as he? Was he at the same time calling forth—constructing through the medium of film—another kind of community, one that is not uniformly or necessarily predisposed to hearing the same message? When the film is interpreted as a heterolingual, rather than simply monolingual (or mononational and monocultural), address, its fantastical narrative transition, with its puzzling juxtaposition of the two apparently incommensurable parts, the "before" and "after," merits interrogation.

If the stigmatization and ostracization faced by Yukie's husband's (Noge's) family is an allegory of the stigmatization and ostracization faced by Japan in the community of nations at the end of the war, it is through unconditional submission and dedication to the goal of renewed, collective self-fashioning—exactly the kind of aggressive affect that bolstered both Japan's militarism *and* the violence of its antimilitarist activism before and during the war—that Noge's family, led by Yukie, now tries to extricate itself from its predicament. Albeit a peaceful corrective, the return to the soil seems in tune with patterns of obsessive mental and physical behavior that were inscribed in Japan's wartime catastrophe in the first place. In both cases, it is about persisting in (re)gaining footing in and recognition by a hostile world, with a stubborn investment in Japan's exceptionalism, as is typically justified in what came to be known as *Nihonjinron* (the discourse on the Japanese).

Viewed as an attempt at heterolingual address, directed not only at a uniform or predictable Japanese audience but also at a postwar international public *occupied* in multiple senses by the United States, the narrative transition that happens between the first and second part of this "Japanese" movie may therefore be grasped as the enunciation of a certain redefined geotemporal politics in relation to America. Made very soon after the war, the film hails the audience as members of a new global configuration—a kind of "us"—dominated by America and its own version of expansionism and Orientalism in the Pacific. Ironically, too, this was the period in which the official, U.S.-led Occupation forbade the representation of Occupation forces in Japanese films: "The American censors tried not only to suppress criticism of it [the Occupation], *but also to hide the very fact that Japan was being occupied at all* and that foreign officials were closely supervising the Japanese media."[7] This active prohibition of reference to a political and military presence meant that (for a filmmaker such as Kurosawa) the historicity of Japan's so-called second chance of the postwar years had to be dealt with by indirect means. To this extent, the strikingly incongruent temporalities of Kurosawa's film narrative can be read—irrespective of Kurosawa's personal convictions and intentions—as a kind of response to this prohibition, a response that takes the form of a silent decoding of the destinies scripted for the Pacific in its postwar transactions with the United States and the rest of the capitalist Western world.

First among these postwar transactions (between Japan and the West) is the inducement of discipline that takes the form of a rationalistic submission and dedication to the work ethic. From the ashes of the war, Japan was to rise to the status of a global economic power through quantifiable capitalist productivity (in the form of industry and manufacture). This phenomenon of a hyperproductionism, encouraged and supported by the United States in its attempt to arrest the spread of communism in East Asia, was to replicate itself in the emergence of the so-called Asian Tigers (Taiwan, South Korea, Singapore, and Hong Kong) in the 1970s and 1980s, and finally, since the 1990s, in the rise in world status of an ideologically capitulating and complicit People's Republic of China.

Second, even though this magical capacity for work is an indispensable ingredient in the postindustrial capitalist vision of economic growth, in *No Regrets for Our Youth* it is enigmatically associated with another kind of time: the time of the peasant, of agriculture, and of country life. As has become clear in the case of contemporary China, the demands and rewards of capitalism always mean the uprooting of countryside populations and massive migrations to urban areas where work opportunities are more abundant. To valorize the work ethic through an affirmation of a return to the soil is thus, as Kurosawa's narrative suggests, to place Japan in an impossible bind: if Japan and the rest of Asia are given recognition as participants in the global present through dedication to work, such dedication is granted intelligibility only as the attribute of a nonpresent time (that is, the attribute of a continuous tradition, an essential Asian-ness).[8]

7. Kyoko Hirano, *Mr. Smith Goes to Tokyo: Japanese Cinema under the American Occupation, 1945–1952* (Washington: Smithsonian Institute, 1992), 54, my emphasis.

8. As a parallel, in Western scholarship on Japanese film, critics are fond of finding essentialist principles (such as the samurai code of honor, the warrior ideal, the

The schematization of the story into two kinds of temporalities, a mere technicality of the plot for some audiences, turns in this manner into a heterolingual and heterocultural manner of addressing—both in the sense of speaking about and in the sense of speaking to—America. To the postwar international public, the address enunciates America, as Spanos suggests in his essay on American studies, as a kind of thinking or language (rather than as a bounded object) whose effects are felt in the form of an ontological rupture—the enigmatic splitting of Japanese society between the two temporalities just described. Enigmatic because it is, within the film diegesis, unclear from where such a splitting could arise: What causes the rupture in the first place? Can the problems of modernity and urbanization be resolved by a return to agriculture and country life? Can Japan abandon its fascism and militarism and simply start over again by growing rice? In retrospect, what is being foregrounded in the narrative transition is the problematic nature of an imaginary effort at cultural recommencement, or cultural reorigination, under the American-centric circumstances after the war.

Considered in this manner, the supposedly forward- but slightly awkward-looking image of Yukie on her final return to the village (as she climbs onto the truck with the help of other villagers) gives us a good clue to Kurosawa's conception of the problems at hand. As the leader of the democratic culture movement—a symbol of hopefulness, willpower, and emancipation—Yukie seems rather out of sync with the villagers, who represent the future yet who are also quite capable of being stuck in bigotry and malice. It is in this complex series of significations, shuttling throughout the film among personal, communal, national, and international levels of intensity, and superimposed on one another to produce Yukie's face itself as a time-image, that we should come to terms with Kurosawa's statement "This woman I wanted to show as the new Japan."[9]

To sum up, my point about *No Regrets for My Youth* is that it may be considered a cinematically mediated heterolingual address, in which the epistemic contradictions and incommensurabilities of imagining Japan's contemporaneity in the postwar world in terms of its rice-growing ritual, its return to a pure, rustic Japaneseness, are plainly acknowledged and

---

Zen sensibility for harmony with nature, and so forth) in modern Japanese scenarios in order to argue the continuity of a Japanese cultural heritage. See Mitsuhiro Yoshimoto, *Kurosawa: Film Studies and Japanese Cinema* (Durham: Duke University Press, 2000), 71–74 and throughout.

9. Cited in Donald Richie, *The Films of Akira Kurosawa*, 3rd ed. (Berkeley: University of California Press, 1998), 40.

staged rather than being suppressed. How would we respond as the recipients of or interlocutors with such an address, especially from the point of view of American studies?

Rhapsody in August

In the second to last film he made in his career, *Rhapsody in August* (1991), Kurosawa dramatizes the problematic of the Japan-U.S. relationship through another, much older female character, Kane, a grandmother of four teenagers who are spending their summer vacation in her farmhouse outside Nagasaki, while their parents (Kane's son, Tadao, and daughter, Yoshie) are in Hawaii visiting an elder brother of Kane's, Suzujiro Haruno, who had emigrated to the United States in 1920. The old woman, we soon learn, is a widow whose husband, a schoolteacher, was among the civilians killed in Nagasaki on 9 August 1945, when the United States dropped the second atomic bomb on Japan. While enjoying their time together with Granny (even though they do not like her cooking) and recalling what happened in Nagasaki at the end of the war, the young people receive a letter from their parents with pictures of their relatives on the other side of the Pacific. Suzujiro, who married a white American woman who is now deceased, is quite ill, and his son, Clark, is managing the family's sizable pineapple business. From the pictures, it is clear that Kane's extended family live the enviable life of the well-to-do in America. Tadao, Yoshie, and Clark all urge Kane to go to Hawaii and see her dying brother.

In an attempt to persuade their mother, Tadao and Yoshie fly back to Japan, only to find on their arrival that Kane has, with the help of the grandchildren, already sent off a telegram to the Hawaii relatives, indicating her willingness to visit after she has attended the annual memorial service for her husband. Anxious that this embarrassing mention of the past might upset the Hawaii relatives and thus spoil their own business prospects in the United States, Tadao and Yoshie become rather agitated, especially when they hear that Clark, on receiving Kane's telegram, has decided to come for a visit himself.

The rest of the film shows the three generations of the family playing host to Clark after he arrives, fussing over making him comfortable, answering his questions about the family and their grandfather (his uncle), and taking him to visit various sites, including the elementary school playground in Nagasaki where schoolchildren were killed by the atomic blast, the commemoration ceremony in the village honoring Grandfather and other victims, and the pond by the waterfall where the children like to spend their time playing (and where Clark receives the news that his father has just died). We also see Clark having a conversation with Kane in which he apologizes for not knowing what had happened to her in the past and she repeatedly responds, "It's all right." After Clark's departure, Tadao and Yoshie are about to take off again, only to notice that something seems to have overtaken Kane's mind, causing her to act as though she were back in 1945. She mistakes Tadao for her elder brother and, at the light and sound of a thunderstorm, hastens to cover the sleeping children's bodies with white sheets so as to shield them from the glare of what she thinks is the atomic blast. The next morning, a neighbor comes with the news that Kane, probably seeing how that day's cloud patterns resemble the cloud patterns on 9 August 1945, has headed off for Nagasaki to look for her husband. The last series of scenes shows the family members running in the storm to try to catch up with her. The scene finally ends with Kane forging ahead, her umbrella turned inside out, while the noise of the wind and rain gives way to a children's choir singing the song "Heidenröselein" (Franz Schubert's setting of Goethe's early nineteenth-century poem of the same name, translated as "The Heathrose"), the tune that one of Kane's grandchildren has been trying to play on her old pedal organ since the beginning of the film.

In contrast to the enigmatic temporal transition in *No Regrets for Our Youth*, the engagement with the Second World War and with America in *Rhapsody in August* takes the form of memory. Although, as in the earlier film, narrative is the key to our grasp of the mise-en-scène, it is less a matter of a progression of external events than a recollection of catastrophic happenings, a recollection that materializes somewhat sporadically, in the children's conversations among themselves and with Kane over the course of several weeks. And even as we become aware of the burden of history that Kane has been bearing for forty-some years, *Kurosawa offers no newsreel footage or direct voice-over journalistic accounts of that history*. The conspicuous absence of such documentary evidence of the original event (reminding us of the absence of any images of the war or any direct reference to the Occupation period in *No Regrets for Our Youth*) renders the act of recollection all the more evocative, as the audience is left to imagine what it was like and what it must have been like. As we visit, first with the children and then with Clark, a scene of the crime—the playground in the elementary school in Nagasaki where Kane's husband was presumably killed together with the schoolchildren, and where the monument of a twisted jungle gym stands as the only visible index to the tragedy of the destruction—the present becomes foregrounded as the time in which both the characters and the audience must come to terms with what is remembered.

Such foregrounding of the present raises the stakes for the heterolingual address to an acute level. Following the narrative that results from memory and recollection, the audience must negotiate its reactions to myriad imbrications: Japan as a victim of the atomic bombs and of America's ultimate acts of aggression; Japan's own record of imperialism and its countless victims in the rest of Asia; Japan's self-reconstruction as a pacifist nation since the end of the war; reactionary Japanese politicians' denial to this day of Japan's war crimes; and the history of Japanese Americans in the United States. By withholding the customary imagistic and narrational reminders, and by focusing our attention on the time of *now*, Kurosawa has, I believe, once again opened up a space, one that is, like that in *No Regrets for Our Youth*, epistemic in import. Whereas in the earlier film the staging of epistemic rupture serves to foreshadow Japan's postwar existence in a global situation dominated by America, in *Rhapsody in August* what is of interest is less the anticipation of geotemporal politics than the portentous yet mundane question of authority and agency in the aftermath of an unimaginable disaster. How are people supposed to behave when their loved ones are seized from them by war? Faced with the aggressor, in this case America, how are an atomic bomb widow and her descendents supposed to survive?

Tadao and Yoshie offer one kind of answer: for them it is better simply to be silent about the past because the former aggressors, citizens of a superpower, must be treated with kid gloves; having cordial relations with them is of vital importance to Japanese self-interest. Kane herself, on the contrary, insists that there is nothing wrong with speaking about the past because there is nothing wrong with speaking truthfully; in that insistence, which seems to be shared (though perhaps not entirely comprehendingly) by Kane's grandchildren, we find a refreshing alternative to the unctuous and obsequious attitudes personified by her son and daughter. Even so, Kane's memory is thrust into a new dimension of complexity by the arrival of Clark. The pain she has been enduring for forty-some years is now unexpectedly brought into sharp focus and subjected to the gaze of an outsider who is, moreover, not just an American but also a blood relative.

Clark is, strictly speaking, a cultural as well as biological hybrid, and his status as half-Japanese and half-American can perhaps be read as an allegory of the inextricably entwined fates of Japan and America in the postwar era. (Entirely left out of Kurosawa's and the Japanese characters' purviews is the ugly history of the U.S. government's internment of Japanese American citizens during the war.) Be this as it may, Clark's visit to the Japanese village and its inhabitants is nothing short of a dramatic entrance, the kind of fictional design that is aimed at or has the potential of bringing about something significant. What exactly is it? If Clark is a stand-in for "ethnic America," what does his brief appearance accomplish?

Clark's sojourn makes it impossible not to think of *Rhapsody in August* as a film about mourning. It is as though Kane's memory, which has hitherto been somewhat blurry (as she at first seems to have forgotten, or so she claims, even about her elder brother in Hawaii), is now—if I may use a term from film technology—remastered with Clark's entry. As her personal loss and suffering acquire the effects of a restored and enhanced film, which has reemerged in its full sensorial immediacy from the fog of old age and antiquated domestic existence, the act of recollection takes on the significance of an inimitable cinematic handling of the past. Yet even as the audience is, like her grandchildren, drawn sympathetically into the mournfulness of Kane's life story, the knowledge of Japan's imperial aggression against its neighbors also looms. For a scholar of Chinese descent such as myself, the compassion Kurosawa so clearly bestows on the victims of Nagasaki is controverted by the film's silence on Japan's war crimes in China, Korea, and southeast Asia.[10] In this respect, is not the film ironically a bit like Tadao and Yoshie, its most callous characters? What could be the rationale for *its* muteness about the past?

The ineluctability of this kind of antagonistic, rather than comfortable or harmonious, reaction among members of the film's audience is, I believe, exactly what lies at the core of Sakai's proposal of the heterolingual address: How to speak responsibly and nonexclusively to the element of the genuinely foreign or alien in our midst? By extension, this question would have to involve not only the demographics of the audience (Japanese, American, Chinese, Korean, men, women, children, and so forth) but also what may come across as politically objectionable or inappropriate language, as for instance *the language of a film*. In the case of a film

10. For a discussion of the critical controversy surrounding the film's seeming dehistoricization of the events that led up to the dropping of the atomic bombs, see Yoshimoto, *Kurosawa*, 364–71. As Yoshimoto writes, "The reception of *Rhapsody in August* (Hachigatsu no rapusodi [kyoshikyoku, 1991]) has been predominantly negative and more important, politically charged" (365).

about a survivor of the Nagasaki bombing, how are we to deal with the existence and eruption of obviously irreconcilable perspectives, such as those stemming from Japanese national chauvinism, on the one hand, and, on the other, our knowledge of Japan's criminal imperialist behavior during the Second World War?

The ingenuity of Kurosawa's handling of this impasse may be glimpsed in several sets of speeches and exchanges within the diegesis.

In an early scene, when the grandchildren suspect that Kane will not want to go to Hawaii because of the way her husband died, Kane clarifies that she does not particularly "like or dislike America" because of what happened, and that rather, "war is to blame." She reiterates this attitude toward war later, when she hears Yoshie scolding her son for writing that awkward telegram to the Hawaii relatives. Taking responsibility for the telegram, Kane lashes out, "They claim they dropped the flash to stop war. It's already been forty-five years now. But the flash hasn't stopped war. They're still killing people! But you know . . . war is to blame. People do anything . . . just to win a war. Sooner or later, it will be the ruin of all of us."

Even in English translation, these simple words are striking in the manner they move from the specific to the general, through the semantic shifts introduced in the third-person plural pronoun, "they."[11] In its collective anonymity, "they" is provocative in this context precisely because it is ambiguous—and ambivalent. While the word does refer straightforwardly, at first, to Americans insofar as they were the ones who dropped the flash, the perspective of Kane's speech steadily broadens to become a criticism of *anyone* who supports fighting a war in order to be triumphant and supremacist: "They're still killing people! . . . People do anything . . . just to win a war." If the identifiable "they" returns us to a nameable other—Japan's national enemy who victimized innocent Japanese (and other) citizens—the anonymous "people" signals rather a general denunciation of war itself, whoever the instigator might be. To put it differently, if "they" remains (localized in or as) the United States, Kane's statement can be interpreted as an anguished rejection of the national enemy, an entity based on the clearly set boundary between "us" and "them": since "they" killed "our" people, we must continue to condemn them. Mourning the dead, in this instance, would amount to a tribal ritual, one that insists on not forgiving or forgetting one's own condi-

11. My thanks to Yuriko Furuhata for her assistance with comparing the English translation with the Japanese dialogue.

tion of being injured, and the attendant act of recollection would serve the purpose of reinstating that boundary between us and them so as to avenge those of our own who have been sacrificed. (The characters Shylock and Shin-ae, as discussed in chapter 5, furnish good examples of this type of mourning and avenging behavior.) Once the notion of "they" is detached from a particular name to become simply "people," however, Kane's statements take on a decidedly different kind of connotation: all those who, like the Americans, provide justifications for the atomic attack (that it would not only end the war but also end war) are precisely those who will continue waging war and killing people indefinitely. Instead of invoking a definitive boundary between us and them as adversaries based on national, cultural, or other types of identities, Kane's statements problematize war itself by pointing to the hypocrisy and delusion of its perpetrators (those who always insist on giving war yet another round of reasoning, yet another chance).

Equally remarkable is the exchange that occurs between Kane and Clark as they sit outside her house under the moonlight. Contrary to Tadao and Yoshie's fears, not only are Clark and his family not offended by the reminder of what happened in Nagasaki, but his father also immediately sent him on a visit so that he can do whatever he can to help his aunt. As he sits face to face with Kane, this is what they say to each other:

Clark: I am terribly sorry for not knowing about Uncle. I'm really sorry.
Kane: That's all right.
Clark: You were born and live in Nagasaki. And still, we didn't realize it. That was wrong of us. We were wrong.
Kane: That's all right.

In the same conversation, Kane says "That's all right" a third time, followed by "This is just fine." She then finishes by saying, in broken English, "Thank you very much," whereupon she reaches out to Clark and shakes hands with him. Once again, Kurosawa has exploited these simple words to their full ambiguous capacity. Is Clark sorry because he and his family had no idea of what happened to Kane, or is he sorry for what the United States did to Japan? Did he come as a member of the extended family to offer an apology to his aunt, or did he come as a representative of the United States, to offer an apology to the Japanese?[12] Although I

12. See Yoshimoto's discussion of the ambiguity of Clark's apology in *Kurosawa*, 367–68. Yoshimoto's own reading, which sees the apology as one offered *within*

tend to agree with the view that there is nothing in Clark's words to suggest that he is delivering more than a personal apology to an elderly relative, the historical relations between Japan and the United States make it difficult to dismiss the loaded symbolic dimensions of his deliverance.

This scene is poignant not because of Clark's words but because of Kane's response: "It's all right." Is she saying it's all right that the relatives in Hawaii did not think of what happened to her husband because they were preoccupied with their own affairs, or is she saying it's all right *despite all her suffering*, because no one in particular, not even an American citizen or a blood relative, can or should be held accountable for the casualties of that perpetual injunction, our love for war?

In Kane's gracious words, the aggression of identitarian politics, with neatly divided positions between aggressor and aggressed on the basis of national boundaries, has quietly unfolded (as a paper boat unfolds into the piece of paper which gives it its erstwhile shape, to paraphrase Walter Benjamin) into a universal refusal of war. (To borrow the words of Julia Kristeva, "Might not [such] universality be . . . our own foreignness?").[13] This process of unfolding through pure linguistic ambiguity turns the ordinary speeches and exchanges in this film into examples of profound heterolinguality, wherein the lifelong sorrow of an elderly widow, speaking only Japanese and residing in the countryside, transforms itself into a sophisticated pacifist, cosmopolitan address. In this transformation, mourning becomes a fore-giving and an embrace: even those who have inflicted irreparable damage on one are offered release from their guilt.

Perhaps this is the reason the film ends the way it does, with all the characters running after Kane in the torrential rain. In their intensity and harshness, the elements strike like an invincible enemy, against whom human resistance by means of a feeble umbrella seems laughable. Yet the

---

the extended family between Japan and Hawaii, is as follows: "As ambiguous as his broken Japanese is, Clark clearly speaks as an extended family member, not as an American. He admits his family's and his own failure to realize what kind of pain the grandmother has been suffering from her husband's death by the atomic blast. They didn't make a connection between the death of Kane's husband and the location of her home, Nagasaki. Instead, they talked only about themselves without paying attention to Kane's circumstances. By urging her to come to Hawaii as soon as possible, they were even unintentionally asking her to miss the anniversary of the Nagasaki bombing and memorial services for her dead husband. . . . This is the reason why Clark apologizes to Kane; it is not at all the case that he apologizes for the American attack on Nagasaki with the atomic bomb" (368).

13. See Julia Kristeva, *Strangers to Ourselves*, trans. Leon S. Roudiez (New York: Columbia University Press, 1991), 168. The question is the title of chapter 8.

film concludes not with the rain stopping or with the characters finding shelter. Instead, after showing various characters slipping and falling on their run, the film concludes when Kane's umbrella has so completely collapsed that it might as well be given up. As she persists by inching forward, her body drenched and exposed in the midst of the downpour, her fragile defense against nature's onslaught becoming utterly useless, the noise of the wind and rain is replaced by children's voices singing these lyrics of the Schubert song:

> And the boy a rose did see, a rose standing in the field.
> Blooming in innocence,
> Awed by the color it did yield.
> A never-ending fascination
> For the crimson color
> of the rose standing in the field.[14]

Is Kane not precisely the bright red rose standing in the field (like the one seen by her little grandson and Clark outside the place of the memorial service for the atomic bomb victims), whose life force demonstrates that war-like defenses are things that cannot and will not last?[15]

In his study of postwar world cinema, Gilles Deleuze writes that Kurosawa is a director whose films are not so much about arriving at meaningful actions in response to a given situation as about discovering large metaphysical questions deeply hidden therein. Deleuze also comments that in Kurosawa's stories, no flight tends to be possible.[16] The way *Rhapsody in August* ends is certainly not a flight in the sense of an escape from the situation; at the same time, it unsettles Deleuze's conclusion, I think, with something rhapsodic. In the transcendence of war as allegorized

14. The lyrics are quite different from the words in Goethe's poem. Kurosawa's remarks about his use of music in filmmaking are interesting to note here: "From *Drunken Angel* onward, I have used light music for some key sad scenes, and my way of using music has differed from the norm—I don't put it in where most people do. Working with Hayasaka [Fumio], I began to think in terms of the counterpoint of sound and image as opposed to the union of sound and image." Akira Kurosawa, *Something Like an Autobiography*, trans. Audie E. Bock (New York: Vintage, 1983), 197.

15. For a different reading, which sees Kane as a brave *warrior* and the dysfunctional umbrella as becoming like a rose, see Yoshimoto, *Kurosawa*, 370–71.

16. See Gilles Deleuze, "Figures, or the Transformation of Forms," *Cinema 1: The Movement-Image*, trans. Hugh Tomlinson and Barbara Habberjam (Minneapolis: University of Minnesota Press, 1986), 188–92, reprinted in *Perspectives on Akira Kurosawa*, ed. James Goodwin (New York: G. K. Hall, 1994), 246–50.

by Kane—war not simply in the sense of reciprocal hostility between warring parties but also in the sense of defensiveness, vengefulness, and self-aggrandizement against others—we find an aesthetic improvisation of a type of postcatastrophe authority and agency, which comes across much less in the form of action and assertion than in the form of letting go. In their de-monumentalization of (the debt of) memory and making-possible of forgiving, Kane's (speech) acts are no longer simply parts of a stubborn old woman's recollection of the past. Rather, they constitute and are enunciated filmically as the potentiality of a heterolingual address, in which we hear a different "we" emerging, hailing a form of co-existence that is yet to be permitted by the human world.

7

Postcolonial Visibilities

Questions Inspired by Deleuze's Method

> Foucault is uniquely akin to contemporary film.
> —GILLES DELEUZE, *Foucault*

> It is a paradox of contemporary image consumption that exactly at the point when domestic television viewing is moving towards high definition and high resolution, audiences are moving towards arguably the most popular new media phenomenon, YouTube, which presents the lowest definition, lowest resolution images and yet attracts a larger audience among younger age groups because of its user-generated content. It is precisely the "low-res" look of YouTube clips which allows us to say that the visual is problematized in this sphere, since every subject is abstracted by the rate of compression, and every clip becomes a kind of quotation, either by being sourced from previously existing material and re-presented or, in the case of original material, simply by being uploaded into a stream of pre-existing material.
> —HELEN GRACE, "Monuments and the Face of Time: Distortions of Scale and Asynchrony in Postcolonial Hong Kong"

Judging from the regularity with which events of captivity and detention occur on the international political theater, it would hardly be an exaggeration to say that the theme of confinement, a hallmark of Michel Foucault's works in the 1960s and 1970s from *The History of Madness* and *The*

Birth of the Clinic to *Discipline and Punish*, has lost none of its critical relevance at the beginning of the twenty-first century. Indeed, in so many ways, the post-9/11 global scene only seems a fantastical set of demonstrations of Foucault's arguments about the omnipresent and omnipotent reach of technological-cum-ideological surveillance under the guises of our neoliberal society. Events such as "Guantánamo" (where innocent men suspected of complicity with terrorist activities are held outside U.S. jurisdiction, so as to block their access to the legal representation that is a constitutional right for anyone being held on U.S. soil) and "Abu Ghraib" (the prison in Baghdad where Iraqi inmates were subjected to physical torture and sexual abuse by U.S. military personnel for purposes of one-upmanship and entertainment), among others, have arguably raised the question of confinement and its implications to an order of magnitude that goes well beyond Foucault's original frames of reference.

Foucault's interest, we remember, has less to do with the cultural, ethnic, and religious conflicts that shape contemporary scenarios like Guantánamo and Abu Ghraib than with his dissection of the historical trajectory by which post-Enlightenment European society organized human social conduct into various generative grids of rationality. Key to this historical trajectory is the close relation established between confinement and visibility, in the sense that the negative experience of being captured and segregated (as in the paradigmatic case of being locked up in prison) was associated by Foucault not with darkness but rather with light—that is, with being turned into a site of institutional and social visibility. Beginning with his massive study of madness (or *déraison*, literally, "de-reason")—a boundless, excessive, undialectical condition of being, gradually delineated as (and disappearing in) the palpable, reduced state of "mental disorder," which in turn necessitates collaborative management and control by the network of apparatuses such as clinics, hospitals, psychoanalysis, the police, and the prison—Foucault's analyses of confinement and visibility remain most memorable in a work such as *Discipline and Punish*, not least because of its famous reference to Jeremy Bentham's Panopticon as a summary image of the architectonics involved in subjugation as a science. Equally thought-provoking is Foucault's emphasis on the discursive linkages between the physically violent acts of arrest and detention, on the one hand, and, on the other, the range of gentle coercions applied on the bodies and souls of prisoners in the form of lenient pedagogy, physical exercise, confession, and other types of regulatory, corrective practices.

Foucault's eloquent accounts of the logistics of confinement and visibility, in other words, are consistent with his theorization of the way power functions: much more than the prohibitive or censorious features of surveillance and punishment, it is the enabling, generative dimensions of soul making and reformation that turn modern incarceration into such an efficient, cost-effective space-time of social control. Insofar as confinement and visibility may be thought of as one of modern society's largest systems of life management, geared toward updating, renovating, and repurposing rather than simply demolishing the human being in the aftermath of crime, Foucault's work on clinics and prisons is deeply resonant with the logics of his writings on sexuality, governmentality, and biopolitics.

At the same time, this work on clinics and prisons also accentuates the increasingly complex relation between the realms of words and of things, the sayable and the visible.[1] As Foucault demonstrates in works such as *The Archeology of Knowledge* and *The Order of Things*, with the progressively widening chasm between words and things, visibility can no longer be treated as the secure opposite of what is hidden, or as the simple unveiling of data that can be accessed similarly in (or that share a straightforward resemblance with) words. Rather, visibility is now caught up in the shifting relations of political sovereignty and in the discontinuities among different representational regimes, which constitute the human sciences and the concept of man that emerges interstitially in their midst. For Foucault, who always emphasized the historical contingency (as opposed to the naturalness) of this state of affairs, visibility is ultimately about the finitude of man.

Deleuze's Foucault

In the context of postcolonial studies, one type of criticism made from time to time of Foucault's work is that it is Eurocentric—namely, that Foucault has paid scant attention to cultures and histories of the formerly colonized, non-European worlds. The point of such criticism can be compelling: If the multifarious social, ideological coercions accompanying Europe's arrival at modern rationalism can be demonstrated by Foucault in such copious detail, is not his relative silence on how such coercions were exercised in Europe's colonies, during exactly the same

1. For an important study on this topic, see Gary Shapiro, *Archaeologies of Vision: Foucault and Nietzsche on Seeing and Saying* (Chicago: University of Chicago Press, 2003).

period when the institutions he studied became consolidated within Europe, indefensible?

The interrogation of Foucault's tendency to focus on Europe proper should obviously not go unheeded, but the criticism of his work on the basis of its subject matter also (if inadvertently) highlights visibility in a specific sense, one that Foucault's work, in fact, helps problematize. How so? Translated into the problematic of visibility, the possible complaint about Foucault just mentioned is that he is allowing only institutions inside Europe the *privilege* of being "seen" and discussed. Visibility in this instance is implicitly analogized to power, hegemony, status, and authority; it is understood as something desirable. In this politicized but largely abstract sense, visibility is less a matter of becoming physically seen than a matter of attaining discursive attention and recognition, of which being visible, so to speak, is simply a metaphor. Everyone wants attention and recognition, or so this thinking goes, but few people get enough of them. Therefore, it follows, it would be necessary to challenge those who have acquired or who own more visibility than others *and* those who seem to bestow visibility on select parts of the world at the expense of others.

Pursued in these metaphorical terms, visibility has much more to do with the ethical concerns of distributive fairness, equality, and justice than with the sensorial or phenomenological event of seeing. In this ethical alignment, importantly, the visible tends to be considered as *continuous with and equitable to* the nonvisible—in particular, the realm of verbal language: to be seen and to be spoken of are believed to be equivalent orders of things, and in both cases, more is better than less.

For Foucault, however, visibility is precisely no longer to be assumed as equivalent to verbal language in this manner, but should be understood as a realm that has become irreducible to the plane of articulation that is words, statements, and the sayable. In Deleuze's reading of Foucault, accordingly, it is this irreducibility of the visible that comes to the fore, though Deleuze does not understand such irreducibility in terms of an innate quality or specificity based on the human sensorium. As Deleuze elaborates, "Visibilities are not defined by sight but are complexes of actions and passions, actions and reactions, multisensorial complexes, which emerge into the light of day."[2] That is to say, the singularity of visi-

2. Gilles Deleuze, *Foucault*, trans. and ed. Seán Hand, foreword by Paul A. Bové (Minneapolis: University of Minnesota Press, 1988), 59. Hereafter all references to this book will be included in parentheses in the text.

bilities needs to be grasped, paradoxically, in the "multisensorial complexes" that constitute them, and it would be a simplification to attribute to them any clearly demarcated origins or individual agents.

Deleuze takes pains to demonstrate how visibilities are often disjointed from nonvisibilities, and that it is such disjunction that, he suggests, Foucault attempted to explore in his writings: "Between the visible and the articulable a gap or disjunction opens up," Deleuze writes.

> But this disjunction of forms is the place—or "non-place," as Foucault puts it—where the informal diagram is swallowed up and becomes embodied instead in two different directions that are necessarily divergent and irreducible. The concrete assemblages are therefore opened up by *a crack* that determines how the abstract machine performs. (*Foucault*, 38, my emphasis)

Deleuze's difficult language of "informal diagram" and "abstract machine" aside, his point is clearly that the discontinuity between the visible and the articulable is the crux of the matter here.

Meanwhile, this "gap," "disjunction," or "crack" between the two semiotic orders is at once a limit and (in our contemporary language) a kind of virtual connectivity that exceeds the readily perceptible, empirical dimension. With characteristically imaginative turns of thinking, Deleuze describes such connectivity as follows:

> As long as we stick to things and words we can believe that we are speaking of what we see, that we see what we are speaking of, and that the two are linked: in this way we remain on the level of an empirical exercise. But as soon as we open up words and things, as soon as we discover statements and visibilities, words and sight are raised to a higher exercise that is *a priori*, so that each reaches its own unique limit which separates it from the other, a visible element that can only be seen, an articulable element that can only be spoken. (*Foucault*, 65)

By "a priori" (which is akin to the "informal diagram" and "abstract machine" just cited), Deleuze is referring, I believe, to something like an immanent condition of possibility that is at once absolute and historical. The last point I'd like to highlight in Deleuze's account of Foucault is thus:

> *There is a "there is" of light, a being of light or a light-being*, just as there is a language-being. Each of them is an absolute and yet historical, since each is inseparable from the way in which it falls into a formation or corpus. The one makes visibilities visible or perceptible, just as the other made state-

> ments articulable, sayable or readable. This holds true to such an extent that visibilities are neither the acts of a seeing subject nor the data of a visual meaning. . . . Just as the visible cannot be reduced to a perceptible thing or quality, so the light-being cannot be reduced to a physical environment. . . . *The light-being is a strictly indivisible condition, an a priori that is uniquely able to lay visibilities open to sight, and by the same stroke to the other senses*, each time according to certain combinations which are themselves visible: for example, the tangible is a way in which the visible hides another visible. (*Foucault*, 58–59, my emphases)

Several conceptual moves are discernible in Deleuze's reading: a refusal to be naïvely empiricist about the visible as something readily accessible; an investment in the disjunction, which is at once the connectivity, between the visible and the verbal; a grappling with the "a priori" that enables the visible to become visible and in that way open to the other senses. In particular, Deleuze reiterates the view that visibility is not to be confused with visible *objects*: "If, in their turn, visibilities are never hidden, they are none the less not immediately seen or visible. They are even invisible so long as we consider only objects, things or perceptible qualities, and not *the conditions which open them up*" (*Foucault*, 57, my emphasis). And again:

> Visibilities are not to be confused with elements that are visible or more generally perceptible, such as qualities, things, objects, compounds of objects. In this respect Foucault constructs a function that is no less original than that of the statement. *We must break things open*. Visibilities are not forms of objects, nor even forms that would show up under light, but rather *forms of luminosity which are created by the light itself and allow a thing or object to exist only as a flash, sparkle or shimmer*. (*Foucault*, 52, my emphases)

In citing Deleuze's statements at length, my goal is not necessarily to suggest that his rendition of Foucault should become definitive but rather to ask: Why is Deleuze so insistent on reading Foucault this way? What is it in this reading that might, arguably, be more Deleuze than Foucault? What I find relevant to think with, especially in the broad context of postcoloniality, is a distinctive method that is oriented toward lines of mutation, mobility, experimentation, emergence, and freedom. Instead of simply corroborating instances of blockage and stasis (such as the weighty reality of incarceration), Deleuze, when confronted with such instances, seeks in them points of departure for an elsewhere, seedlings for a metastasis. Exactly where Foucault's analytics seems to settle starkly on the inescapability of imprisonment as the way to define modern life, Deleuze reconfigures that settlement into a possible transit point, a novel flight path.

To underscore this, let us recall more precisely the way Deleuze delineates visibility as it appears in *Discipline and Punish*. Deleuze argues that visibility is what constitutes (or is the a priori to) the very architectonics of the event of locking up someone:

> Prison, for its part, is concerned with whatever is visible: not only does it wish to display the crime and the criminal but in itself it constitutes a visibility, *it is a system of light before being a figure of stone*, and is defined by "Panopticism": by a visual assemblage and a luminous environment (a central tower surrounded by cells) in which the warder can see all the detainees without the detainees being able to see either him or one another. (*Foucault*, 32, my emphasis)

This reading is, of course, entirely in concert with Foucault's critical stresses, which in the section on Panopticism bluntly conclude that "visibility is a trap."[3] In other words, in tandem with his ongoing investment in the institutionalization of social relations that takes the forms of asylums, hospitals, schools, and the police, Foucault associated the processes of making-visible with an intensifying order of collectively enforced aggression against the human individual. Light—and with it the Enlightenment values of clarity and rationality—is theorized by Foucault not as a medium of emancipation but explicitly as a medium of entrapment: precisely as it enables one to be seen, it also enables one to be caught.

Much as he reads his friend and ally responsively and faithfully, Deleuze also restores in Foucault's otherwise bleak emphasis a dialectical movement. In his rendition, Deleuze first transcends the strictly empirical status of the visible by reinstating the vital linkage between the visible and the invisible in nonvisible terms: "The abstract formula of

3. The statements leading up to this conclusion are: "The panoptic mechanism arranges spatial unities that make it possible to see constantly and to recognize immediately. In short, it reverses the principle of the dungeon; or rather of its three functions—to enclose, to deprive of light and to hide—it preserves only the first and eliminates the other two. Full lighting and the eye of a supervisor capture better than darkness, which ultimately protected. Visibility is a trap." Michel Foucault, *Discipline and Punish: The Birth of the Prison*, trans. Alan Sheridan (New York: Vintage, 1979), 200.

Panopticism is no longer 'to see without being seen' but *to impose a particular conduct on a particular human multiplicity*" (*Foucault*, 34).

Then, in an inimitably illuminating stroke, Deleuze goes on to propose that confinement is only one (subordinate) step to a larger set of concerns. From within the tracks of Foucault's preoccupation with the prison, from which there appears little possibility of escape, Deleuze plots an alternative route:

> Foucault has often been treated as above all the thinker of confinement (the general hospital in *Madness and Civilization*, the prison in *Discipline and Punish*). But this is not at all the case, and such a misinterpretation prevents us from grasping his global project. . . .
>
> In fact, Foucault has always considered confinement as a secondary element derived from a primary function that was very different in each case. . . . The imprisonment of madmen was imposed like an "exile" and took the leper as its model, while the confinement of delinquents was carried out by "partitioning" and took its model from the plague victim. . . . But exiling and partitioning are first of all precisely functions of exteriority which are only afterwards executed, formalized and organized by the mechanisms of confinement. . . . As Maurice Blanchot says of Foucault, "*confinement refers to an outside, and what is confined is precisely the outside*. . . . It is by excluding or placing outside that the assemblages confine something, and this holds as much for physical interiority as physical confinement." (*Foucault*, 42–43, my emphasis)

It is such visionary methodical cracking open of the seemingly secluded or locked-up spaces that leads Deleuze to conclude that "nothing in Foucault is really closed off" (*Foucault*, 43).[4]

For this reason, Deleuze's method can be highly suggestive for postcolonial studies. Returning now to the viable criticism that Foucault has (inadvertently or deliberately) reinforced a certain boundary between the inside and outside of Europe, and thus cut off the study of European institutions of knowledge production from Europe's colonial and imperialist histories, we can say that Deleuze's method shows how this visible foreclosure, this confinement of European history to a presumed interiority, should be taken precisely as the beginning for a divergent engagement. Where Foucault is clearly concentrating on the mechanisms

4. For an astute analysis of Deleuze's visionary reading of Foucault, see Paul A. Bové, "Foreword: The Foucault Phenomenon: The Problematics of Style," in Deleuze, *Foucault*, vii–xl, in particular the discussion beginning on xxxii.

and apparatuses of social control inside Europe is thus also, we might say, a plane of disjunction, where Europe proper has to be grasped in a relation of exclusion, as the illusory interiority produced by a function of exiling and partitioning (others). *Europe's visibility in Foucault's work, in other words, is none other than the visibility of a space of confinement, constituted by an excluded outside.* Following Deleuze's lead, it would be eminently logical for scholars to embark on an affirmative postcolonial studies, one that is less anxiously preoccupied with the mechanisms and apparatuses of European exclusion, perhaps, and more substantively engaged with the transformative potential of the ongoing encounters between Europe and the rest of the globe.

Although it only constitutes a small part of his large body of work, therefore, I believe Deleuze's study of Foucault's writings on confinement and visibility is a key to the kind of enabling conceptual engineering he performs (even as certain epistemic predicaments remain unresolved, as they tend to in most thinkers, in ways that are symptomatic of larger issues of our time). Central to such conceptual engineering is Deleuze's manner of wresting even the interiority of a space-time of blockage and social death from what might otherwise come across as a pessimistically conclusive reading. This turn away from epistemic foreclosure is also traceable to Deleuze's other projects. From the rejection of Freudian psychoanalysis (with its historically and economically specific ways of perpetuating the patriarchal neuroses of Oedipus) and the description of the positivity of schizophrenia, to the engagement with the libidinal potentialities of a perversion such as masochism, the listening for a language's becoming-minor in Kafka's German writing, and the terms he generates for conceptual experimentation such as becoming, deterritorialization, assemblages, multiplicities, affects, virtualities, bodies without organs, nomads, the rhizome, and so forth, Deleuze's signature utopianism offers infinite inspiration for the postcolonial as a type of liberatory thought.[5]

5. The works in question include but are not limited to the following: Gilles Deleuze and Félix Guattari, *Capitalism and Schizophrenia*, vol. 1: *Anti-Oedipus*, trans. Robert Hurley, Mark Seem, and Helen R. Lane (Minneapolis: University of Minnesota Press, 1983), and vol. 2: *A Thousand Plateaus*, trans. Brian Massumi (Minneapolis: University of Minnesota Press, 1987); Deleuze, *Masochism*, trans. Jean McNeil (New York: Zone, 1989); Deleuze and Guattari, *Kafka: Toward a Minor Literature*, trans. Dana Polan (Minneapolis: University of Minnesota Press, 1986). Deleuze has expressed reservations about the term "utopia" because of the mutilated meaning given it by public opinion (see Gilles Deleuze and Félix Guattari, *What Is Philosophy?*, trans. Hugh Tomlinson and Graham Burchell [New York:

Battling for the Commodified Media Frame: "Postcolonial" in Another *Sense*

Indeed, in the writings of the past several decades by notable thinkers such as Frantz Fanon, Albert Memmi, Edward Said, Gayatri Chakravorty Spivak, Stuart Hall, Homi Bhabha, Paul Gilroy, Robert Young, and others, postcolonial theory and criticism have tended to share the emancipatory spirit of anticolonial political struggles. And while it is true that there are significant differences among these thinkers, some of whom are more old-fashionedly humanistic while others are deconstructive in their approaches to language and identity, it is fair to say that the range of issues that remains central to postcolonial debates, from the racial violence experienced by the wretched of the earth, to the problematics of Orientalism, subaltern representation, and subject formation based on class, gender, ethnic, and religious differences, is consistently about resistance. Albeit not always stated, then, the cultural logic at work in postcolonial thought in general is that of repression, understood both in the political and psychoanalytic senses.

Even so, should the term "postcolonial" continue to be defined exclusively according to this cultural logic? Just as it behooves us, from the perspective of postcolonial consciousness, not to forget the "outside" that is constitutive of Europe's institutions of knowledge production, so is it salutary to take a closer look at how the postcolonial, as a form of thinking, may exceed the repressive-liberatory terms which have hitherto so powerfully dominated its reasoning. The point here is not simply to attempt to "trump" postcolonial thinking with the help of Foucault's critique of the repressive hypothesis (attributed by Foucault to Freudian psychoanalysis) or Deleuze and Guattari's critique of the related interpretative hermeneutics encrypted in the Western bourgeois family romance of Oedipus (a legacy they also attributed to Freud).[6] Rather, it is to show how, even as it holds on to certain sympathetic political aspirations, the term "postcolonial" as such cannot function in isolation from a web of current discursive articulations in the twenty-first century.

The 1960s, arguably the period that saw the beginnings of many of the

---

Columbia University Press, 1994], 100). However, insofar as he also defines utopia as "*what links* philosophy with its own epoch" and as a word that "designates *that conjunction of philosophy, or of the concept, with the present milieu*" (99, 100), I tend to think it is an apt description of his own work.

6. See Michel Foucault, *The History of Sexuality*, vol. 1: *An Introduction*, trans. Robert Hurley (New York: Pantheon, 1978); Deleuze and Guattari, *Anti-Oedipus*.

postcolonial debates remaining current to this day, was a period marked by populist moral fervor and political activism around the world. But the 1960s also saw the beginnings of a different kind of social struggle. Alongside the demand for an end to Western imperialism and military violence, the demand for national independence among former colonies, the demand for women's equality and liberty, and the demand for civil rights to disenfranchised populations (together with the idealism attached to a non-Western regime such as Mao Zedong's China), large-scale mass demonstrations of that period were increasingly energized by a new type of battle, the battle for what might be called the media frame. In the midst of the political messages about universalisms such as equity, rights, and justice was another message—namely, that equity, rights, and justice, fought on grounds of class, gender, race, ethnicity, and other identity-related particularisms, were themselves thoroughly enmeshed with and indistinguishable from the production and dissemination of media spectacles. Indeed, one may go so far as to say that the 1960s was the period in which the theater of political activism went through a significant shift in the very concept of struggle—from the plane of physical actions and conflicts, which many continue to want to believe as real, to a political economy of representation and performance, whose actions and conflicts often preemptively determine the way we imagine our relation to the real nowadays. In many ways, the media frame has, since the 1960s, become the actual, omnipresent political battleground.

With the emphasis on the media frame, we can see that the multifarious postcolonial insurgencies of the 1960s were, from the outset, confronted with a contradictory set of conditions of possibility as well as urgent political tasks. Such struggles must, on the one hand, discredit and dismantle the agency of some groups while celebrating agency as it was placed with other groups (for example, women instead of men; blacks instead of whites; independent new nations instead of former colonizers). What does this mean in terms of visibilities? If, following the cultural logic of resistance to patriarchal, capitalist, and racial repression, the point of such struggles was to take apart the wrongful public images and representations of the groups-to-be-vindicated, it was nonetheless only by actively seizing media attention—and competing for the right to own and manage the visual field, to fabricate the appropriate images and distribute the appropriate stories—that such insurgencies could fulfill their obligation to emancipate the respective groups. Once this process of fighting for the media frame—by acquiring the maximal and optimal visibility—was set in motion, however, postcolonial activists had to face up to the fact that (their) particularist claims are never final or exclusive but always relative and *serial*, and that still more particularist claims, in the name of still more divergent causes, can be advanced, ad infinitum, for media attention.

If media representation is analogized to what Marx described and critiqued as the commodity (that is, a product of labor that receives its stamp of value from a source other than itself, from circulation rather than intrinsic use), what Marx's argument serves to underscore is not only laborers' alienation but also the very process in which what is hitherto presumed to be mere representation (the commodity), secondary and inferior to the authentic something ("labor," "the body," "reality," "history,"), is steadily assuming center stage as *the* event in the late capitalist social fabric. Rather than simply denouncing the commodity on moral grounds, therefore, the legacy of Marx's observations lies in their intimation of a future in which the artificiality, artifactuality, and potency of the commodity—precisely in the form of repeatable visibilities—will usurp the significance of the "original" that is human labor. In this future, even the most precious truths about human life, such as people's identities and histories, and their agency, will need to compete for legitimacy as commodities, as visibilities. (The aforementioned criticism of Foucault's Eurocentrism belongs as well in this competition.)

As a thinker with major works produced during and after the 1960s, Deleuze, though seldom described as postcolonial, shares important affinities with the emancipatory aspirations and objectives of postcolonial thought. At the same time—and this is why he can be so intriguing to think with—he was, of course, explicitly critical of, and distanced himself from, the cultural logic of repression-resistance that genealogically burdens even the most theoretically sophisticated varieties of postcolonial debates. The present discussion of visibilities is a good case in point: Deleuze's method is poised at the crossroads among multiple visibilities in different *senses* of the postcolonial. From the Foucauldian prison, its system of luminosity, and its "a priori," to the spectacles of mass protests and demonstrations for rights, and their imbrications with the commodified media frame (itself oftentimes a kind of trap), the proliferation of visibilities since the 1960s has called forth a new definition of postcoloniality, one that will need to go beyond the conventional, chronological connotations of the term as being the resistance to and aftermath of official colonialism. What must now be recognized as embedded in the postcolonial as such are the thresholds, limits, and potentialities of visibilities, of visibilities as the "multisensorial complexes" of shifting social relations.

In this light, the endeavor, characteristic of postcolonial struggles, to fight for the media frame and contend for the right to be properly imaged, mirrored, and represented may be understood anew as a cultural-political practice in an ever-expanding field of visibilities, with the protesting human being herself occupying the status of fetish, rhetorician, artist, and performer all at once, while the rebuke of (incorrect) images must go hand in hand with the massive generation and circulation of more and more images—be those images about classes, races, nations, religions, or persons of different sexual orientations.

The articulation of postcoloniality to visibilities in these conflicting senses, tending both toward liberation from repression *and* toward desire for inclusion in the commodified media frame (which in turn involves ever more occasions for repression), could be one reason Deleuze was invested in a media form like cinema. In cinema, these conflicting, indeed antagonistic senses of visibilities converge in a collective practice that is as rooted in extradiegetical commercialism as it is in the transformations internal to film semiotics (which Deleuze addresses in the form of the movement-image and the time-image in his two volumes on film, using the Second World War as a rough dividing timeline).[7] To isolate what he calls cinematographic concepts, Deleuze at times writes as though he is aestheticizing visibility through familiar avant-garde techniques such as montage, rupture, contrapuntal relations, deframing (wrenching figures and movements from their conventional spaces of representation for a sensation of de-figuration and de-nomination), and the like.

Such aestheticization of the filmic image should, nevertheless, be seen in the context in which cinema, including art house cinema, is thoroughly immersed in processes of commodification, the substantial (numerical) scale of which, from production costs to the salaries commanded by movie stars and famed directors, and the profits or losses incurred in worldwide market distribution, could not have been lost on Deleuze. While he accentuates cinematographic concepts that are consistent with European avant-garde theorizations of film, therefore, I think he is at the same time accentuating the question of such concepts' ability to survive in the midst of ever proliferating postcolonial visibilities. That is to say, such concepts need to be explored in the form of their limits as well as their linkages to the visibilities and discourses of commodifi-

7. Gilles Deleuze, *Cinema I: The Movement-Image*, trans. Hugh Tomlinson and Barbara Habberjam (Minneapolis: University of Minnesota Press, 1986); *Cinema II: The Time-Image*, trans. Hugh Tomlinson and Robert Galeta (Minneapolis: University of Minnesota Press, 1989).

cation, confinement, and freedom, all of which together define our contemporary virtual public sphere. It is in this sense of limit-cum-linkage that we may finally understand Deleuze's description of the relation between the visible and the verbal in Foucault, and of the kinship Foucault, according to Deleuze at least, shares with film: "And yet the unique limit that separates each one is also the common limit that links one to the other, a limit with two irregular faces, a blind word and a mute vision. Foucault is uniquely akin to contemporary film" (*Foucault*, 65).

In the end, Deleuze's creative manner of thinking visibility also makes it necessary to question his own thesis about postwar cinema, namely, that there is a fundamental distinction between the types of images produced before and after the Second World War. In making such an argument, Deleuze, despite his insights about the mutual implicatedness—literally, mutual in-foldings—between cinematic time and cinematic image as immanent, twinned formations, seems to have fallen back on an external historical happening (the war) as the way to account for changes *in* the film image. This surprising slippage on Deleuze's part (using a chronological timeline as an organizing principle) is critiqued by Jacques Rancière in a perceptive engagement with Deleuze's argument. Distrusting the circularity of Deleuze's chronological logic, Rancière displaces the question of time back into the image itself. The two types of images described by Deleuze are, for Rancière, not so much opposed as two different points of view on the image, points of view that, in fact, share basic techniques of snatching from bodily states, imposing a screen logic, arresting movements, reordering, and restitution. All in all, these basic techniques are so many (old or new) gestures of capturing:

> The passage from the infinity of matter-image to the infinity of thought-image is also a history of redemption, of an always thwarted redemption. The filmmaker takes perception to images by snatching them from bodily states and placing them on a plane of pure events; in so doing, the filmmaker gives images an arrangement-in-thought. But this arrangement-in-thought is always also the re-imposition of the logic of the opaque screen, of the central image that arrests the movement in every direction of other images to reorder them from itself. *The gesture of restitution is always also a new gesture of capture.*[8]

8. Jacques Rancière, "From One Image to Another? Deleuze and the Ages of Cinema," *Film Fables*, trans. Emiliano Battista (Oxford: Berg, 2006), 107–23; the quoted passage is on 116, my emphasis.

By insisting on the inextricable, yet ever shifting, relation between the act of redemption or restitution and the act of capture, Rancière has put his finger on what is perhaps the most crucial issue that has surfaced in the age of the new media: Which of the two acts is, epistemically speaking, the before, and which the after? Although Rancière's discussion, like Deleuze's, is still based in film, it also signals profound transitions taking shape in that relation, in what may be termed the *postcinematic entanglement of time and image*. To see this, we will need to take our discussion in the direction of more contemporary screen technologies.

Capture in the Age of Shadow Media

Although Deleuze did not write about technologies such as cell phones, Palm Pilots, videophones, portable cameras, text messaging, GPSs, and so forth, I believe his method has vast implications for such visibilities, if only because of the paradox of their often minuscule sizes (that is, their extreme individuation and atomization) and their hypercapacities for connectivity and interactivity.

Given the steadily diminishing sizes of screens on these portable little machines, have not postcolonial visibilities arrived at yet another conceptual threshold? It might no longer be sufficient to think of visibilities as a system of luminosity (surveillance) in which we are trapped, or even as an ever-commodifiable form of power (such as the media frame) which we all desire to acquire. *It has also become necessary to come to terms with visibilities as information-objects we can hold in our hands and disseminate widely in a matter of moments.* (To pick an egregious example, the scandal of Abu Ghraib came to public attention because the acts of torture and abuse committed by U.S. military personnel were recorded on cell phones and circulated on the Internet.) What, then, is the import of capture on a tiny screen?

In a study of the emergence of such new visibilities in contemporary Hong Kong (a Special Administrative Region of the People's Republic of China), where citizens have in recent years staged political protests against their government's demolition of historical monuments, the photographer, filmmaker, and new media producer Helen Grace refers to "a strange new domestication of history" in our "era of image over-production." Unlike Deleuze's study of film, which approaches the image largely as an aesthetic or semiotic form (as it evolves from the movement-image to the time-image in different directors' works), Grace's focus is rather on the affective engagements in moments of expressiveness that lead to the production of images of local significance, on popular sites such as YouTube and Flickr. The important difference, according to Grace, is that instead of becoming a memorial to a past time (as many images, such as photographs, tend to become the instant they are produced), the image seized by the new media technologies serves rather as a way of enacting and performing the present precisely through the small act of capture:

> The ubiquitous image [in contrast to the memorial act of analogue photography] . . . has a much more tenuous link to the present, which it does not necessarily accept as real; rather, *it is the act of "capture" which brings the present into existence*, because ubiquitous image-making belongs to a world in which the real *in itself* is so thoroughly mediated that it does not exist without at the same time producing an image of itself—and it is this image which secures the lived reality in which the image-maker is situated. This does not mean that the performative and the memorial are opposed; rather it indicates that memory is also secured via the image and, in its embodied form, is brought forth in action and performance.[9]

Grace's observations are illuminating because they are attuned to the effects of the collapse of time lag (or, technically, time shifting), a factor that used to define how reproductive technologies serve the purpose of memorializing the past. In such memorializing—what Rancière in his passage, quoted earlier, calls redemption and restitution—reality and its image are differentiated and hierarchized on the basis of the time lag between them, with the image always being considered second best because it is a mere copy (signifying what is irredeemably lost). With the advancement in techniques of instant replay, live coding, live processing, and real-time documentary making, the memory of the past, which is, arguably, always a product of time shifting, is fast becoming conceptually outmoded. In place of memory, to which techniques of capture have always played a subordinate, subservient role, capture now emerges as the primary action and event. As Grace puts it, "It is the act of 'capture' which brings the present into existence." Capture is what activates reality, what makes reality happen (as in a live performance) in the transitory

9. Helen Grace, "Monuments and the Face of Time: Distortions of Scale and Asynchrony in Postcolonial Hong Kong," *Postcolonial Studies* 10.4 (2007): 473, first emphasis mine.

and vanishing movements of the click, the tap, the pinch, and the finger-swipe.

Insofar as she is interested in the *ephemeral coextensiveness of the image and the present*, a coextensiveness that is brought forth by the mere pressing of a button or a key, Grace's observations sidestep the large, systemic connotations of visibility-as-confinement that Foucault delineates. Instead, she inserts visibilities into the mundane motions and stoppages of the everyday, replete with the risk (and the certainty) that many of them will remain unnoticed and unseen in the dense strata of online material, except by those with a vested interest in local happenings. This apparent focus on the local (in this case, the mass political movements in Hong Kong after 1997) notwithstanding, Grace's manner of conceptualizing the present as a collective but diffused assemblage of enunciation, one that may be snatched in bits at a time and then plugged into a mutating plenitude of virtualities, is eminently Deleuzian because of the fluidity and mobility—indeed, the immanent recyclability—between images and life that she so evocatively suggests. Likewise is her sense of the blurring of distinctions between heterogeneous categories of knowledge that results from such captured images' incessant flow, crisscrossing, and *becoming*:

> The taking of images amidst everyday action blurs the distinction between significant and insignificant moments, so that every image becomes a variety of family snapshot—from the simple outing to the amateur footage of a train crash, used on the evening news, to the riot, and the overthrow of a regime. Any of these images can be recycled beyond the domestic sphere to become news footage—legitimate records of an event which official news management deems un-newsworthy.[10]

Grace describes this contemporary state of visibilities-in-flux, made up of user-generated, often mediocre-quality images, in terms of "shadow media" (a phrase she borrows from Patricia Spyer): "the tangential, mobile infrastructure of a counter-discourse to conventional national and international broadcasting."[11]

In addition to the battles for the media frame, then, the conceptualization of the postcolonial needs, at this juncture, to address these newly

10. Grace, "Monuments and the Face of Time," 472.

11. Grace, "Monuments and the Face of Time," 472; the work by Patricia Spyer cited by Grace is "Shadow Media and Moluccan Muslim VCD's," *9/11: A Virtual Case Book*, ed. Barbara Abrash and Faye Ginsburg (New York: Center for Media, Culture, and History, Virtual Case Book Series, 2002). See also New York University website for possible updates.

multiplied visibilities and the global and local constituencies that are formed and unformed in relation to the so-called shadow media. Should the users of these minuscule screens be described as subjects of confinement in the Foucauldian sense (in that the atomized screens, in being used, are de facto surveillance *embodied*, by none other than the persons using them as "cool" gadgets)? How does the existence of channels of communication such as YouTube, together with the entry and exit possibilities they inject into everyday life (from postings of video vigilantism to movie premieres and amateurish performances), complicate and transform the notion of freedom? Or, has the ubiquity of such commodified visibilities replaced freedom's relevance altogether, in an age in which human existence seems inconceivable without viral media-dependency, which therefore must be recognized as nothing less than a vital force—literally, a life link? Finally, to return to the other term we invoked with capture: Is redemption or restitution now simply a matter of technological recyclability?

Offshoots from ready-formed shapes of thought, these rhizomic—and schizoid?—questions about visibilities, agglomerating diverse cognitive, gestural, mimetic, and perceptive acts across semiotic chains, organizations of power, and historical struggles, are clearly some of the potentially fertile contact zones waiting to materialize between Deleuze and postcoloniality. Indeed, we may think of the numerous pathways from Deleuze's work as part of an extensive media network, with the exciting capability of collaborating with a postcolonial studies reconceived against shifting trajectories of global political power and, in particular, against the ambiguities, opacities, and uncertainties of postcolonial visibilities.

8

Framing the Original

Toward a New Visibility of the Orient

> *Every social community reproduced by the functioning of institutions is imaginary*, that is to say, it is based on the projection of individual existence into the weft of a collective narrative, on the recognition of a common name and on traditions lived as the trace of an immemorial past (even when they have been fabricated and inculcated in the recent past). But this comes down to accepting that, under certain conditions, *only* imaginary communities are real.—ÉTIENNE BALIBAR, "The Nation Form: History and Ideology"

A friend, long deceased, once told me how he had decided to specialize in Japanese literature. In the early 1970s, he heard a talk by a well-known Japanologist, who contrasted China study and Japan study by citing the opening lines of two primers for foreign students. The Chinese primer began with the line "I am hungry"; the Japanese primer began with the line "The cherry blossoms are falling from the sky." My friend chose to go the way of the cherry blossoms.

Like most stories about origination, this one bears a mythic dimension, which resonates beyond the mere empirical data: important boundary lines are drawn, marking territories of (re)cognition and potentiality. In this case, the binary construction signals that in the study of the Far East during the cold war era, what mattered were two players, China and Japan. This foreclosure of other Asian cultures allowed the stakes and possibilities involved to be cast in terms of a fundamental difference between infra- and superstructure, between material scarcity and aesthetic (or ideological) cultivation. Japan was rising from the ashes of defeat in the Second World War. Dominated by the United States and intent on establishing a new self-image as a peace-loving nation, Japan offered the prospect of quietist contemplation of the beauty of the natural world. China, on the other hand, was closed off to the West in its trajectory of self-determination as a new communist nation. As an object of study, China was apprehended predominantly in the language of political economy, which highlighted its conditions of physical hardship, such as starvation. This stark epistemic and disciplinary divide between China and Japan also meant that for a long time during this period, *modern* Chinese literature and culture would be consigned to a spectral, because ghettoized, existence, without cultural capital and thus largely negligible. (It shared this status with other ghettoized fields and subfields of the time, such as African American studies, Asian American studies, and women's studies.) The Chinese literature and art that were deemed worthy of study belonged instead in the respectable realm of sinology, in which poetry, fiction, art, music, and other types of cultural production gained esteem on account of their remoteness from the present known as modernity. To study China as a venerable producer of truly beautiful things, or so this thinking went, one needed to go back to its grand imperial past.

With the rise of the People's Republic of China to the status of an economic superpower in the late twentieth century, this cold war paradigm for studying China, Japan, and the rest of East Asia is undergoing a significant shift. What does it mean for Western knowledge production when China can no longer be imagined and approached with the line "I am hungry"? In the following discussion, I will explore one aspect of this paradigm shift, using as my primary example the transnational event of contemporary Chinese cinema.[1]

Drawing on the associations of impoverishment, illiteracy, and technical dissonance with the rest of the world—in brief, the familiar constituents of human subalternity—mainland Chinese directors known as the fifth generation (Chen Kaige, Zhang Yimou, Tian Zhuangzhuang, and their contemporaries) produced films that captured international attention in the 1980s and the first half of the 1990s. (Among the best-known examples are *Yellow Earth*, *Red Sorghum*, *Judou*, *Raise the Red Lantern*,

1. The next three paragraphs have been adapted, with modifications, from a related discussion of contemporary Chinese cinema; see my "Afterword: Liquidity of Being," *The Chinese Cinema Book*, ed. Song Hwee Lim and Julian Ward (London: British Film Institute / Palgrave Macmillan, 2011), 194–99.

Farewell My Concubine, *To Live*, and *The Blue Kite*.) For audiences who have some knowledge about China, these films carry the import of an exercise in cultural redemption, compelling reflection on Chinese history through a focus on the underprivileged, often rural masses who remain on the margins of modern Chinese society. In more general theoretical terms, one could say that these films invest in a kind of nativism or indigenism, presented in various versions of an ancient folk, the communist revolution, a socialist collective livelihood, and so forth.

In hindsight, however, what the fifth generation filmmakers' redemptive gestures helped to inaugurate was an unprecedented economic-semiotic transfer. Filmmaking meant that the philosophical and aesthetic investments in Chinese nativism and indigenism were set in motion at a steady pace of deterritorialization, in which the native or indigene, signifying the rooted, local knowledge that is associated with China and Chineseness, took on the exchange value of a marketable, because circulatable, transnational exhibit. This remarkable lesson is not unique to China, but in the case of Chinese cinema it crystallizes the intercultural politics of visibility because of the rapid change in contemporary China's global status within a few decades. Through the deployment of innovative moving images in the works of the fifth generation directors, the organic intellectual efforts to remember the Cultural Revolution and the founding aspirations of Chinese communism—letting the subalterns speak, vindicating and empowering the downtrodden classes—metamorphosed into a commodification and spectacularization of subalternity as a type of late capitalist cinematic sign. To compete for the world's attention, their films suggest, even socialist utopian visions must adopt the same tools as capitalism's; even destitute subalterns must appear as glamorous screen images.

To that extent, it can be said that the story of contemporary Chinese cinema that began with films about poor Chinese peasants, such as *Yellow Earth* and *Red Sorghum*, culminated in the spectacle of the opening ceremony of the Beijing Olympics of 2008, under the artistic direction of Zhang Yimou. In flawlessly coordinated performances designed for television and Internet audiences as well as tourists from around the world, traditional symbols such as calligraphy, book learning, music, chess, and choreography showcased Chinese civilization as an equal if not superior partner in international sports. With this extravaganza of China's superpower, the economic-semiotic transfer inscribed in contemporary Chinese cinema's ethnographic gaze at the subalterns had come full circle. If China was once a subaltern among nations—enduring social inequality, disenfranchisement, and underrepresentation or unrepresentability—as a result of the globally mediatized transactions since the 1980s, it now talks back fluently and stares back proudly in languages and images of high tech, futuristic architecture, and finance capital. This economic-semiotic transfer is corroborated in the first decade of the twenty-first century by blockbuster films such as *Crouching Tiger, Hidden Dragon*, *Hero*, *The House of Flying Daggers*, *The Promise*, *The Curse of the Golden Flower*, and *Red Cliff*, in which a masculinist moral universe (as evidenced in the patriarchal codes of imperial governance and martial arts) is packaged for the big-budget cinematic screen with bestselling contemporary ingredients like naturalized heterosexuality, fetishized female body parts, computer-enhanced cinematography, and special effects.

In the academic pursuit of China, the older, neoliberal, and politically progressive orientation toward those who are hungry now needs to work side by side with the newer impetus of the *subaltern-turned-spectacle*. This paradigm shift, one that transforms the production of knowledge from stable disciplinary divides (say, political economy on one side and aesthetics and performance on the other) into a hegemony of the glossy picture, is intensified, in the age of digitization, by the proliferating and ever-improving technologies of image-capturing and distribution. If the much debated concept of national allegory has been a prevalent mode of approaching the cultural productions of China, the rest of Asia, and other non-Western areas, what is increasingly allegorized these days, it seems, is not so much the nation as what may be called, in the vocabulary of contemporary philosophy and media theory, the event of emergence, an event that is (not necessarily but) often conveniently configured in relations of visibility.

What are some of the constituents of such emergence? As an example, let me briefly discuss the film *Se, jie* (*Lust, Caution*, 2007), by the renowned director Ang Lee. An overwhelming box office success in the Chinese-speaking world, where it has provoked substantive intellectual and popular debates across old and new media, the film also commanded warm receptions around the globe, especially among art house cinema audiences.[2]

2. For a few examples among an uncountable number of debates in the Chinese language alone, see discussions by acclaimed scholars and cultural critics such as the following: Chang Hsiao-hung, "Ai de bukeneng renwu: *Se, je* zhong de xing—zhengzhi—lishi" / "The Mission Impossible of Love: Sex—Politics—History in *Lust, Caution*," *Chungwai Literary Monthly* 38.3, no. 426 (2009), 9–48; Dai Jinhua, "Shenti, zhengzhi, guozu—cong Zhang Ailing dao Li An" (Body, politics,

Adapted from a short story of the same title by Eileen Chang (Zhang Ailing), *Se, jie* (a title that may also be translated as "Sex, prohibition") is, in a nutshell, the story of a trap turned against itself.[3] It is set in the period 1938–42, when Japan had invaded and occupied strategic areas in China. A group of patriotic students at the University of Hong Kong decide to embark on a clandestine plot to capture a national traitor, Mr. Yee, who is working for the collaborationist government under Japan. The bait is the conventional lure of sex: Wang Chia-chih, a freshman, is assigned the task of seducing Yee and stringing him along until they can assassinate him. Much of the film revolves around the details of this plot, including the appearances of Wang (in the role of "Mrs. Mak," the wife of a businessman) in the social circle of Yee and his wife, the relationships among the student patriots, and the various characters' movements between Hong Kong and Shanghai. Finally, the time is ripe: Wang and Yee, now lovers, are at a jewelry shop picking up an expensive diamond ring for her,[4] while Wang's accomplices lurk nearby. In the split second before the snap of the trap, Wang finds herself unable to proceed as planned and instead tells Yee to run.[5] After making his narrow escape, Yee has Wang and the others tortured and executed.

I offer this rather reductive summary to pinpoint the crux of my concern—several scenes of rough sex between Wang and Yee in the film that are not in Eileen Chang's story. These scenes are controversial on account of the licentiousness of the sex being depicted (they were edited from the

---

nation—from Eileen Chang to Ang Lee), *Zuoan tegao*, 13 December 2007, accessed on 11 May 2010 from the website Wuyouzixiang; Leo Lee, "Ang Lee's *Lust, Caution* and Its Reception," *boundary 2* 35.3 (2008), 223–38, and *Di Se, jie: Wenxue, dianying, lishi* (Hong Kong: Oxford University Press, 2008); Long Yingtai, "Wo kan *Se, jie*," *Mingpao Daily* (North American ed.), 27 September 2007.

3. See Zhang Ailing, "Se, jie," *Wangran ji* (Taipei: Crown, 1983), 13–44. For a discussion of the possible meanings of the two characters *se* and *jie*, see Ang Lee's remarks in Li Dahan, *Yi shan zou guo you yi shan* (A Journey of Ang Lee: From *Brokeback Mountain to Lust, Caution*) (Taipei: Ruguo chubanshe, 2007), 436, 442, 449. In the Chinese language, as Lee points out, *se* carries the connotations not only of sex but also of the emotions, desire, and ambition, while *jie* may refer to a ring, an artifact signifying a warning and a necessary boundary.

4. Obviously, much can be made of the metaphoric and plot significance of this ring, which seems as much about "lust" as it is about "caution" (see previous note): it makes Wang vulnerable at the thought that Yee seems to really love her, a thought that, we surmise, causes her fatal change of mind.

5. For a discussion of this moment in terms of what she terms contingent transcendence, see Haiyan Lee, "Enemy under My Skin: Eileen Chang's *Lust, Caution* and the Politics of Transcendence," PMLA 125.3 2010), 640–56.

version of the film released in the PRC). In particular, critical interest tends to settle on the fatefulness of Wang's apparent enjoyment of her dangerous liaison with Yee. Intended as the bait, Wang ends up caught in the snare of Yee's desire (for her); *jouissance*, in the sense of a rapturous loss of control over oneself, proves to be Wang's undoing. For many, the appeal of *Lust, Caution* lies in the scandal—and truth—of this liberation of the flesh on the part of the woman, which brings about a fatal reversal of her patriotic act.[6]

In advancing female jouissance—deemed to be the breaking forth of an involuntary force—as the heart of the intrigue, members of the audience often cite a line from Eileen Chang's story as an instruction for their interpretation: "到女人心裏的路通過陰道" ("The route to a woman's heart is through her vagina").[7] Chang's text, however, is anything but straightforward. With the use of free indirect discourse and reported references, the stylistic effect created around this assertion about female anatomy is one of hearsay:

> 又有這句諺語:「到男人心裏去的路通過胃。」是說男人好吃，碰上會做菜款待他們的女人，容易上鉤。於是就有人說:「到女人心裏的路通過陰道。」據說是民國初年精通英文的那位名學者說的，名字她叫不出，就曉得他替中國人多妻辯護的那句名言:「只有一隻茶壺幾隻茶杯，哪有一隻茶壺一隻茶杯的?」
>
> 至於什麼女人的心，她就不信名學者說得出那樣下作的話。她也不相信那話。

> And there was this idiom: "The route to a man's heart is through his stomach." It refers to how men love to eat, and how they may be easily caught by women who can entertain them with good cooking. Hence some people also say: "The route to a woman's heart is through her vagina." Reportedly this was said by that famous scholar from the early Republican years who had superb English. She [Wang] could not remember his name, but knew the famous saying with which he had defended Chinese polygamy: "We have only seen a teapot accompanied by several teacups; when have we ever seen a teapot with just a single teacup?"
>
> As for whatever it is about a woman's heart, she simply did not believe

6. An interesting exception is Dai Jinhua, who argues that the story should be understood first and foremost as a spy story about the cold war era. See Dai, "Shenti, zhengzhi, guozu."

7. See, for instance, Long Yingtai, "Wo kan *Se, jie*"; Long sees sex as the key to the story.

that the famous scholar had said such a vulgar thing. Nor did she believe that line herself. (Chang, "Se, jie," 36, my translation from the Chinese)[8]

Although the literary text is tentative in presenting the link between the female heart and the vagina, Lee's film adaptation and many audiences seem ready to overlook such linguistic caution. The issue at stake is not, however, one of mistranslation:[9] rather, it is an act of "clarification," a decision that I'd term a framing of the original. From an open-ended, hesitant reflection on female sexuality in the literary text, in which utterances are relayed through other people's talk, reported anonymously, and narrated with doubt and incredulity, the film and its critics cut to one quoted remark, treating it as though it were a reality laid bare and a foolproof index to the woman's lustfulness. Why? What motivates, energizes, and legitimates the resoluteness, the faith, behind that cut, which fills the gaps of saying with the fullness of seeing?

As in Lee's other box office successes (for instance, *The Wedding Banquet* and *Brokeback Mountain*), the film narrative of *Lust, Caution* hinges on what Michel Foucault calls the repressive hypothesis, the popularized Freudian assumption that the truth about sexuality and human society in general can only be accessed through an understanding of repression.[10] This assumption propels the plot insofar as the woman's loss of self-control over an illicit affair—itself supposedly a fake—is spotlighted as the ultimate secret or truth that, once revealed, causes the decisive break in the action. Whereas the aforementioned Chinese primer be-

8. The translation of these paragraphs by Julia Lovell has altered Chang's text somewhat; nonetheless it clearly conveys the tentative nature of the assertion about the female heart and the vagina. See Eileen Chang, *Lust, Caution*, story by Eileen Chang, screenplay by Wang Hui Ling and James Schamus, preface by Ang Lee, trans. Julia Lovell (New York: Pantheon, 2007), 36–37.

9. On the contrary, Ang Lee's attitude toward the original literary text is sensitive and thoughtful. For instance, he acknowledges, with modesty, that Chang's writings tend to defeat any attempt to translate them into film, while also asserting perceptively that *Lust, Caution* as a text was already written with filmic methods (see Lee's remarks in Li Dahan, *Yi shan zou guo you yi shan*, 437). Lee's attentiveness to Chang's text suggests that his bypassing of Chang's linguistic caution (by adding the conspicuous sex scenes) is not a matter of linguistic incompetence or carelessness.

10. For a more detailed discussion, see Rey Chow, "Sexuality," *A Concise Companion to Feminist Theory*, ed. Mary Eagleton (Oxford: Blackwell, 2003), 93–110. For a set of historically informed and informative comments on the significance of repression in Ang Lee's work in general, see Leo Lee, "Ang Lee's *Lust, Caution* and Its Reception" and *Di Se, jie: Wenxue, dianying, lishi*.

gins with the line "I am hungry," the message conveyed by Lee's film is rather "I am hungry . . . to be desired." This revelation of the secret or truth leads not only to the sabotage of the collective goal; it also spells the woman's destruction. In accordance with the logic of the repressive hypothesis, Wang's jouissance is therefore at once a coming and a coming-out—of an animal-like being breaking loose from behind the honorable façade of the patriotic agent. This coming and coming-out amount to a suicide.

The Second Coming

In this instance, jouissance is not only the narrative content pertaining to a particular character but also the form of filmic enunciation. Contrary to Chang's story, in which the scenes of sex do not exist, the film stages them (puts them on, as it were) like a prosthesis, whose conspicuousness evokes a certain imaginary, a liminal zone involving an inside and an outside. If Wang, as the bearer or the site and sight of jouissance, can be understood as the liminal zone between her accomplices and Yee, cannot the scenes of Wang and Yee's sexual encounters be similarly understood as a liminal zone, one that divides the Chinese and the non-Chinese? (In the film, the plot to catch Yee is preceded by a stage play performed by the same group of students, culminating in the unison of characters and audience shouting "China cannot fail!"). At this second level, jouissance can no longer be equated simply with an individual character's sexual climax, in the form of an eruption of nature in all its untamable animality. Still, how are we to account for the excessiveness of these scenes? What is made manifest, what is confessed? In accordance with the repressive hypothesis, it would be something like a secret—but what or whose secret? Here the problem is in part compounded by medium specificity, for film, of course, tends to make everything look like a public display—that is, tends always already, by virtue of its demonstrative character, to seem like a confession. Even so, Ang Lee's handling of the story has gone much further than this defining condition of the film medium. The manifest "confession" of the scenes is the outcome of something else.

The scenes of sex in question are delivered in such a manner as to become virtually indistinguishable from conventional pornography, and the excessiveness of the scenes, like that of pornography, suggests that the point is perhaps not sex per se but *what can be made visible in ways that defy all possible reservations and boundaries*. Under Lee's direction, in other words, the camera itself is given over to jouissance, in the sense of a violent prying-open of the possibilities of visualization. The camera demands that audiences look in places where some might, in fact, prefer to avert their gaze.[11]

In the second volume of *The History of Sexuality*, *The Use of Pleasure*, Foucault refers briefly to the case of premodern China in terms of the thematic complex of the regulation of sexual behaviors and pleasures.[12] Foucault's turn to the ancients, we recall, was part and parcel of an interrogation of the systematization of sexuality that, with the ascendency of Christianity in the West, had become increasingly aligned with a truth that lies lurking in the human individual. For Foucault, the so-called *ars erotica* of the ancient world served as a nontranscendent approach to sexuality that was premised not on truth but on practices (including social customs, habits, regimens, and dietetics). In contrast, he tells us, the modern West specializes in developing a *scientia sexualis*, one that, by paradoxically treating sex both as a secret and as something we incessantly talk about, has led to the proliferation of knowledge under conditions of discipline and surveillance. In this scenario of a society governed by the power of multiplying discourse networks, a scenario in which Jeremy Bentham's Panopticon is the eponymous blueprint for incarceration by light, Foucault famously equates visibility with a trap.[13]

With Foucault in the picture, the problematic of jouissance as posed by the film *Lust, Caution* needs to be taken quite a bit further than natural female lust. In the light of world cinema (or world literature, or world art), what might have been construed as a Chinese story is bestowed with a visibility that transcodes what looks like *ethnic* ars erotica into something akin to a scientia sexualis. Instead of being couched in metaphors or indirect language—as in the allusions commonly found in ancient Chinese sex manuals[14]—ethnic sex or erotic art is now presented in the form of an aggressively spectacular, technologically impeccable production-cum-exposé. Sensational details, from the characters' genitalia to their contorted facial expressions and their tortuous manners of

11. I remain indebted to Linda Williams's instructive study of the aesthetics and politics of pornography; see her classic *Hard Core: Power, Pleasure, and "the Frenzy of the Visible,"* expanded ed. (Berkeley: University of California Press, 1999).

12. Michel Foucault, *The Use of Pleasure*, trans. Robert Hurley (New York: Vintage, 1986), 137.

13. Michel Foucault, *Discipline and Punish: The Birth of the Prison*, trans. Alan Sheridan (New York: Vintage, 1979), 200.

14. For a Western-language reference, see R. H. Van Gulik, *Sexual Life in Ancient China* (1961; Leiden: Brill, 1974).

seizure, penetration, copulation, climaxing, and release, are shown with methodical finesse and screen polish. In terms of visibility, *there seems to be no (more) repression*, only skillful professional manipulation (of camera angles): nothing is withheld; everything is rendered in and as plain sight. If these lurid images have outdone the most fanciful orientalist depictions of a debauched Orient, it is because the Orient is no longer a veiled mystery but an infinitely visualizable surface, one that embodies the potency—and promise—of being stripped naked, of being opened up in the most unmentionable of perspectives.

This other jouissance—not of the human characters but rather of the film's machinic mode of actively producing what used to be deemed debased, shameful, or representationally off-limits, this strip search of the past, in a conscientious endeavor to make the formerly untouchable (or, what amounts to the same thing, the lamentably vanishing) yield its secrets, to make the subaltern (in this case, sexuality) speak, as it were—is fundamental to the framing of the original in this context.

Interestingly, as has become typical of films about past eras, the capture of the original China of the 1930s and 1940s had to be made partly in locales of the diaspora: in addition to Shanghai and Hong Kong (where the story takes place), major scenes were actually shot on location in Malaysia, where the frenzy of demolitions and reconstructions had been occurring at a somewhat slower pace, and public architecture, shop fronts, and street ambience resembling those in China from several decades before were still to be found. Among the tidbits drawn from the production process, it is reported that Lee took pains to re-create precise historical details of the film's setting, down to the type of desk and stationery likely to be used by a man like Yee at his office, the type of tree growing in the appropriate neighborhood in Shanghai, the measurements of the license plate (together with the numbers on the plate) of the type of rickshaw transporting the characters around town, and the construction materials used in building the film set.[15] According to Lee, this was all part of an effort to carry out the mission of restoring the world of a bygone China, the China of his parents' generation.[16] This effort to "rescue history" (*qiangjiu lishi*) from oblivion seems in parallel with the effort to bare the secrets of sex to their utmost in the monstrous sex

15. See Li Dahan, *Yi shan zou guo you yi shan*, 322 and following; see also Long, "Wo kan *Se, jie*."

16. See the interview with Ang Lee, in English, included in the DVD version of *Lust, Caution* (Focus Features Spotlight Series, Universal Studios, 2008) released in the United States.

scenes.[17] In both cases, the aim is, literally, to make believe—to manufacture authenticity, to manage its looks and effects through what can be called, in the vocabulary of animation, compositing,[18] in order to reveal, to suggest, that things were really like that.

The phrase "framing the original," then, should be understood both in the sense of providing the original with a representational frame and in the sense of incriminating the original with contrived evidence and witnessing that, precisely on account of their ambition to be documentary, are indistinguishable from consummate artifice. Formulated in these terms, in which rescuing history from oblivion is inextricable from a deliberate production or active display of *signs* of originality and authenticity, framing can be linked conceptually to the more familiar phenomena of nativism and primitivism, which typically invest, retrospectively and nostalgically, in the irretrievable original meanings of the past. Conversely, nativism and primitivism, as ideologies, can themselves be articulated as variants of jouissance in the manner I have explicated. In this light, despite apparent divergences, *Lust, Caution* seems an uncanny rejoinder to the works of the fifth generation directors about China's rural populations.

The conceptual affinity of nativism and primitivism to Lee's framing of the original becomes all the more clear when we notice that the sensations of seeing conveyed by *Lust, Caution* are quite different from those derived from the more classic perversion of voyeurism. Whereas voyeurism is based on the structural interplay between concealment and revelation, the modes of framing offered by Lee's film are, strictly speaking, not about visibility's oscillation and uncertainty, but rather about visibility as an extreme artifactuality (or, to borrow the title of a popular U.S. television program, an extreme makeover). The sex scenes in question do not so much intimate a gentle lifting of the curtain, tantalizing the audience with a peek, as confront them with a type of nakedness whose effect can only be described as brutal.

How should such brutality be understood? Is it the combined effect of pornography and Orientalism, dominant modes of visualizing otherness in modernity that have become thoroughly incorporated into the processes of non-Western ethnic self-presentation? Could the sensation of brutality be attributed in part to the inarticulate, invisible historicity

17. The phrase is used by Long; see her "Wo kan Se, jie."

18. I owe my knowledge about compositing to a discussion with Thomas LaMarre.

of watching oneself (and one's culture) being watched and treated *as a lowly, violated object*, a historicity that cannot be grasped through the empirical facts of documented history alone (for instance, Japan appointing itself, in the context of modern European imperialism, the leader of the Greater East Asia Co-prosperity Sphere; the attacking of China by Japan as well as by Western powers; the concentration of criminal and revolutionary activities alike in colonial or semicolonial enclaves such as Hong Kong and Shanghai)? Instead, *brutality and historicity ask to be grasped as a force of imaging, one that infects and pervades the very process of objectification*, in narrative as much as in images.

From this perspective, what is most remarkable about the story of *Lust, Caution* is not so much the female lead's enjoyment of sex as her masochism, her capacity for ecstasy at being seized, abused, and dehumanized as an animal or object—and that by a man who, the immense pleasure he can have with her notwithstanding, has no compunction about eliminating her when his self-interest is at stake. The scandal of Wang's self-annihilating bonding with Yee is that it is not singular but may be seen as an extension of the masochism required of her (and her fellow students) by the Chinese resistance, which dignifies such masochism as heroism (martyrdom). Even more unthinkable, perhaps, is that this collective masochism in relation to China also bears an eerie kinship to Yee's masochism in relation to the Japanese. Whether in the role of patriot or traitor, hero or villain, each actor must excel in what Yee, alone with Wang at a Japanese restaurant in one scene, calls whoring. The actor must play his or her role with body and soul, in full submissiveness to the cause (saving China, serving Japan), even as the cause remains elusive—indeed, treacherous in its indifference to the actor's personal grievances and its readiness to betray and sacrifice him or her.[19] Last but not least, are not Ang Lee's fastidious efforts as director also masochistic, in that although he believes he is carrying out a mission to restore the bygone China of his parents' generation, the mission can never be accomplished, no matter how hard he tries, and the splendid dress rehearsal of the past he delivers for the world to see—otherwise known as the film *Lust, Caution*—is therefore, at best, a knockoff?[20]

19. According to Leo Lee, in this scene the two characters are shown by Ang Lee to be bound by an awareness of their "shared victimization . . . in one momentary escape into sentimentality" ("Ang Lee's *Lust, Caution*," 233); see also Leo Lee, *Di Se, jie*, 98.

20. See Chang Hsiao-hung, "Ai de bukeneng renwu," for an insightful discussion

The supplementary questions about this *masochism series*—questions conjuring all the identificatory stakes of loyalty and betrayal, of becoming-other and self-immolation, and enmeshed with the ubiquitous social media technologies for (self-)imaging, (self-)announcement, and (self-)display typical of the communications of our age—are a seldom discussed but, to my mind, nonnegligible aspect of the paradigm shift taking place today in the study of Asian cultures in a globalized academy. As a considerable number of ethnically Asian scholars and students, "minorities" raised in Asian and non-Asian languages, join what used to be an esoteric Western academic establishment (Asian studies) dominated by white (and mainly male) researchers, this extra dimension of the historicity of having-been-rendered-object needs to be recognized as a dimension of intellectual and artistic creativity, one that bears a sticky, messy historical imprint—namely, a claim to a (collective) memory of being aggressed against *and* the masochistic pleasures and pains that typically accompany such a claim. To this extent, we may view a film such as *Lust, Caution* finally as a kind of high-tech search engine, whose design is not so much for finding or relocating the past (as its director earnestly supposes) as it is for assembling or compositing the past in the form of an artifact, replete with libidinal, machinic, and historical bits and pieces, as outlined here. The emergence of such artifactual installations, together with the inexhaustible webs of discourses that unfold and circulate around them, is likely to define the terms for a new visibility of the Orient in the twenty-first century.

---

of the "mission impossible" of love, in particular love of the nation (patriotism), in the film.

Postscript

Intimations from a Scene of Capture

The Anti-Lure

A common enough sight: a decal in the shape of a bird spreading its wings, hung or pasted on a window to prevent birds from crashing into the glass.[1]

A different kind of story begins to unfold when one remembers that the glass is, first and foremost, a line of demarcation and a barrier, shielding a man-made interior from the outside. The glass at once prohibits entry and masks the violence of such prohibition; its transparency is in effect a trompe-l'oeil, a lure that can deceive the birds. To call attention to this imminent state of danger, a supplemental sign is put up—a benevolent warning, humans tell themselves, that would forestall disaster for their avian friends.

On the "No Entry" encrypted in the glass, thus, the *Vogelscheuche* is added as a visible, second No.[2] This No is the vigilant pose of the Anti-Lure—rational, self-conscious, and full of goodwill. Like a mute gatekeeper guarding a sanctuary, the Vogelscheuche signals to the (already barred, already banned) outsiders: STOP.

1. These pictures were taken inside a science and technology museum, where an exhibit included the windmill seen outside the window.

2. The equivalent of "scarecrow," "Vogelscheuche" literally means "bird-shoo-away."

Julian Rohrhuber,
Vogelscheuche
(Four Photographs, 1995).
Courtesy of the artist.

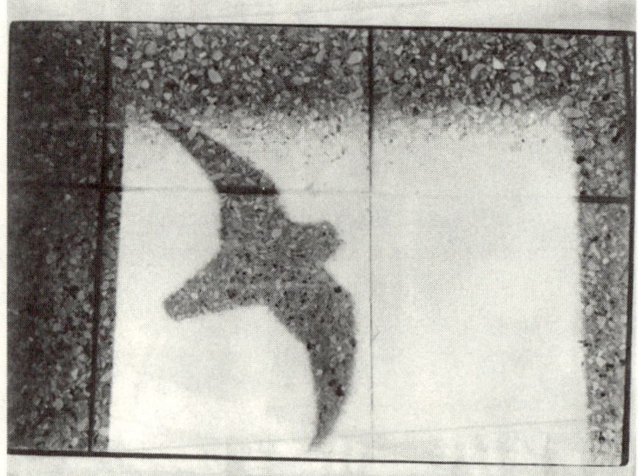

Abduction by the Sun

Unperturbed by the cares and cautions of the human world, the sun streams through the glass, abducting the Vogelscheuche along the way, then laying it down on the stone floor like a fugitive from another world. By this process of a literal photo-graphy, a writing by light, a bird now appears on the inside. The artifact series that begins with the Vogelscheuche has acquired a new extension: a shadow bird, a bird shadow.[3] Looking at it from a distance, it is difficult to tell if the shadow is not that of a live bird.

Into the Open

Superimposed on the grain of the stone, the shadow forms part of a mosaic, an assemblage of forces in transit, elemental and geological, but also lingual and imagistic.

Is not the name Vogelscheuche, in its onomatopoetic spirit, the performance of a fundamental ambivalence? A shooing-away, an instruction to the other to disappear, is expressed as a kind, apotropaic wish: "Sh, sh, birdies, away, away! We expel you but we want you to live; we forbid you to enter but we must protect you from disaster, from yourselves . . ."

And why does this shooing-*away* of birds have to take the *appearance* of a bird? (Do birds need to recognize this bird-like shape to know they should fly off?) This mock resemblance announces an excess, an allurement of another order. In this make-believe form, the space-clearing logic of the Anti-Lure becomes enmeshed in the imitative habit of imaging. To whom is the Vogelscheuche really addressed?

Is not the bird series (decal, shadow, image of shadow . . .) a line of sacrificial surrogates, birds that are caught instead, that take the place of live birds crashing on the glass? These overlapping semiotic folds—each a stand-in for another, each hollowing another out from within, each shooing another away—can only be described as entanglements, whose transmedial character intensifies in a second-order photography, this set of frames.

What exactly is captured in these frames? The ambivalence suggested by the name Vogelscheuche? The intermediary status of the artifact, the hinge to imbrications of enclosures and exclusions? The border between

3. In Chinese, "photography" is 攝影 (sheying): literally, the taking or capturing of shadows.

life and death (between the live birds, scattered and invisible because banished to the outside, and the ever looming chance of a catastrophe, warded off by a surrogate)? What has been barred from entry and shooed away shows up on the ground of the interior as a spectral presence: a weightless bird flickering in the sun.

Should not this shadow be viewed as the exhibit of a conceptual drift—of an anti-lure intention ensnared in mimesis and hovering, momentarily, over an inanimate plane doubling as a reflective screen? Where is the shadow heading? From within the state of visibility, its trap, might this bird yet leap forth—and soar, through night's darkness, back into the open?

Index

REY CHOW is Anne Firor Scott Professor of Literature at Duke University. Among the numerous works she has authored are *Woman and Chinese Modernity* (1991), *Writing Diaspora* (1993), *Primitive Passions* (1995), *Ethics after Idealism* (1998), *The Protestant Ethnic and the Spirit of Capitalism* (2002), *The Age of the World Target* (2006), and *Sentimental Fabulations, Contemporary Chinese Films* (2007). *The Rey Chow Reader*, ed. Paul Bowman, was published in 2010. Chow's scholarly writings have appeared in ten languages.

Library of Congress Cataloging-in-Publication Data
Chow, Rey.
Entanglements, : or transmedial thinking about capture / Rey Chow.
p. cm. — (A John Hope Franklin Center book)
Includes bibliographical references and index.
ISBN 978-0-8223-5216-7 (cloth : alk. paper)
ISBN 978-0-8223-5230-3 (pbk. : alk. paper)
1. Culture. 2. Mass media. 3. Humanities. 4. Psychology and literature.
5. Postcolonialism—Philosophy. 6. Violence. 7. Aesthetics.
I. Title. II. Series: John Hope Franklin Center book.
GN357.C446 2012
306—dc23 2011041898

CARDIFF UNIVERSITY
PRIFYSGOL CAERDYDD